# Felix Frankfurter
## THE JUDGE

*Also edited by Wallace Mendelson*

FELIX FRANKFURTER: A TRIBUTE

# Felix Frankfurter
## THE JUDGE

*Edited by*

### Wallace Mendelson
*University of Texas*

★★

REYNAL & COMPANY
*New York   1964*

One could read everything that he has written—a formidable task from several points of view—and still have little more than an inkling, if that, of why this man has evoked in so many such passionate devotion and exercised for half a century so profound an influence. I can think of no one in our time remotely comparable to him. . . .

DEAN ACHESON

# Contents

# Introduction

Felix Frankfurter is, in sum, the most vital and creative person I have ever known. . . .
—Reinhold Niebuhr

Posterity may or may not take our word for it that Felix Frankfurter had more influence on more lives than any man in his generation.
—Archibald MacLeish

This is the second of a two-volume study. The first—*Felix Frankfurter: A Tribute*—was designed to convey some conception of F.F.'s personality and pre-judicial career. The present volume deals with his work on the bench. Each contributor describes what he saw—each working independently of the others. Yet it seems to me there is a common theme—as Lincoln put it: "Why should there not be a patient confidence in the ultimate justice of the people? Is there any better or equal hope in the world?"

Wallace Mendelson

# Felix Frankfurter
## THE JUDGE

# Separation of Powers: The Justice Revisits His Own Casebook

Nathaniel L. Nathanson, *Professor of Law, Northwestern University*

Professor Frankfurter's conception of separation of powers, as illustrated by the first 457 pages of the original Frankfurter and Davison *Cases and Other Materials on Administrative Law*, published in 1932, was obviously a house of many mansions. So many, indeed, that some of the more irreverent (or functionally minded) of his students were known to harbor the suspicion that it was designed to accommodate all those great cases of American constitutional history, and a few of their English kinsmen, which the professor was particularly fond of teaching. Be that as it may, it seems appropriate to consider for the purpose of this occasion what opinions of the Justice would be fitting companions for those which originally inhabited the house the professors built and how radically, if at all, its character would be altered by their taking up residence.

## I. LEGISLATIVE POWER:

The first case in the original casebook, Calder et Wife v. Bull et Wife,[1] decided by the United States Supreme Court in 1798, involved the question whether the Connecticut legislature could, without violation of the *ex post facto* clause of the federal Constitution, set aside a decree of the Probate Court and grant a new hearing with the right of appeal, after the ordinary time for appeal had expired. The Justices delivered opinions seriatim in the English, and occasionally Frankfurtian, rather than the Marshall tradition, but it is only the opinion of Mr. Justice Chase which is reproduced, apparently more for the dicta than the explicit holding. The holding was simply that this was not an ex post facto law because the resolution and the new hearing "took away no right of property vested in Calder and wife."[2] The dicta were as broad as the holding was narrow:

> ... An act of the legislature (for I cannot call it a law) contrary to the great first principles of the social compact, cannot be considered a rightful exercise of legislative authority. .... The legislature may enjoin, permit, forbid, and punish; they may declare new crimes, and establish rules of conduct for all citizens in future cases; they may command what is right and prohibit what is wrong, but they cannot change innocence into guilt; or punish innocence as a crime, or violate the right of an antecedent lawful private contract, or the right of private property. To maintain that our Federal, or State Legislature possesses such powers, if they had not been expressly restrained, would, in my opinion, be a political heresy, altogether inadmissible in our free republican governments.[3]

Although it is hard to find an exact modern counterpart for Calder et Wife v. Bull et Wife, the next case, Cooper v. Telfair,[4] brings us one step further along the road of a natural progression, as constitutional challenge is leveled against an act passed by the legislature of the state of Georgia entitled "An Act for Inflicting Penalties on and Confiscating the Estate of Such Persons as are therein declared Guilty of Treason, and for other purposes therein mentioned." Again the challenge failed, primarily because, as Mr. Justice Washington said: "The constitution of Georgia does not expressly interdict the passing of an act of attainder and confiscation by the authority of the legislature."[5] In absence of such a specific prohibition reliance had been placed upon more general articles of the state constitution (the case had originated in the federal courts), such as the provision: "The legislative, executive, and judiciary, departments shall be separate and distinct, so that neither exercise the powers properly belonging to the other."[5] To this contention, Mr. Justice Paterson boldly replied: "I consider it as a sound political proposition, that wherever the legislative power of a government is undefined, it includes the judicial and executive attributes."[6]

Having thus teased us with lofty generalities relating to separation of powers, and some passing references to the specifics of *ex post facto* laws and bills of attainder, the casebook passes on to some other aspects of retroactive application of law, without criminal characteristics. It does not pursue further the *ex post facto* and bill of attainder themes, until they reappear much later, under the heading of Executive Power, in *Ex parte* Garland,[7] complicated by the application of the President's pardoning power to disqualification from membership in the Supreme Court bar resulting from inability to take a test oath reciting among other things that "the deponent has never voluntarily borne arms against the United States since he has been a citizen thereof." It was upon this decision, and the companion case of Cummings v. Missouri,[8] that the majority of Mr. Justice Frankfurter's colleagues relied in United States v. Lovett[9] for "the proposition that legislative acts, no matter what their form, that apply either to named individuals or to easily ascertainable members of a group in such a way as to inflict punishment on them without a judicial trial are bills of attainder prohibited by the Constitution."[10] Of course, the concurring opinion of Mr. Justice Frankfurter, in which Mr. Justice Reed joined, questioned neither the validity of the general proposition nor the soundness of Cummings and Garland, but rather the applicability of the proposition to the particular facts presented in Lovett, i.e., an appropriation rider providing that no part of an appropriation to any department agency or instrumentality of the United States should be used to pay the salary of certain named individuals, unless they were appointed by the President with the advice and consent of the Senate.

No one at all familiar with Justice Frankfurter's personal philosophy can doubt the sincerity of his suggestion that this early emanation from the Un-American Activities Committee "may imply notions that are abhorrent to us as individuals or policies we deem harmful to the country's well-being."[11] Consequently, the Justice's opinion in the Lovett case presents a classic example of his scrupulous separation of "personal views" from his responsibilities as a judge, particularly when dealing with what he regarded as "very specific provisions of the Constitution." The following passage is revealing, not only because of the historical approach to the meaning of the bill of attainder clause of the Constitution but also because of the way that it fitted into a general conception of separation of powers:

> The prohibition of bills of attainder falls of course among these very specific constitutional provisions. The distinguishing characteristic of a bill of attainder is the substitution of legislative determination of guilt and legislative imposition of punishment for judicial finding and sentence. "A bill of attainder, by the common law, as our fathers imported it from England and practised it themselves, before the adoption of the Constitution, was

4

an act of sovereign power, in the form of a special statute . . . by which a man was pronounced guilty or attainted of some crime, and punished by deprivation of his vested rights, without trial or judgment *per legem terrae.*" . . . It was this very special, narrowly restricted, intervention by the legislature, in matters for which a decent regard for men's interests indicated a judicial trial, that the Constitution prohibited. It must be recalled that the Constitution was framed in an era when dispensing justice was a well-established function of the legislature. The prohibition against bills of attainder must be viewed in the background of the historic situation when moves in specific litigation that are now the conventional and, for the most part, the exclusive concern of courts were commonplace legislative practices. . . . Bills of attainder were part of what now are stable judicial functions which legislatures then exercised. It was this part of their recognized authority which the Constitution prohibited when it provided that "no Bill of Attainder . . . shall be passed." Section 304 lacks the characteristics of the enactments in the Statutes of the Realm and the Colonial Laws that bear the hallmarks of bills of attainder.[12]

The Lovett case also presented a special problem of statutory construction. Undoubtedly the House of Representatives had adopted the rider in response to the view of its committee that the named individuals were unfit to hold positions of trust in the government because of their "subversive activities." The Senate, however, reluctantly accepted the rider after having rejected it several times, and "after the fifth conference report showed that the House would not yield."[13] And the President, when he signed the bill, explained: "The Senate yielded, as I have been forced to yield, to avoid delaying our conduct of the war. But I cannot so yield without placing on record my view that this provision is not only unwise and discriminatory, but unconstitutional."[14] This chain of legislative events satisfied the majority that the provision "was designed to force the employing agencies to discharge respondents and to bar their being hired by any governmental agency" and more broadly "to 'purge' the then existing and all future lists of government employees of those whom Congress deemed guilty of 'subversive activities' and therefore 'unfit' to hold a federal job."[15] But Mr. Justice Frankfurter was equally satisfied that "to hold that a measure which did not express a judgment of condemnation by the Senate and carried an affirmative disavowal of such condemnation by the President constitutes a bill of attainder, disregards the historic tests for determining what is a bill of attainder."[16]

I have often wondered how the Justice would correlate this particular exercise in statutory interpretation with the usual search for legislative intent or statutory meaning. I would suppose that ordinarily the intent of one house, in originating a particular provision, would be determinative of legislative intent, to the extent that such intent was relevant, if it also clearly appeared that the other chamber and the President, without attaching any other purpose or meaning to the provision in dispute, reluctantly accepted the provision in order to break a legislative log jam. I would also suppose that the Justice would himself accept this as a general principle of statutory interpretation, but would deny its applicability to the particular problem of legislative intent presented in the Lovett case. There, it might be said, the question was not how the provision was to operate, because that was clear and not in dispute; the disbursing officers were not to pay the salaries of the named individuals. The question was rather how this legislative command should be characterized, for constitutional purposes, and in this connection the reason for the legislative action was asserted to be relevant. In this framework, the Justice's answer was that the conflicting reasons or motives of the House, the Senate, and the President could not supply the unequivocal "legislative verdict of guilt" which is the hallmark of a bill of attainder.

Whether one is persuaded by the Justice's argument perhaps depends, more than anything else, upon how whole-heartedly one accepts his basic premise that "the most funda-mental principle of constitutional adjudication is not to face constitutional questions but to avoid them if at all possible."[17] The Lovett case, as the Justice would have disposed of it, was an especially beautiful example of that principle in action, for his opinion was not a dissent but rather an explanation, for him-self and Mr. Justice Reed, of their concurrence in the judg-ment of the Court. They reached the result that the plaintiffs were entitled to a judgment in the Court of Claims on the ground that prohibition of the rider "merely prevented the ordinary disbursal of money to pay respondents' salaries," but "did not cut off the obligation of the Government to pay for services rendered."[18] Under either the majority or the concur-ring view, the result of the judgment was to remit to the Con-gress the further question whether monies should be appropri-ated to pay the judgment of the Court of Claims.

I have adverted elsewhere[19] to the subsequent debate in the House of Representatives on the question whether the appropri-ation for the Court of Claims was to include these particular judgments, and the argument that it should out of respect for the Supreme Court's opinion holding the rider unconstitutional, which apparently provided the narrow margin of victory for such inclusion. I have also raised the question whether the de-cision of the Court would have been equally persuasive had it rested on the narrow ground taken by Justices Frankfurter and Reed. I did not mean to suggest, however, that this happy (from the plaintiffs' viewpoint) denouement necessarily established that the majority was right and the concurring Justices wrong. It might be suggested, for example, that the very closeness of the margin (one vote) by which the Court's decision escaped being flouted completely shows how wise it would have been to avoid a decision which could so easily be rendered nugatory by the refusal of Congress to honor it. Or it might be suggested that the fundamental decencies of democratic behavior would have been better served if the congressional debate had proceeded without benefit of the Court's pronouncement and the Senate and the President had had another opportunity, relieved of the pressure of wartime appropriations, to insist that such decencies be observed. In these respects the Lovett case presents in microcosm some of the questions with respect to the role of the Court in a democratic polity which have concerned Professor and Mr. Justice Frankfurter throughout his professional life—the extent to which it should hesitate to declare more than it can confidently count on being enforced, and the extent to which it should risk its own prestige and public acceptance by throwing the weight of its moral judgments into the scales of deeply divisive issues of public conscience.

Perhaps it is only coincidence that the Lovett case arose out of the early activities of the Un-American Activities Committee, which was destined to contribute so much to the law of congressional investigations and so to the living doctrine of separation of powers. In our casebook the problems of legislative investigations were presented through Kilbourn v. Thompson,[20] McGrain v. Daugherty,[21] and Attorney General v. Brissenden,[22] a Massachusetts case which, insofar as it involved the use of the attorney general of the state, instead of a committee, as the investigating arm of the legislative, is partially comparable to Sweezy v. New Hampshire.[23] The attitude of Professor Frankfurter toward these cases was doubtless consistent with that reflected in an article entitled "Hands off the Investigations," published in *New Republic* in May 1924, and cited by Mr. Justice Clark in his dissent in Watkins v. United States.[24] The concluding paragraph of that article was a sweeping one:

> The procedure of congressional investigation should remain as it is. No limitations should be imposed by congressional legislation

or standing rules. The power of investigation should be left untrammeled, and the methods and forms of each investigation should be left for the determination of Congress and its committees as each situation arises. The safeguards against abuse and folly are to be looked for in the forces of responsibility which are operating from within Congress and are generated from without.[25]

This paragraph must be read, however, in the context of what preceded, which contained, for example, the following sentences: "Of course, the essential decencies must be observed, namely opportunity for cross-examination must be afforded to those who are investigated or to those representing issues under investigation. Despite Daugherty's statement to the contrary, the opportunity has been scrupulously given by the Brookhart Committee."[26]

It should be remembered that all three of the casebook cases, including even Kilbourn, were concerned essentially with governmental operations; the affairs of private individuals were being inquired into only for the light that they would shed upon affairs of government. It was not until the decision in United States v. Rumely[27] that the Court dealt directly with the "informing function of Congress" as applied to private as distinguished from governmental affairs. Speaking for the Court, Mr. Justice Frankfurter, after quoting the famous sentences of President Wilson, "The informing function of Congress should be preferred even to its legislative functions," explicitly recognized the new dimensions of the problem presented:

> Although the indispensable "informing function of Congress" is not to be minimized, determination of the "rights" which this function implies illustrates the common juristic situation thus defined for the Court by Mr. Justice Holmes: "All rights tend to declare themselves absolute to their logical extreme. Yet all in fact are limited by the neighborhood of principles of policy which are other than those on which the particular right is

9

founded, and which become strong enough to hold their own when a certain point is reached." Hudson Water Co. v. Mc-Carter, 209 U.S. 349, 355. President Wilson did not write in light of the history of events since he wrote; more particularly he did not write of the investigative power of Congress in the context of the First Amendment. And so, we would have to be that "blind" court, against which Mr. Chief Justice Taft admonished in a famous passage, Child Labor Tax case, 259 U.S. 20, 37, that does not see what "[a]ll others can see and understand" not to know that there is wide concern, both in and out of Congress, over some aspects of the exercise of the congressional power of investigation.[28]

Here again, as in Lovett, the Justice found both a reason and a way to avoid the constitutional question, the asserted prohibition of the First Amendment upon inquiry into the area of private opinions. As he put it, "Whenever constitutional limits upon the investigative power of Congress have to be drawn by this Court, it ought only to be done after Congress had demonstrated its full awareness of what is at stake by unequivocally authorizing an inquiry of dubious limits."[29] The particular question of interpretation was whether the House of Representatives, when it directed its Select Committee on Lobbying Activities "to conduct a study and investigation of (1) all lobbying activities intended to influence, encourage, promote, or retard legislation," had in mind only "lobbying in its commonly accepted sense"—that is, " 'representation made directly to the Congress, its members, or its committees' "—or whether it also meant to reach "attempts 'to saturate the thinking of the community.' "[30] Personally, I find it difficult to question seriously the Court's choice of the more restricted meaning, even without the aid of the Justice's supporting principle: "So to interpret is in the candid service of avoiding a serious constitutional doubt."[31] This time it was Justices Douglas and Black who joined in a concurring opinion, which found the restricted interpretation implausible and insisted upon facing the constitutional issue. In the light of subsequent developments, it is of some interest that their opinion found support for the broader interpretation, not so much in the language of the resolution itself or its own antecedent history, but rather in the House debate on whether the contempt citation should issue. This use of legislative history subsequent to the hearing at which the alleged contempt was committed suggests the question, later highlighted in Watkins, whether the witness was not entitled to have the standard of pertinency made clear before he was required to comply with the subpoena or accept the risk of criminal indictment for contempt.

It was this very point that Mr. Justice Frankfurter emphasized in his concurring opinion in the Watkins case: that "Prosecution for contempt of Congress presupposes an adequate opportunity for the defendant to have awareness of the pertinency of the information that he had denied to Congress"; and that "The basis for such awareness must be contemporaneous with witness' refusal to answer."[32] The same point was also made by the Chief Justice, speaking for the Court, when he said: "The problem [the need for a standard of pertinency] attains proportion when viewed from the standpoint of the witness who appears before a congressional committee. He must decide at the time the questions are propounded whether or not to answer."[33] But the specific problem which neither the opinion of the Chief Justice for the Court, nor the concurring opinion of Mr. Justice Frankfurter, addressed themselves to, was how introductory statements by the chairman of the Committee could be allowed to supply a standard of pertinency which was wholly lacking in the authorizing resolution. Perhaps this question did not have to be answered in Watkins, because the finding was that the introductory statement of the chairman failed to supply such a standard. But the assumption of the Chief Justice's opinion in

Watkins seemed to be that it might have done so; and the subsequent holding in Barenblatt v. United States[34] was partly justified by Mr. Justice Harlan, speaking for the Court, on the ground that "The subject matter of the inquiry had been identified at the commencement of the investigation as Communist infiltration into the field of education."[35] This statement by Mr. Justice Harlan did not convince the Chief Justice, who, joining in Mr. Justice Black's dissenting opinion, apparently adopted the view that it was the standard of the authorizing resolution—in this case Rule XI of the House of Representatives—which was determinative, and not anything that was said in announcing or opening the hearing. Thus, in a sense, the Chief Justice rejected the narrower ground, which his own opinion had suggested as the possible basis for Watkins, while Mr. Justice Frankfurter, joining in the opinion of Mr. Justice Harlan, was apparently satisfied that the required standard of pertinency lacking in the original authorizing resolution could be supplied at the opening of the hearing by the committee itself.

If I may borrow again from my own previous commentary, I have already suggested that this apparent inconsistency may be resolved, at least partially, by analogizing the investigatory authority of the Committee to the delegated authority of administrative agencies to establish by regulation the elements of conduct which will constitute a crime in violation of the authorizing statute.[36]. It is apparent that the standards of the statute authorizing the administrator to act may be considerably more indefinite than the regulations of the administrator defining the crime; in other words the standards of vagueness applicable to determine whether there has been a valid delegation of authority to the administrator are properly more relaxed than those applicable for determining whether there has been sufficient definition of the crime to constitute fair notice to the potential defendant for the purpose of due process. For example, the standards for fair and equitable prices, contained in the Emergency Price Control Act and sustained against the challenge of unlawful delegation in the Yakus v. United States,[37] would hardly have been sufficient to sustain a criminal prosecution, despite the recent decision of the Court sustaining an almost equally vague proscription of unreasonably low prices in the Robinson-Patman Act.[38] It was only after the price administrator translated "fair and equitable" into more explicit directives through price regulations that an appropriate basis was laid for criminal prosecution.

Professor Bickel, taking note of the analogy, suggests that it fails because, even in Watkins, the chairman of the Committee, by directing the witness to answer, "afforded notice of what the Committee thought it was inquiring into and of what it deemed pertinent."[39] Recognizing this difficulty, I would still defend the applicability of the analogy on the ground that the direction to answer a particular question is more like the threat of prosecution for a particular course of conduct, e.g., for charging a particular price. It does not supply a general standard of conduct applicable to all those within a defined area. In the administrative process, this is supplied by general regulations; in the legislative investigations, it may be supplied by the Committee's announcement of the general scope of its inquiry. But the significant consideration lies more in the substance than in the form of the analogy. Surely, the Court was justified in concluding that the standing committees of Congress must operate under broad grants of investigatory authority which would give only the vaguest hint of a standard of pertiency for particular questions. The rule of Watkins, as applied in Barenblatt, would permit such delegations of investigating authority to continue, subject to the qualification that they must be spelled out by the Committee itself, for the purposes of each particular investigation, sufficiently to provide the witness with some point of reference by which to judge his obligation to respond. With this portion of the Barenblatt opinion and with Mr. Justice Frankfurter's concurrence therein, it seems to me there can be no serious quarrel. Whether, even so, the prosecution should have failed on account of violation of the First Amendment, on a theory comparable to that espoused by the Justice himself in the Sweezy case, is a line of inquiry which I am happy to relinquish into other hands.

The final case in this subdivision of our casebook must have had a special personal interest for Professor Frankfurter, since it concerned a clash between Governor Roosevelt and the New York State legislature with respect to budgetary powers.[40] However, I do not recall that he expressed any attitude with respect to the governor's triumph in securing the invalidation of the legislature's attempt to devolve upon committee chairmen some share in the authority to approve specific allocations in appropriations made for more general purposes. Whatever his views on the merits of the question, he must have been amused by the governor's exulting comment, quoted in the footnote,[41] which read in part:

> The Court of Appeals upholds in its decision the sacred, time-honoured American principle of the separation of the judicial, legislative and executive departments of government.
> Every school child has been taught that this is the fundamental division of our governmental powers. Many attempts have been made in the past to break this clear division down.
> The highest court of the State of New York sustains this sacred American principle. And from now on I trust that, instead of constant bickerings and efforts to throw monkey-wrenches into the machinery, we shall have a better cooperation and closer understanding of the governmental powers in Albany.

## II. EXECUTIVE POWER

The next subdivision of the casebook, entitled Executive Power, opened with Myers v. United States,[42] which had not yet been qualified by the Humphrey's case.[43] There is little doubt where Professor Frankfurter's sympathies lay so far as Myers was concerned, and that he must have welcomed Humphrey's, despite its rebuke to the President. Nevertheless, in the Justice's opinion in Wiener v. United States[44] there is not the slightest indication of desire to discredit Myers, any further than the qualification already imposed by Humphrey's, which, as the Justice said, "narrowly confined the scope of the Myers decision to include only 'all purely executive officers.' "[45] Although Wiener was, in a sense, more difficult than Humphrey's because the statute contained no provision at all with respect to removal, it was also, in another sense, easier because the War Claims Commission, of which Wiener was a member, had only one task to perform—to adjudicate claims for compensating internees, prisoners of war, and religious organizations who suffered personal or property damage at the hands of the enemy in connection with World War II. This was a task, the Justice explained, which "Congress could of course have given . . . to the District Courts or to the Court of Claims. The fact that it chose to establish a Commission to 'adjudicate according to law' the classes of claims defined in the statute did not alter the intrinsic judicial character of the task with which the Commission was charged."[46] But ever wary of the pitfalls of overgeneralization, as exemplified in Myers, the Justice's opinion was also careful to point out: "We have not a removal for cause involving the rectitude of a member of an adjudicatory body, nor even a suspensory removal until the Senate could act upon it by confirming the appointment of a new Commissioner or otherwise dealing with the matter."[47] These may be problems of another day.

Of course, any discussion of executive power would now be dominated by the steel seizure case, Youngstown Sheet & Tube Co. v. Sawyer,[48] rather than Myers, although the casebook editor might have difficulty in deciding just where to put it. If one looks primarily to Mr. Justice Black's opinion, it might be regarded as an introduction to the entire subject of separation of powers, albeit an extraordinary oversimplification. It may have been this oversimplification which prompted Mr. Justice Frankfurter to say in the opening sentence of his opinion: "Before the cares of the White House were his own, President Harding is reported to have said that government after all is a very simple thing."[49] Yet the Justice was also careful to avoid disassociating himself entirely from Justice Black's opinion, prefacing his own with an introductory statement which said in part: "Although the considerations relevant to the legal enforcement of the principle of Separation of Powers seem to me more complicated and flexible than may appear from what Mr. Justice Black has written, I join his opinion because I thoroughly agree with the application of the principle to the circumstances of this case."[50]

It may sound frivolous to say that what stands out most sharply in the Justice's opinion are the appendices which detail in tabular form all instances of legislative authorization of seizure of industrial property and all instances of presidential seizures, accompanied by analysis of the relevant circumstances. These tables may, however, appropriately be described as the pictorial representation of the philosophy of the Justice's opinion. As he put it: "The Founders of this Nation were not imbued with the modern cynicism that the only thing that history teaches is that it teaches nothing. They acted on the conviction that the experience of man sheds a good deal of light on his nature. It sheds a good deal of light not merely on the need for effective power, if a society is to be at once cohesive and civilized, but also on the need for limitations on the power of governors over the governed."[51] This emphasis upon the teachings of history is a familiar theme, which illumines many of the Justice's opinions, especially those concerned with separation of powers.

Other familiar themes run through the Youngstown opinion. It is obvious, for example, that of all the members of the Court the Justice was the most concerned that perhaps the merits of the question did not have to be reached at all. "To start with a consideration of the relation between the President's powers and those of Congress—a most delicate matter that has occupied the thoughts of statesmen and judges since the Nation was founded and will continue to occupy their thoughts as long as our democracy lasts—is to start at the wrong end. A plaintiff is not entitled to an injunction if money damages would fairly compensate him for any wrong he may have suffered."[52] Professor Freund has developed in detail the reasons why this may indeed have provided the most appropriate ground for disposing of the case, or at least for refusing to issue a preliminary injunction,[53] despite the Justice's reluctant conclusion to the contrary; and I have sometimes wondered whether, if the division of the Court had been close enough to make his own vote decisive, the Justice might not have been content to dispose of it upon that ground. Perhaps as he watched the long strike which followed the Court's decision, without Congress lifting a finger to provide a solution as the Justice in his closing paragraph hopefully anticipated it would, he too may have wondered whether this may not have been another instance for the application of his oft-repeated principle: "A basic rule is the duty of the Court not to pass on a constitutional issue at all, however narrowly it may be confined, if the case may, as a matter of intellectual honesty, be decided without even considering delicate problems of power under the Constitution."[54] Equally characteristic was the Justice's reliance upon "Marshall's admonition that 'it is a Constitution we are expounding,' "[55] and upon the aphorism of Holmes J., dissenting in Springer v. Philippine Islands:[56] "The great ordinances of the Constitution do not establish and divide fields of black and white."[57] In keeping with these admonitions, the Justice made no attempt "to define the President's powers comprehensively . . . to delineate what belongs to him by virtue of his office beyond the power even of Congress to contract; what authority belongs to him until Congress acts; what kinds of problems may be dealt with either by the Congress or by the President or by both, cf. La Abra Silver Mng. Co. v. United States, 175 U. S. 423; what power must be exercised by the Congress and cannot be delegated to the President."[58]

The main thrust of the opinion was that this particular power had been jealously guarded by the Congress and had been deliberately withheld, not only when the Labor Management Relations Act of 1947 was adopted, but also when the Defense Production Act of 1950 and its amendments were passed and the needs of the Korean conflict were reasonably apparent. The underlying assumption of the Justice's opinion was, nevertheless, necessarily the same as that of Mr. Justice Black: this was a power the President could not exercise in direct opposition to the will of Congress. This is made clear in another quotation from the dissenting opinion of Mr. Justice Holmes in Myers: "The duty of the President to see that the laws be executed is a duty that does not require him to achieve more than Congress sees fit to leave within his powers."[59] And if there is a general principle which informs the whole opinion, it is that drawn from the dissent of Mr. Justice Brandeis in Myers:[60]

The doctrine of the separation of powers was adopted by the Convention of 1787, not to promote efficiency but to preclude the exercise of arbitrary power. The purpose was not to avoid friction, but, by means of the inevitable friction incident to the distribution of the governmental powers among three departments, to save the people from autocracy.[61]

No wonder that Chief Justice Vinson, in his dissenting opinion, complained: "Although more restrictive views of executive power, advocated in dissenting opinions of Justice Holmes, McReynolds and Brandeis, were emphatically rejected by this Court in Myers v. United States . . . members of today's majority treat these dissenting views as authoritative."[62]

## III. JUDICIAL POWER

Returning to the casebook, we find a natural transition from the last case of the second subdivision *Ex parte* Grossman,[63] to the first case of the third subdivision, Evans v. Gore,[64] both concerning themselves with the independence of the judiciary, the one from executive dominance through the exercise of the pardoning power in regard to contempt of court, and the other with "legislative encroachment" through the imposition of an income tax on judicial salaries. But the master stroke is the introduction of the subject of judicial power with a statute of William III, enacting that judges' commissions be made "quandiu se bene gesserint," followed by an excerpt entitled "George III, Speech Respecting the Independence of the Judges, March 3, 1761." For most of us it was the first "good thing" we had ever heard about George III. After Evans v. Gore, appropriately footnoted with reference to the contrary views taken in Australia and South Africa, we turn to one of Professor and Mr. Justice Frankfurter's most abiding preoccupations, the nature of the judicial power and particularly the limitations implicit in "case or controversy" as developed from Hayburn's case,[65] through United States v. Ferreira Admr.,[66] Gordon v. United States,[67] and Muskrat v. United States.[68]

Probably the most controversial application of the principle appears in the declaratory judgment cases, beginning with Liberty Warehouse Co. v. Grannis[69] and culminating, for the time being at least, in Poe v. Ullman.[70] The casebook included, of course, Mr. Justice Brandeis' famous opinion in Willing v. Chicago Auditorium Association,[71] in which he said: "What the plaintiff seeks is simply a declaratory judgment. To grant that relief is beyond the power conferred upon the federal judiciary."[72] To most of us this seemed, and still seems, as one example where Homer nodded, particularly in suggesting, as Mr. Justice Stone's concurring opinion noted, that there was a constitutional obstacle to the exercise of such power. For Mr. Justice Frankfurter, however, this opinion, properly understood, was very likely only another example of Brandeisian prescience. To support this view, declaratory judgment must be read in the same sense as it was used by Mr. Justice Sanford in the Grannis case, the determination of a hypothetical rather than a real controversy; in short, an advisory opinion. Subsequent opinions, it is true, give the term a different meaning, limiting it to an additional procedural device available only within the conventional constitutional limits of case or controversy, and later, even more drastically, within the traditional limits of equity jurisdiction. This limited view was emphasized by the Justice in his own opinion in Colegrove v. Green,[73] when he said: ". . . the test for determining whether a federal court has authority to make a declaration such as is here asked is whether the controversy 'would be justiciable in this court if presented in a suit for injunction,'" quoting from Mr. Justice Stone in Nashville C & St. L Ry Co. v. Wallace,[74] and "The Declaratory Judgment

Act 'only provided a new form of procedure for the adjudication of rights in conformity' with 'established equitable principles;'" quoting from Mr. Justice Stone in Great Lakes Dredge & Dock Co. v. Huffman.[75]

With the possible exception of United Public Workers of America v. Mitchell,[76] the most crucial illustration of these principles in action appears in the Justice's own opinion in the Connecticut birth control case, Poe v. Ullman.[77] Speaking for himself and three other members of the Court, the Justice in effect justified dismissal of the suit on the ground that there was insufficient reason to believe that the plaintiffs were faced with a realistic threat of prosecution if they used contraceptives, or gave advice with respect to their use, in violation of the statute. This brought the Court back almost full circle to the Grannis case, where the plaintiffs had also alleged in general terms that they were threatened with various civil and criminal punishments and penalties for violation of the Act whose constitutionality they challenged, but where the Court found no semblance of any adverse litigation with the defendant, the Commonwealth Attorney. In Poe, as in Grannis, the plaintiffs gave no indication that they had violated, or planned to violate, the statute before a determination by the Court as to its validity; consequently there could be no threat of imminent prosecution. This was apparently what the Justice had in mind when he said: "The lack of immediacy of the threat described by these allegations might alone raise serious questions of non-justiciability of appellants' claims."[78] But the Justice did not rest on the broad ground that there could be no case or controversy unless the plaintiffs were willing to subject themselves to the risk of prosecution by violating the statute before a determination of its validity. Instead he relied upon an "undeviating policy of nullification by Connecticut of its anti-contraceptive laws throughout all the long years that they have been on the statute books," which he thought bespoke "more than prosecutorial paralysis."[79] It is somewhat ironic that, in thus choosing the narrower ground for decision, the Justice nevertheless exposed himself to criticism, as the dissenting opinions forcefully pointed out, by overstating the case for Connecticut's "undeviating policy of nullification." Connecticut had in fact indicated that a policy of obvious challenge to the law by openly operated birth control clinics would be sufficient to stimulate prosecution.[80] Thus the issue became whether there was sufficient adversity between the particular parties when measured against a policy of enforcement with respect to certain types of violation, and nullification with respect to others. Since the plaintiffs' proposed action clearly came within that class of violations which the state had apparently shown no disposition to prosecute, there was much justification for regarding the case as one of those "which disclosed a want of a truly adversary contest, of a collision of actively asserted and differing claims."[81]

Nevertheless, there was, as the dissenting opinions, particularly that of Mr. Justice Harlan, demonstrated, considerable to be said on the other side. This was not an obvious case of desuetude, involving a statute remaining on the books simply because it was forgotten and no one had bothered to repeal it. Nor was it one where the plaintiffs could have much hope of establishing an estoppel against the state if it did choose to prosecute, because of failure to prosecute others.[82] So, at least, the dissenters assumed and there is nothing in Justice Frankfurter's opinion to suggest the contrary. In one sense, at least, the policy of Connecticut did require a kind of obeisance to the law; namely, that it was not to be openly flouted. Whether a claim to such respect, as opposed to the claim of right to do candidly what one was allowed to do clandestinely, presented a sufficiently antagonistic assertion of rights to justify constitutional adjudication could not be resolved either by appeal to established general principles of case or controversy or by reliance upon prior decisions. That one as convinced as the Justice has been of the wisdom of avoiding constitutional adjudication whenever "intellectual honesty" permits should have found the case lacking in true adversity is not surprising, just as he should not be surprised if many who agree with him in principle doubt the soundness of the application in this particular instance.

This subdivision of our casebook also explored the practice of the advisory opinion, as distinguished from the declaratory judgment, in England, Canada, and Australia, including an editorial from the London *Times* warning against the dangers of using "Judges as Official Advisors," drew heavily upon the dissenting opinion of Mr. Justice Brandeis in International News Service v. Associated Press[83] and Pennsylvania v. West Virginia[84] for an exposition of those kinds of matters which should more wisely be left to legislative or administrative, rather than judicial, resolution, and finally closed with observations by Judge Kellogg, of the Permanent Court of International Justice, in the case of the Free Zones of Upper Savoy and the District of Gex (Second Phase),[85] on the importance for the Court of confining itself to the "determination of the legal rights of the Parties" and of avoiding "political questions" in passing upon which "there is no rule or principle of law, no norm of equity, justice or even of good conscience which the Court can apply." Thus the theme first introduced in Luther v. Borden,[86] under the rubric of executive power, is picked up again from the point of view of judicial power. Of course, it would now have to be further developed to include Coleman v. Miller,[87] Colgrove v. Green[88] and Baker v. Carr.[89]

Speaking before the decision in Baker v. Carr, at the Harvard conference celebrating the bicentennial of John Marshall, Mr. Justice Frankfurter adverted, almost in passing, to the doctrine of political questions, conscious perhaps that it would soon again be knocking at the threshold of the Court:

"It is not for me to find the common denominator of these judicial abstentions, or to give the contour and content of what questions are 'political,' in the sense of precluding judicial examination. But I do venture to believe that no judge charged with the duty of enforcing the Due Process Clauses of the Fifth and Fourteenth Amendments and the Equal Protection of the Laws Clause of the Fourteenth Amendment, can free himself from the disquietude that the line is often very thin between the cases in which the Court felt compelled to abstain from adjudication because of their 'political' nature, and the cases that so frequently arise in applying the concepts of 'liberty' and 'equality.' "[90]

One wonders whether the Justice was conscious that the thin line might soon be moved sharply to include under equal protection what had theretofore been regarded as "political." At any rate, what he so carefully eschewed at the Harvard Conference, the Justice resolutely attempted in his dissent in Baker, in support of his profound conviction that the Court had just suffered a "self-inflicted wound," comparable in its seriousness even to Dred Scott. The depth of the Justice's concern was manifested in his opening paragraph:

. . . Such a massive repudiation of the experience of our whole past in asserting destructively novel judicial power demands a detailed analysis of the role of this court in our constitutional scheme. Disregard of inherent limits in the effective exercise of the Court's "Judicial Power" not only presages the futility of judicial intervention in the essentially political conflict of forces by which the relation between population and representation has time out of mind been and now is determined. It may well impair the Court's position as the ultimate organ of "the supreme Law of the Land" in that vast range of legal problems, often strongly entangled in popular feeling, on which this Court must pronounce. The Court's authority—possessed of neither the purse nor the sword—ultimately rests on sustained public confidence in its moral sanction. Such feeling must be nourished by the Court's complete detachment, and by abstention from injecting itself into the clash of political forces in political settlements.[91]

Despite the firmness of his conviction that the validity and fairness of the apportionment of electoral power through the creation of electoral districts was not appropriate for judicial determination, the Justice has never pretended that the application of the label "political question" to such controversies was anything more than "a form of stating this conclusion." Apart from the immediately applicable precedents involving electoral districting, his search was for the "unifying considerations" which have underlain the classification of certain types of problems as political questions. Speaking of cases concerning war or foreign affairs, his explanation is essentially the same as that of Judge Kellogg in the Free Zones case: "A controlling factor in such cases is that, decision respecting these kinds of complex matters of policy being traditionally committed not to courts but to the political agencies of government for determination by criteria of political expediency, there exists no standard ascertainable by settled judicial experience or process by reference to which a political decision affecting the question at issue between the parties can be judged."[92] Insofar as the Justice relies upon authority for this proposition, he finds it in the opinion of Chief Justice Hughes, in which he did not join, in Coleman v. Miller, where the Chief Justice found the dominant consideration to be "the lack of satisfactory criteria for a judicial determination."[93] If we ask how we are to know what are satisfactory criteria for judicial determination, the answer must be, presumably, from the lessons of our experience.

There are other themes which play a supporting role in the analysis. The Justice refers, for example, to "The reluctance to interfere with matters of state government in the absence of an unquestionable and effectively enforceable mandate," and the "unwillingness to make courts arbiters of the broad issues of political organization historically committed to other institutions and for whose adjustment the judicial process is ill-adapted."[94] Apparently the Justice had in mind both the hazards of eventual enforcement in the event of legislative recalcitrance, and the difficulty of adequately assessing, through the judicial process, the competing claims of different interest groups.

This suggests still another strand of the Justice's argument, which appears in both the Colegrove and Baker opinions. He refers to it as "the policies underlying the requirement of 'standing'; that the litigant who would challenge official action must claim infringement of an interest particular and personal to himself, as distinguished from a cause of dissatisfaction with the general frame and functioning of government—a complaint that the political institutions are awry."[95] Apparently the Justice doubts the reality of the claim that the individual litigant has standing in his own right, not as representative of a group interest, but because of the "dilution" or "debasement" of his own vote. "Talk of 'debasement' or 'dilution' is circular talk. One cannot speak of 'debasement' or 'dilution' of the value of a vote until there is first defined a standard of reference as to what a vote should be worth."[96] One simple answer is that it should be worth as much as anyone else's: i.e., that all districts must be equal in population or elections must be held at large. Such an answer the Justice would characterize as a choice "among competing bases of representation—ultimately, really among competing theories of political philosophy."[97] Yet it is the only answer which can be regarded as directly responsive to the claim of debasement or dilution of the individual vote. Taken literally rather than figuratively, the claim can only mean that the mathematical likelihood that the individual's vote will be decisive in any election is reduced in inverse proportion to the size of the electorate. As far as I am aware, no plaintiff has yet been willing to stake his "standing" simply upon this indisputable principle of mathematical probabilities. But if this is indeed the claim, Mr. Justice Frankfurter's answer is made clear in the final sections of his opinion. As in Youngstown, the appeal is to history, to demonstrate that the claim is contrary to the whole course of the development of Anglo-American political institutions.

It is too early to say whether the Justice's opinion in Baker v. Carr will go down in history as the last great defense of a lost cause, somewhat like Mr. Justice Sutherland's dissent in Home Building & Loan Ass'n v. Blaisdell,[98] or as prophetic warning of the shoals ahead upon which the Court's ill-starred venture into the storm-tossed waters of electoral reform is bound to founder.[99] Indeed at present writing no one can tell just how far the Court will eventually be tempted to carry its dangerous voyage. Mr. Justice Brennan, writing for the Court, purported to decide only that "the complaint's allegations of a denial of equal protection present a justiciable cause of action upon which appellants are entitled to a trial and decision."[100] Mr. Justice Stewart, in his concurring opinion, objected to the broad interpretation of the decision implicit in some of the concurring and dissenting opinions and emphasized his understanding that the complainants had established only that they were entitled to a hearing on the merits of their claim that "Tennessee's system of apportionment is utterly arbitrary— without any possible justification in rationality."[101] Even if this should be the eventual limit which the Court places on the scope of its new doctrine, it would not thereby deflect the main thrust of the Justice's dissent; he would still insist that, in this area where the only test of rationality afforded is the ability of contending interest groups to compromise their differences, there are no "satisfactory criteria for a judicial determination." Nevertheless, such a limitation upon the scope of Baker v. Carr, implemented in the modest spirit which Mr. Justice Stewart's concurring opinion implies, may itself provide a viable compromise, in practical terms, between the sense of injustice and frustration which has stimulated the continued assault upon the principle of Colegrove and the Justice's resolute defense of that embattled fortress.[102]

## IV. IN CONCLUSION

Our casebook had still another subdivision curiously entitled Admixture of Powers, but I trust that I will be forgiven for passing over it lightly, just as the Justice was wont to skim lightly over a goodly half of the casebook in the last session of any course he taught. Suffice it to say that this section emphasized a little more explicitly what had already been implied throughout the three preceding sections, and what was especially emphasized in the Justice's concurring opinion in Youngstown—that the American doctrine of separation of powers is not to be applied in a spirit of cast-iron, inflexible categorization, but rather as guiding principle which permits of an innumerable and unpredictable variety of individual adjustments and combination of functions, so long as "we . . . keep in mind that the great end of the theory is, by dispersing in some measure the centers of authority, to prevent absolutism."[103] If there is any specific area of the general subject where the Justice might conceivably be accused of emphasizing the "thou shalt nots" at the expense of the permissiveness of the principle, it is obviously in the self-imposed limitations which he has been so thoroughly convinced the judiciary must scrupulously observe. As the Harvard lecture makes clear, this emphasis is in no small sense related to the Justice's concern that the distinctive power of constitutional adjudication should not become overextended to the point of a fatal weakness. Whether or not this concern has occasionally been carried beyond the limits of a healthy prudence the Justice would doubtless cheerfully leave to his favorite arbiter, history, to decide.

# Mr. Justice Frankfurter and the Reading of Statutes

## Henry J. Friendly*

### I.

To quarry from Mr. Justice Frankfurter's wisdom on the reading of statutes is, if we may borrow his own metaphor, "not to pick plums from a pudding but to pull threads from a pattern."[1] The pattern has been woven over a lifetime of teaching and judging; and his own credo, the Cardozo lecture, "Some Reflec-

---

* Judge Friendly studied under Professor Frankfurter at the Harvard Law School, 1924–27, and was nominated by him to be law clerk to Mr. Justice Brandeis at the October Term, 1927. He was appointed to the United States Court of Appeals for the Second Circuit in 1959.

Frank I. Goodman, Harvard, LL.B. 1959, and Stephen R. Barnett, Harvard, LL.B. 1962, have made helpful suggestions concerning this paper.

tions on the Reading of Statutes,"[2] is a rich and enduring tapestry. To be sure, that lecture purported to be in large measure a distillation from the views on statutory construction entertained by three of his illustrious predecessors—Holmes, Brandeis, and Cardozo. But the lecture amply bears out Professor Freund's perceptive remark, "It is frequently true of memorial addresses that they provide a truer insight into the mind of the speaker than into the mind of the deceased"[3]; indeed, many passages only paraphrase opinions of the Justice's first decade.

Why then should an epigone attempt to annotate what the hero himself has written? Why try to reconstruct the recipe by sampling the sauce when we have it in Brillat-Savarin's own hand? And why do again what the editor of this volume has already done so well?[4] Yet it would be an inexcusable gap if this collection were to contain nothing on such a central theme of the Justice's life and works; and we can now view his "Reflections" of 1947 in their own reflection—the scores of opinions in which the teacher indelibly impressed his teachings on the United States Reports through nearly a quarter century. Hence I have endeavored to scan his opinions on statutory construction in Volumes 306-369 and to set down some thoughts gathered in the process. I use the word "scan" deliberately, since the time that could be eked out from other tasks has not permitted even a "reading" of those opinions *Frankfurterweise*—much less a thorough study of them, which ought also to have embraced his votes in cases where he did not write. But it is all I have been able to do, and the process, in one of Mr. Justice Brandeis' favorite terms, has been "instructive."[5] If these notes, partial as they necessarily are, should convey a small portion of what I have learned, and should serve as a prolegomenon to the work in depth that more competent hands will someday perform, they will have accomplished their purpose.

The centricity of statutory construction to the work of a

federal judge is, as I have indicated elsewhere,[6] an inevitable result of the nature of federal "law." Frankfurter came to the Supreme Court when, on the one hand, the power of federal judges to create general common law had just been curtailed by Erie R. Co. v. Tompkins[7] and, on the other, the flood of New Deal legislation was starting to spill over the dam for interpretation—when, in his words, "cases not resting on statutes are reduced almost to zero."[8] No judge before him, including the three greats of his Cardozo lecture, arrived at the task of statutory construction so well prepared. His whole legal life had been lived with statutes. He had come to the bar in the Roosevelt I era of new federal legislation, had gone on to Washington with Stimson, had continued there through the most fruitful legislative part of the Wilson administration, had pioneered the teaching at the Harvard Law School of such statutory subjects as federal jurisdiction, administrative law, and federal regulation of business, and had been the counselor and friend of Roosevelt II in the most productive period of the New Deal. It was simple truth to describe himself as "one for whom the statutes at large constitute his staple reading."[9] When, as a Justice, he was obliged to interpret the Interstate Commerce Act, this was no craggy mass looming into view for the first time, but rather a friendly mountain whose slopes he had trod, with understanding and delight, for many a year.[10]

Can anyone imagine Holmes or Cardozo saying that the statutes at large had constituted his staple reading? Holmes would have rejected such a diet as speedily as he did Brandeis' suggestion that he devote a summer to reading reports on the Massachusetts textile industries.[11] True, when Holmes had to deal with statutes, he displayed the genius that he did in everything, and some of his aphorisms, of which "A word is not a crystal, transparent and unchanged, it is the skin of a living thought"[12] must serve for the present as a solitary example, will live as long as our law. But Holmes's enduring significance will be as the author of *The Common Law*, of path-breaking legal essays, and of great constitutional opinions, not as a construer of statutes. Cardozo will be known to the generations as a common law judge; for him, as Frankfurter owned, "statutory construction was an acquired taste," although in his too brief years in Washington "he came to realize that problems of statutory construction had their own exciting subtleties and gave ample employment to philosophic and literary talents,"[13] and the opinions he has left us show what might have been. Brandeis had Frankfurter's relish for statutes, but he was their valiant defender against constitutional attack and niggling construction, rather than their sensitive interpreter. He was prone to "invoke the additional weight of some 'rule' of construction," as Frankfurter acknowledges,[14] and, with his magnificent freedom from doubt, to ride the horse of the moment a bit too hard.[15] If I were obliged to pick a rival contender, it would be none of these three Justices but rather Judge Learned Hand. No one has written of the task of statutory interpretation with deeper perception,[16] and Hand, in his fifty-two years on the federal bench, extending from Taft to the New Frontier, had many a statute to construe. But Hand did not have Frankfurter's love for legislation; he took statutes as a rather painful part of his job—leaving in his mind, as he somewhat exaggeratedly said, in speaking of the Internal Revenue Code, "only a confused sense of some vitally important, but successfully concealed, purport, which it is my duty to extract, but which is within my power, if at all, only after the most inordinate expenditure of time."[17] In Frankfurter there is a happy union of Brandeis' appreciation and knowledge of statutes and Hand's insight into the interpretive task.

## II.

Anyone who has given serious thought to the interpretation of statutes must be conscious of a Faustian conflict between adherence to the words and search for the will—a search, moreover, that often is not for the will that was but the will that would have been. Many judges have stopped with the words, or at least have professed to do so. Others have hurdled the words and proceeded directly to the purpose, as revealed by legislative history or some private process of divination. Indeed, the same judges—even very great ones—give differing emphasis at different times to the two souls that dwell within their breasts. Thus Holmes, whom Frankfurter quoted as saying of legislators, "I don't care what their intention was. I only want to know what the words mean,"[18] wrote also that "the general purpose is a more important aid to the meaning than any rule which grammar or formal logic may lay down,"[19] and even that "the meaning of a sentence is to be felt rather than to be proved."[20] Judge Hand, whose definition of interpretation as "the art of proliferating a purpose"[21] Frankfurter feared "might justify interpretations by judicial libertines, not merely judicial libertarians,"[22] had such fears himself; he warned the judge to beware of pushing too hard in an effort "to find out what the government would have intended which it did not say," since by doing so "he will usurp the office of government, even though in a small way he must do so in order to execute its real commands at all."[23] Frankfurter has his own formulation of the basic problem: "the troublesome phase of construction is the determination of the extent to which extraneous documentation and external circumstances may be allowed to infiltrate the text on the theory that they were part of it, written in ink discernible to the judicial eye."[24]

Although this puts the question, the Justice would readily agree that it yields no answers. It leaves open "the extent" to which non-textual factors "may be allowed to infiltrate"; some judicial eyes will be keener to discern non-textual significances than others; and the same eye, no matter how hard its owner may strive for objectivity, is likely to be a bit keener when it does not care overmuch for what it sees in the text. But the formulation raises a more basic issue. Why should there be a limitation on "the extent" to which non-textual matters may be considered?

I take it that the Justice's defense of this concept of the text as the center of a magnetic field from which the judge must not stray too far[25] would run along three main lines. One is his view that the "judge's role should be limited, to protect against willful judges who lack humility and self-restraint,"[26] with its corollary —the fear of popular reaction against undue indulgence in law-making by judges of the sort described.[27] A second, not so loudly articulated in his opinions but surely there, is the need that citizens should be able to rely on what they see in the statute book—a consideration whose force, at least in civil matters, will vary with the degree to which the statute *sub judice* may have induced planning. Third, there is the doubt how far non-textual bases can be relied on as showing a true consensus of the lawmakers.[28] Turning to the opinions without further ado, let us begin with Frankfurter's emphasis on the text and then consider how far and under what circumstances he has allowed "extraneous documentation and external circumstances . . . to infiltrate" it.

### III.

It is significant that the Justice took as the title of his Cardozo lecture, not the "Construction" or the "Interpretation" of statutes, but the "Reading" of statutes. The *double entendre* was surely not accidental. If we would arrive at the meaning of a statute, we must first read it—a homely truth which ought to be self-evident but which, like so many of its kind, is too often honored in the breach, however rewarding in the observance. "Though we may not end with the words in construing a disputed statute," he said in his lecture,[29] paraphrasing one of his opinions,[30] "one certainly begins there." It was to enforce this "hoary platitude" that, as a teacher, he had developed his threefold imperative to law students: (1) Read the statute; (2) read the statute; (3) read the statute! The lesson was of crucial importance at the Harvard Law School in the 1920s when his courses were the few where statutes were not viewed, in his later phrase, "as wilful and arbitrary interference with the harmony of the common law and with its rational unfolding by judges"[31]—best kept veiled from the aspirant. Yet, although that attitude has passed, the lesson remains vital. Few judges, I suspect, could honestly deny how often reading even the most familiar statute—*really* reading it, as Frankfurter used to emphasize—has disclosed a meaning never discerned when the mind had been directed, not to what the legislature had said, but to what the judge recalled it as having said or to what he would have said in its place.

There are times when adherence to this simple rule can be not only the first step in the interpretive process but the last. However, this will not usually be so. "Legislation by even the most competent hands . . . is subject to the frailties of the imagination. Concentration on the basic aims of a reform . . . inevitably overlooks lacunae and ambiguities which the future reveals and which the future must correct."[32] Hence the careful reading of the statute generally is only the lustration of the judge's mind, like the cleansing of the surgeon's hands before the tissues are laid bare.

Although presumably no one would quarrel with the admonition to begin by reading the statute, the Justice has occasionally used sterner tones, more subject to debate. "An elaborate process of implications should not be invented to escape the plain meaning" of a statute which provided for judicial review in some instances but not in that *sub judice*.[33] In construing a provision of the Railway Labor Act for court review of money awards, "We are pointed to no aids to construction that should withhold us from giving the familiar term 'money award' any other than its ordinary meaning as something that awards money"—rather than as including one that denies it.[34] In construing "a definite procedural provision" in the Emergency Price Control Act, a court will "do well to stick close to the text and not import argumentative qualifications from broad, unexpressed claims of policy."[35] Even on a difficult question of the meaning of the loss of status provision in Section 8(d) of the National Labor Relations Act, "While literalness of construction does not conclude ascertainment of a statute's meaning"—and surely did not in the Justice's opinion—"it certainly is the beginning."[36]

Before turning to what may seem another side of the Frankfurter reading coin, it is well to set down some of the Justice's hints on how to read. "Ordinary words should be read with their common, everyday meaning when they serve as directions for ordinary people," as, for example, in the Selective Service Act.[37] A different principle applies to technical expressions: "Tax language normally has an enclosed meaning or has legitimately acquired such by the authority of those specially skilled in its application."[38] Words that have a well-defined meaning in general speech may have a different sense in a particular context: "The recognized practices of an industry"—here motor carriage—"give life to the dead words of a statute dealing with it."[39] Again, "The Taft-Hartley Act is not an abstract document to be construed with only the aid of a standard dictionary." Although the "ordinary English words" that it uses, such as "national or international labor organization," may carry "to the ordinary ear . . . a meaning different from that which they carry in the domain of industrial relations," the courts are bound to apply the latter.[40]

Another important reading aid is to remember the kind of statute we are reading. At one end of the spectrum are "enactments such as the Sherman Law that embody a felt rather than defined purpose and necessarily look to the future for the unfolding of their content, making of their judicial application an evolutionary process nourished by relevant changing circumstances,"[41] or statutes empowering an agency to regulate under broadly defined criteria.[42] Statutes of this sort are to be read somewhat as the Constitution itself—they are open rather than closed-ended, although even here expansion is limited "to the extent that the words with which [the] purpose is conveyed fairly bear such expansion."[43] At the opposite extreme is a statute which, in effect, was a century-old land grant from the government to a railroad; such "a specific grant . . . does not gain meaning from time. Its scope today is what it was in 1862, and the judicial task is to ascertain what content was conveyed by that section in 1862."[44] Another variant is the strongly worded prohibitory enactment, qualifying language or exceptions in which must not be read so broadly as to stultify the declared end.[45] One whose knowledge of Frankfurter's approach to statutory interpretation was limited to the opinions reviewed up to this point might be surprised to learn that no judge in history has attacked the "plain meaning" doctrine more strongly. In his early years on the Court, when still somewhat suspect by the profession, he wrote, in a passage much criticized at the time: "The notion that because the words of a statute are plain, its meaning is also plain, is merely pernicious oversimplification."[46] Years later there was scarcely a ripple when he returned to the charge, saying: "The notion that the plain meaning of the words of a statute defines the meaning of the statute reminds one of T. H. Huxley's gay observation that at times 'a theory survives long after its brains are knocked out.' "[47] He has inveighed against "the tyranny of literalness,"[48] by yielding to which "the Court creates its own verbal prison,"[49] as when it read the provision in 28 U.S.C. Section 1404(a) restricting transfer to a district in which the action "might have been brought" so as to preclude transfer at the instance of defendants to a district as to which, although they could have had a suit dismissed for lack of jurisdiction and improper venue, they now submitted. Reminding that "It is true also of Acts of Congress that 'The letter killeth,' " he has adjured against reading legislation in "a decimating spirit unless the letter of Congress is inexorable. . . . Its laws are not to be read as though every *i* has to be dotted and every *t* crossed."[50] We must not construe the grant of law and equity jurisdiction in cases arising under the federal Constitution, laws, or treaties in the Judiciary Act of 1875 as "inert language, lifeless words detached from the interpretive setting of history, legal lore, and due regard for the interests of our federal system"; to read that grant so as to confer jurisdiction in maritime cases on the "law side" would be using words as "playthings."[51]

While this juxtaposition of some phrases emphasizing the text and others attacking literalism creates a verbal contradiction, it is verbal only; to such extent as reconciliation is needed, history will supply it. Although the "plain meaning" rule never scaled such dizzy heights in this country as in England,[52] it nevertheless needed to be put in its place. Olympian pronouncements, like Mr. Justice Day's famous one that "the language is plain and admits of no more than one meaning,"[53] often represented only a subjective and arbitrary view of the opinion-writer. It was thus necessary that a great judge should say, as Mr. Justice Frankfurter did, "Generalities regarding the effect to be given to the 'clear meaning' of a statute do not make the meaning of a particular statute 'clear.' "[54] The potential for solipsistic decision inherent in the "plain meaning" rule was enhanced by the corollary which sealed off all other aids to construction when a "plain meaning" was thought to exist—in such cases, Mr. Justice Day pontificated, "the duty of interpretation does not arise and the rules which are to aid doubtful meanings need no discussion."[55] It was thus necessary that a great judge should remind that "Anything that is written may present a problem of meaning," and that judges always have the task of resolving the "contest between probabilities of meaning" save when "only literary perversity or jaundiced partisanship can sponsor a particular rendering."[56] Yet, as is usual in law, reaction went too far; the words of a statute often became only a springboard for judicial improvisation. Illogical though it was to hold that a "plain meaning" shut off access to the very materials that might show it not to have been plain at all, it was equally wrong to deny the natural meaning of language its proper primacy; like Cardozo's "Method of Philosophy," it "is the heir presumptive. A pretender to the title will have to fight his way."[57] Moreover, in Frankfurter's view, although courts may sanction the yielding of much ground to the pretender, they must never permit the words wholly to succumb; the outcome of the battle must always be in some degree consistent with the language—save in the rare case when the words are read out "to avoid patent nonsense or internal contradiction."[58] Hence, as he has told us, "[T]he 'policy' of a statute should be drawn out of its terms, as nourished by their proper environment, and not, like nitrogen, out of the air."[59] And so it is that we constantly find him calling us back to the text—even talking of "plain meaning," although never in the watertight compartment sense of fifty years ago, and sometimes resting primarily on that basis a decision amply supportable on other grounds.[60]

## IV.

The first step which the Justice would take after a thorough reading of the governing words would cause little flurry even in the dovecotes of Westminster. No one on either side of the Atlantic would argue against Lord Blackburn's position "that we are to take the whole statute together,"[61] or against Cardozo's admonition that "the meaning of a statute is to be looked for, not in any single section, but in all the parts together...."[62] In Frankfurter's phrasing, a court is bound "to find that interpretation which can most fairly be said to be embedded in the statute, in the sense of being most harmonious with its scheme and with the general purposes that Congress manifested"[63]; its duty "is to give coherence to what Congress has done within the bounds imposed by a fair reading of legislation."[64] A judge may go further and seek to derive meaning "not from specific language but by fashioning a mosaic of significance out of the innuendoes of disjointed bits of a statute"; but he must realize that "this is subtle business, calling for great wariness lest what professes to be mere rendering becomes creation and attempted interpretation of legislation becomes legislation itself."[65] For Frankfurter there is no presumption that study of the entire scheme of the statute will lead to a reading more expansive than would be suggested by the words immediately applicable; the result may be quite the contrary. As he wrote in his concurring opinion in the steel seizure case, "It is one thing to draw an intention of Congress from general language and to say that Congress would have explicitly written what is inferred, where Congress has not addressed itself to a specific situation. It is quite impossible, however, when Congress did specifically address itself to a problem . . . to find secreted in the interstices of legislation the very grant of power which Congress consciously withheld."[66]

Frankfurter has rarely relied on canons of construction

which, he has followed Holmes in emphasizing, "are not in any true sense rules of law" and have worth only to the extent that they are "generalizations of experience."[67] Thus, *expressio unius* has gotten short shrift from him; too often that rule would "shrivel a versatile principle to an illustrative application."[68] In addition to the occasional, and partial, resort to the "plain meaning" rule already noted, there seem to be only two "canons" of which he has made significant use—the "rule of lenity" as to penal statutes, and the body of doctrines with respect to the effect of the Constitution on statutory construction.

The Justice is "no friend of . . . artificially restrictive interpretations" of criminal statutes, a practice developed by judges in the distant past "to soften the undue rigors of the criminal law."[69] In declining to dismiss a conspiracy indictment of husband and wife because of the supposed medieval view that "they are but one Person in law and are presumed to have but one Will,"[70] he emphasized the need to "free our minds from the notion that criminal statutes must be construed by some artificial and conventional rule."[71] On the other hand he reminds that: "There are surely deep considerations of policy why the scope of criminal condemnation should not be extended by a strained reading."[72] Thus stated, the principle scarcely advances matters; what *are* the statutes that should "be extended by a strained reading"? In Bell v. United States declaring that it is "a presupposition of our law to resolve doubts in the enforcement of a penal code against the imposition of a harsher punishment,"[73] he refused to countenance a two-count indictment under the Mann Act for transporting two women for an immoral purpose at the same time; and he would have applied the same "presupposition" to the definition of a crime, the stealing of an automobile under the Dyer Act.[74] His adherence to the "rule of lenity" does not rest on any naïve assumption "that offenders against the law carefully read the penal code before they embark on crime"[75]; he does not articulate what it does rest on—presumably the instinctive distaste against men languishing in prison unless the lawmaker has clearly said they should.

A still later opinion, Callanan v. United States,[76] holding that extortion and conspiracy to extort are separate offenses under the Hobbs Act, may be thought to indicate some disenchantment with the rule. There he tells us, in language of the mechanical sort he generally eschews, that the rule of lenity, "as is true of any guide to statutory construction, only serves as an aid for resolving an ambiguity; it is not to be used to beget one"—a feat of procreation which he thought the dissenting Justices were unable to accomplish without the rule's help. "The rule," he says, "comes into operation at the end of the process of construing what Congress has expressed, not at the beginning as an overriding consideration of being lenient to wrongdoers."[77] One might question the utility of the rule if there are such dubieties about its exits and its entrances; the problem of deciding whether the rule may legitimately be used becomes as hard as the issue itself. Three Justices saw no ambiguity in *Bell* where Frankfurter did; four were able to see one in *Callanan* where he could not.[78] To me the rule has utility whenever the interpretation it favors is fairly admissible[79]; very likely that is all the Justice meant by his step-by-step *Callanan* formula. Whether the considerations marshaled by the dissenters sufficed to bring their construction of the Hobbs Act into that range, as against the established view as to "The distinctiveness between a substantive offense and a conspiracy to commit" it,[80] was indeed questionable.

I have referred to the "body of doctrines" relating to the effect of the Constitution on the construction of statutes, since there are several principles, sometimes not sufficiently distinguished. One is that the Constitution is itself a datum in the interpretation of a statute; "construction should go in the direction of constitutional policy"—in that case "the constitutional concern for trial in the vicinage"—"even though not commanded by it."[81] A second principle of unquestionable validity is that if one permissible reading will be constitutional and another will not be, the former must be chosen, since courts should not assume the legislature would have intended to act vainly. However, there is a rather apparent slide when the Justice, dissenting from the Court's holding that a suit under Section 301 of the Taft-Hartley Act may be brought in a federal court as one arising under a law of the United States, goes from one sentence saying, "Legislation must, if possible, be given a meaning that will enable it to survive," to another declaring, "This rule of constitutional adjudication is normally invoked to narrow what would otherwise be the natural but constitutionally dubious scope of the language."[82] He has passed from a rule of construing to avoid unconstitutionality to another designed to avoid doubts as to constitutionality. It does not seem in any way obvious, as a matter of interpretation, that the legislature would prefer a narrow construction which does not raise constitutional doubts to a broader one which does raise them. For there is always the chance, usually a good one, that the doubts will be settled favorably, and if they are not, the conceded rule of construing to avoid unconstitutionality will come into operation and save the day. People in such a heads-I-win, tails-you-lose position do not readily sacrifice it; the idea that Congress must use strong language to show it wanted the Supreme Court even to consider the constitutional question—very likely just what Congress thinks the Justices are paid to do—seems rather fanciful. Probably because of such considerations Frankfurter has been careful to refer to the rule, not as one of statutory interpretation, but as one of "constitutional adjudication"[83]—a principle coming in from outside and dictating an interpretation which otherwise might not be the most accurate estimate of the legislature's meaning. Yet, even as thus stated, the principle has its difficulties; in two rather recent dissents, the Justice declined to take shelter in it,[84] declaring in the later case that "Respect for the doctrine demands and only permits that we extract an interpretation which shies off constitutional controversy, *provided* such interpretation is consonant with a fair reading of a statute."

Although questioning the doctrine of construction to avoid constitutional doubts[85] is rather like challenging Holy Writ, the rule has always seemed to me to have almost as many dangers as advantages. For one thing, it is one of those rules that courts apply when they want and conveniently forget when they don't —some, perhaps, would consider that to be a virtue. Although a true rule of law ought to be assertable regardless of the vote in a particular case, it seems somewhat ludicrous to find this principle invoked by a minority, as in *Lincoln Mills*, when we know the doubts have been resolved and the constitutional story is going to have a happy ending. Some considerations advanced in its favor, such as the awesome consequences of "a decree of unconstitutionality,"[86] overlook that if the Court finds the more likely construction to be unconstitutional, another means of rescue—the principle of construing to avoid unconstitutionality —will be at hand. The strongest basis for the rule is thus that the Supreme Court ought not to indulge in what, if adverse, is likely to be only a constitutional advisory opinion. While there is force in this,[87] the rule of "construing" to avoid constitutional doubts should, in my view, be confined to cases where the interpretation that avoids the doubt is well within the range of permissible choice apart from the "rule," and even then it should be used to prefer a less likely reading only when the doubt is exceedingly real. Otherwise this rule, whether it be denominated one of statutory interpretation or, more accurately, of constitutional adjudication—still more accurately, of constitutional non-adjudication—is likely to become one of evisceration and tergiversation.[88]

## V.

We have now read the words directly applicable in the context of the statute as a whole. We have—or have not—applied the few canons of construction whose authenticity Frankfurter will admit. But the great problem—the "extent to which extraneous documentation and external circumstances may be allowed to infiltrate the text"—is still before us. As he is fond of emphasizing, we must not be content with the legislature's words but must seek its purpose. "Legislative words are not inert, and derive vitality from the obvious purposes at which they are aimed. . . ."[89] Statutes . . . are not inert exercises in literary composition. They are instruments of government. . . ."[90] But no matter how felicitously the Justice puts the point, and no one has ever put it better,[91] this again states the goal but does not tell us how to reach it. Perplexities abound—where do we find the purpose; what if we cannot find it; what if we find several conflicting ones; what will satisfy the requirement that there be at least "implicit residues or . . . hints of purpose" in the statutory language?[92] In short, are there any principles in this business of interpretation, or is the process purely emotive and intuitive[93] although draped with verbal trappings which conceal rather than reveal what truly occurs in the judge's mind?

No one who has been faced with the task of interpretation can honestly deny that intuition plays a part. This is implicit in Holmes's saying that "the meaning of a sentence is to be felt rather than to be proved,"[94] and is made explicit in Judge Learned Hand's statement, "At times one is more likely to reach the truth by an unanalyzed and intuitive conclusion from the text as a whole, than by following, step by step, the accredited guides."[95] When the oracles have been consulted but are silent or in conflict, judgment must make the ultimate determination, and the judge's trained intuition plays a part in formulating that judgment. But the Frankfurter opinions eloquently prove what a world of difference there is between arriving at an interpretation by pursuing the search for purpose carefully and without *parti pris*, even though the data are incommensurable and the result is rarely susceptible of absolute demonstration, and making a wholly intuitive determination incapable of rational explication. "In matters of statutory construction also it makes a great deal of difference whether you start with an answer or with a problem."[96]

Professor Frankfurter was fond of preaching from the resolutions in *Heydon's* case[97]; Mr. Justice Frankfurter has been no less so.[98] He tells us, in language that would have found ready acceptance from the barons of Elizabeth I although avowedly not from the law lords of Elizabeth II, that "The starting point for determining legislative purpose is plainly an appreciation of the 'mischief' that Congress was seeking to alleviate."[99] The statute must be given its place in history. Words, Frankfurter wrote, in sentences that Maitland would have cherished, "must be read with the gloss of the experience of those who framed them"[100]; "words acquire scope and function from the history of events which they summarize."[101] And, more extensively, "The meaning of . . . a statute cannot be gained by confining inquiry within its four corners. Only the historic process of which such legislation is an incomplete fragment—that to which it gave rise as well as that which gave rise to it—can yield its true meaning."[102] This last adds a new dimension; we must consult not only what went before but what came after—the statute must be read as part of a continuum.[103]

It would be a gross understatement to say that Justice Frankfurter would have been a great historian. He has been one—not only in his book, *The Business of the Supreme Court*, and in many law review articles, but in the opinions themselves. His knowledge of history, especially of American history, is deep and broad; some of his opinions on the construction of statutes contain historical essays in miniature.[104] Only a few examples of his fruitful use of history as an aid to the interpretation of statutes can be given here. Congress' continued and considered denial of compulsory merger powers to the Interstate Commerce Commission with respect to solvent railroads forbade a construction "that such was the *sub silentio* effect of §77 [of the Bankruptcy Act], an emergency statute hurriedly enacted with scarcely any debate."[105] The overtime provisions of the Fair Labor Standards Act must be read in the light of "the facts of industrial life" on the waterfront of New York Harbor where longshoremen work for different employers and have made satisfactory agreements to handle the problem; to do otherwise, as the majority did, is to treat the words of the Act "as though they were parts of a cross-word puzzle."[106] Section 8(b)(4) of the Taft-Hartley Act must be given an interpretation consistent with the purpose of Congress, disclosed by the relevant history, not to seek an end of all secondary boycotts but only of the most dangerous.[107] When provisions of the Railway Labor Act are claimed to forbid the use of union dues for political activities, courts must look to "the background and presupposition of what is loosely called political activity of American trade unions in general and railroad unions in particular."[108] The long absence of belief that the general grant of federal question jurisdiction in 1875 permitted maritime suits to be tried on the "law side" renders suspect "the claim of a sudden discovery of a hidden latent meaning in an old technical phrase. . . . Our legal history does not . . . offer a single archeological discovery of new, revolutionary meaning in reading an old judiciary enactment. The presumption is powerful that such a far-reaching, dislocating construction . . . was not uncovered by judges, lawyers or scholars for seventy-five years because it is not there."[109] Historical considerations are of special force as to an amending statute. "An amendment is not to be read in isolation but as an organic part of the statute it affects"; the legislators "did not inadvertently add a colonial wing to a gothic cathedral."[110]

The Justice has long stressed the use not only of history in this general sense but of legislative history. American law students of the 1960s may be surprised that this was ever a subject of debate. Yet it was the occasion of vigorous academic controversy three decades ago,[111] and a partial negative position was later to find a persuasive spokesman in Mr. Justice Jackson,[112] whose arguments that the congressmen who pass a bill and the President who approves it cannot realistically be charged with knowledge of reports they have never seen and debates they have never heard, and that citizens and their lawyers ought be able to rely on what can be found in the statute book, should at least warn against the kind of worship of legislative materials which leads to looking at them even before the text is carefully reviewed. But it is equally unrealistic to suppose that all the legislators and the Chief Executive have made a meticulous study of the text of such complex measures as the Internal Revenue Code or the Immigration and Nationality Act; very likely most of them knew only of the general purpose, relied for the details on members who sat on the committees particularly concerned, and were quite willing to adopt the latters' will on subordinate points as their own.[113] Hence, if an intent clearly expressed in committee reports is within the permissible limits of the language and no construction manifestly more reasonable suggests itself, a court does pretty well to read the statute to mean what the few legislators having the greatest concern with it said it meant to them.[114]

Frankfurter has found aid to statutory construction in committee reports,[115] in conference reports,[116] in statements of congressional sponsors,[117] and in the action of one chamber in rejecting a provision inserted by the other.[118] Indeed, he is grieved when Congress fails to furnish courts with enough legislative history "to enable them to enforce its true will."[119] But he is not one to engage in "safaris into legislative documents that succeed only in flushing a phrase here and a sentence there whose connection with the will of Congress is questionable at best."[120] He protested against the use of an exhibit showing the understanding of general counsel for an agency sponsoring legislation—"to attribute to Congress familiarity with, let alone acceptance of" a sentence of a 60,000-word memorandum at a hearing before one house is "to defy the actualities of the legislative process"; by regarding such material as pertinent, "hitherto unsuspected opportunities for assuring desired glosses upon innocent-looking legislation would . . . be afforded."[121] Even the statements of congressional sponsors are not always reliable guides:

> To allow inexplicit remarks in the give-and-take of debate to contradict the very terms of legislation and the history behind it is to put out the controlling light on meaning shed by the explicit provisions of an Act in its setting.[122]

The excursion into legislative history is not inevitably rewarding; when the material unearthed is "sufficiently ambiguous . . . to invite mutually destructive dialectic, but not strong enough either to strengthen or weaken the force of what Congress has enacted,"[123] the courts should disregard it.

Although it is not too difficult to justify a court's drawing from appropriate legislative materials a reading that would be a bit dubious "if one had only the words . . . to go on,"[124] it is far more debatable whether such materials can justify a construction that would otherwise seem downright impossible. The Justice crossed that divide in Commissioner v. Acker.[125] Section 294 (d)(1)(A) of the Internal Revenue Code of 1939 as amended in 1943 provided that, if a taxpayer failed to make and file a declaration of his estimated tax, there should be added to the tax 5% of each installment due and unpaid, plus 1% of such unpaid installment for each month except the first, but not to exceed 10% of such unpaid installments; Section 294(d)(2) provided that, in the case of a taxpayer who had filed a return substantially underestimating the tax, there should be a different penalty—either the underestimate below the permitted tolerance or 6% of the excess of the tax over the estimated tax, whichever was less. Acker filed no estimate, thereby admittedly attracting the penalty of Section 294(d)(1)(A). The Commissioner sought also to collect the penalty for underestimate, under the purported authority of a regulation that "In the event of a failure to file the required declaration, the amount of the estimated tax for the purposes of [Section 294(d)(2)] is zero." The majority refused to sustain this, saying that the regulation was "no more than an attempted addition to the statute of something which is not there."[126] Frankfurter thought the opposite on the basis of a clear statement in the Senate and Conference Reports on a prior act, which in effect would have authorized the regulation; he conceded that

> No doubt to find failure to file a declaration of estimated income to be a "substantial underestimate" would be to attribute to Congress a most unlikely meaning for that phrase in §294 (d) (2) *simpliciter*.[127]

I should say rather that it would be a wholly unnatural and impossible meaning, *simpliciter* or any other way. Here, as it seems to me, the Justice went beyond his precept that "While courts are no longer confined to the language, they are still confined by it," even with the qualification that it is permissible to depart radically from the words if "no doubt can be left that the legislature has in fact used a private code, so that what appears to be violence to language is merely respect to special usage."[128] The legislative reports here were no "private code," such as Mr. Justice Holmes meant when he said that "If Congress has been accustomed to use a certain phrase with a more limited meaning than might be attributed to it by common practice, it would be arbitrary to refuse to consider that fact when we come to interpret a statute"[129]; there was no evidence of a general usage by Congress or even by the Bureau of Internal Revenue that filing no return was equivalent to filing a return showing a zero.[130] Here Congress said one thing in the statute and another in the Senate and Conference Reports; if the search is for what Congress meant by what it said, rather than for what it meant *simpliciter*, the *Acker* majority was right.[131]

VI.

The Justice's most original contribution to the interpretation of statutes has lain exactly where one would expect from a judge "for whom the statutes at large constitute his staple reading."[132] When a particular Act came before him for construction, he saw it, not in isolation, but as a part of the historic unfolding of federal statute law—an unfolding with which he was intimately familiar and in which, for two decades prior to assuming judicial office, he had played no unimportant part. Thus nothing could have been more natural than for him to have become the most significant exponent of the thesis that each statute must be read in the light of the policy expressed in others. "Statutes, even as decisions, are not to be deemed self-enclosed instances; they are to be regarded as starting points of reasoning, as means for securing coherence and for effectuating purpose."[133]

The Justice lost no time in planting this thought in the United

States Reports. He did it in one of his first opinions, Keifer & Keifer v. R.F.C.,[134] delivered on February 27, 1939, just a month after his induction. Writing for a unanimous Court, he denied sovereign immunity to the Regional Agricultural Credit Corporation, a subsidiary of the Reconstruction Finance Corporation, although the statute providing for its creation had made no provision to that end as a great variety of similar statutes had done. He summed up the guiding principle in words now familiar but still meriting quotation:

> The Congressional will must be divined, and by a process of interpretation which, in effect, is the ascertainment of policy immanent not merely in the single statute . . . but in a series of statutes utilizing corporations for governmental purposes and drawing significance from dominant contemporaneous opinion regarding the immunity of governmental agencies from suit. . . . To give Regional an immunity denied to more than two score corporations, each designed for a purpose of government not relevantly different . . . is to impute to Congress a desire for incoherence in a body of affiliated enactments and for drastic legal differentiation where policy justifies none. A fair judgment of the statute in its entire setting relieves us from making such an imputation of caprice.[135]

There has been little disagreement with *Keifer & Keifer.* There was every basis for the inference that Congress, having declared its will so often, even as to Regional's parent, would expect the courts to see what it was "driving at"[136] without the need of constant repetition, and almost no sensible basis for the contrary inference. But no such concord prevails as to the Justice's next and much bolder venture of this sort, United States v. Hutcheson,[137] holding that the scope of the Sherman Act in making certain types of conduct criminal must be determined not only in the light of Sections 6 and 20 of the Clayton Act, which were applicable by their terms but had become largely ineffective as a result of their construction in Duplex Co. v. Deering,[138] but also in the light of the Norris-LaGuardia Act, which gave no indication on its face that it was intended to do more than deprive federal courts of "jurisdiction" to grant injunctions in labor disputes. "It would be strange indeed," said the Justice for a majority of six:[139]

> . . . that although neither the Government nor Anheuser-Busch [the employer] could have sought an injunction against the acts here challenged, the elaborate efforts to permit such conduct failed to prevent criminal liability punishable with imprisonment and heavy fines. That is not the way to read the will of Congress, particularly when expressed by a statute which . . . is practically and historically one of a series of enactments touching one of the most sensitive national problems. Such legislation must not be read in a spirit of mutilating narrowness. On matters far less vital and far less interrelated we have had occasion to point out the importance of giving "hospitable scope" to Congressional purpose even when meticulous words are lacking.[140]

Others might think it strange, as the dissenters did, that if Congress had wanted to take another try at limiting the effect of the Sherman Act on strikes and boycotts it had not gone about this by making Sections 6 and 20 of the Clayton Act sufficiently explicit so that the Court would understand them as Congress did, rather than relying on the Court's antennae being so sensitive as to pick up an uncertain message from a statute that did not purport to amend the anti-trust laws at all. True, the Norris-LaGuardia Act contained a broad declaration of policy, Section 2, but this concluded: ". . . therefore, the following definitions of and limitations upon the jurisdiction and authority of the courts of the United States are enacted"—all relating to temporary restraining orders and injunctions. Indeed, Frankfurter himself was soon to say that the Norris-LaGuardia Act "altered a long process of judicial history, but altered it by a scheme of complicated definitions and limitations."[141] So far as one can gather, the "mischief" at which the Norris-LaGuardia Act was aimed was not criminal prosecution or treble-damage suits but labor injunctions granted by federal judges.[142] Moreover, it is straining more than a little to convert a prohibition on federal judges' enjoining certain conduct into "elaborate efforts to permit such conduct." Apart from the silence of the Act as to federal criminal prosecutions and private suits at law, it did not attempt to dictate to the states either by substantive legislation or even by outlawing state court injunctions as to labor disputes affecting interstate commerce. Very likely the reason for confining the Norris-LaGuardia Act to a withdrawal of jurisdiction of the federal courts to grant injunctions was a desire not to run afoul of Truax v. Corrigan[143]; but, for whatever reason, the Act was so confined. One wonders also why Hutcheson's case should not have been disposed of on the simple but seemingly sufficient basis stated in Mr. Justice Stone's concurrence,[144] or, if a bolder stroke was desired, why Duplex Co. v. Deering and Bedford Cut Stone Co. v. Journeymen's Stone Cutters' Association[145] should not have been held to have been erroneously decided on the basis of the Clayton Act alone, for the reasons there expressed in Mr. Justice Brandeis' dissents—a position for which, one would guess, a court could easily have been assembled. Perhaps the Justice shrank from the latter course for the reasons to be examined under the head of his regard for precedent; perhaps also he saw in *Hutcheson* a striking opportunity to further the methodology of *Keifer & Keifer*.

Fortunately the Justice is far too urbane to have been perturbed when, only a fortnight after *Hutcheson*, he found himself accused by Mr. Justice Douglas, speaking also for two other members of the *Hutcheson* majority, of failing to "construe one of a series of legislative acts dealing with a common or related problem in light of the integrated statutory scheme. See *United States v. Hutcheson, ante,* p. 219."[146] As a piece of "verbal logic"[147] only, the accusation had some force. The issue was whether the Federal Trade Commission could prohibit an intrastate manufacturer from engaging in an unfair trade practice which, it found, enabled him to compete unfairly in the same market with interstate sellers whom the Commission had barred from using the identical practice. True, the "commerce" protected from unfair competition by the Federal Trade Commission Act of 1914 was defined as interstate or foreign commerce. But the Interstate Commerce Act had said no more in 1914 when the Shreveport case was decided,[148] although it was later amended to make explicit the power which that decision had found implicit before.[149] Yet it can hardly be doubted that Frankfurter was on sound ground when he denied the validity of the analogy, saying that "The construction . . . urged by the Commission would thus give a federal agency pervasive control over myriads of local businesses in matters heretofore traditionally left to local law. Such control bears no resemblance to the strictly confined authority growing out of railroad rate discrimination." It was not to be lightly assumed that Congress would depart so far from basic principles of our federal system—a consideration Frankfurter has often invoked as an aid to construction.[150] Although the Federal Trade Commission Act used the same terms as the Interstate Commerce Act, the two statutes did not in fact deal "with a common or related problem" or represent parts of the same "integrated statutory scheme"—as a statute dealing with the rates of motor or water carriers would have done; there is a tremendous difference between prevention of a discriminatory public utility rate in intrastate commerce, usually offered by a carrier operating interstate as well, and a broadside proscription of "unfair methods of competition" by local enterprises generally.[151] Once this distinction was recognized, the Justice was able to turn his method against his detractors. "When in order to protect interstate commerce Congress has regulated activities which in isolation are merely local, it has normally conveyed its purpose explicitly."[152]

Another case in which the Justice's principle of looking to the thought immanent in a series of statutes was applied against him is Stark v. Wickard,[153] where the Court upheld the right of milk producers to challenge a regulation of the Secretary of Agriculture by suit in a district court, although the Act, containing many provisions for judicial review of other types of orders, was silent as to this one. The majority drew heavily on the prevalence of statutes providing for judicial review; to Justice Frankfurter, in dissent, these proved nothing:

> Were this list of illustrations extended and the various regulatory schemes thrown into a hotchpot, the result would be hopeless discord. And to do so would be to treat these legislative schemes as though they were part of a single body of law instead of each being a self-contained scheme.[154]

In a sense this is true enough. Review of Interstate Commerce Commission orders by a suit in equity before a three-judge district court plus review of Federal Trade Commission orders by a court of appeals do not add up with arithmetical certainty to review of an order of the Secretary of Agriculture by a single district judge. But were not the myriad review provisions manifestations of "a single body of law," namely, that "judicial review is the rule," so that "the intention to exclude it must be made specifically manifest"?[155] So, at least, the critics have thought, and so the course of decision has lain.[156]

The Justice has been rather sensitive to differences in language as between cognate statutes; he starts from the premise that, just as when Congress employs the same word, it normally means the same thing,[157] when it employs different words, it usually

57

means different things.[158] Thus, when Congress has failed to use the words that it commonly uses to invoke the whole sweep of the commerce power, the inference is that Congress did not intend to go so far.[159] But black squares and white squares are as absent from his opinions here as elsewhere. He reminds us that "the process of construing a statute cannot end with noting literary differences. The task is one of finding meaning; and a difference in words is not necessarily a difference in the meaning they carry. The question is not whether these provisions are different, but whether there is significance in the difference."[160]

## VII.

Thus far we have been dealing in the main with the language of the statute and the light cast upon it by events contemporaneous with or prior to its enactment. Illumination may come also from later developments.

One such is construction by an agency especially charged with the statute's administration. The problem has several aspects; I shall be brief here lest I trench on Professor Jaffe's territory.[161] There is the open-ended statute where Congress, in Mr. Justice Jackson's phrase, did not "bring to a close the making of the law,"[162] but largely left the content to be filled in by an administrative agency. Here, as would be expected from one so understanding of the administrative process, the Justice tends to accord the agency wide latitude. But here also there are no absolutes. The degree of deference to be afforded the agency, he helpfully explained in one of his late opinions, is the resultant of various factors—"the precision of the statutory language, the technical complexity of the relevant issues, the need for certainty as against experimentation, and the likelihood that Congress foresaw the precise question at issue and desired to express a foreclosing judgment on it."[164] Hence, when Congress, instead of using "broad language," formulated "exceptions, catalogued with particularity . . ." he held that "exemptions made in such detail preclude their enlargement by implication" by the administrator.[165]

Frankfurter has also been in the forefront of judges who respect the agency's interpretation of a statutory term having a technical meaning; he has gone so far as to say that a court should affirm the agency's "definition if that definition does not appear too farfetched."[166] Such respect seems to rest on a firm foundation, indeed on several. The statute can be construed as granting latitude to the agency to define technical terms, as to which Congress may expect the agency to know more than it does. The agency, with its experience in administering the statute, should be able to select a meaning, within permissible bounds, that will effectuate the basic purpose better than can a court, necessarily far removed from the daily battle. Finally, if the construction has been long continued, we encounter some of the considerations as to legislative "adoption" that will be analyzed when we come to the role of judicial precedent and the significance of silence or re-enactment by the legislature.

Still another problem is the weight to be assigned to an agency's continued failure to assert a power later claimed to have been granted. Here the Justice has again demonstrated his objectivity[167]—he is not "pro-agency" but "pro" regard for what the agency has chosen either to do or not to do. Thus, in denying the Federal Trade Commission's belated assertion of power over certain intrastate enterprises, "Authority actually granted by Congress of course cannot evaporate through lack of administrative exercise. But just as established practice may shed light on the extent of power conveyed by general statutory language, so the want of assertion of power by those who presumably would be alert to exercise it, is equally significant in determining whether such power was actually conferred."[168] Further proof of the Justice's regard for administrative construction is found in his lamentations over the absence of prior administrative process when the Court has been obliged to define the scope of the Fair Labor Standards Act[169]—although it has never been entirely clear to me how much administrative decision would have aided on the basic issue of the kind of commerce to which the Act relates or why, if it would have, the administrator's construction, even though reached without prior adversary process, did not at least partially fill the bill.[170]

Adherence to precedent has its usual claims in questions of statutory construction, but also some added ones. The Justice struck both notes in protesting against what he deemed a novel interpretation of the Interstate Commerce Act:[171]

> One would suppose that four uniform decisions of this Court, rendered after thorough consideration of a statutory scheme, constitute such a body of law as not to be overruled, wholly apart from any argument that this Court's construction of legislation is confirmed by Congress by reenactment without change.

One may be permitted to wonder how far either the general policy considerations underlying *stare decisis* or the argument as to re-enactment were properly applied to the precise issue there *sub judice*—whether an order of the Interstate Commerce Commission *denying* a reparations claim was subject to judicial review. Shippers and railroads had scarcely conducted their dealings on the basis that such orders would not be reviewable— whatever regrets the decision may have caused shippers who in the past had failed to take their grievances to court, after a turn-down by the Commission, in the belief that no such recourse was available. In the absence of specific evidence, which was not cited, it is somewhat unrealistic to suppose that the Congress, which had to deal with the grave problems incident to returning the railroads to their owners after World War I and with the many innovations embodied in Transportation Act, 1920, had given much thought to Supreme Court rulings on judicial review as to reparations—a subject on which even the members of the Interstate Commerce Committees might not have achieved an "A" grade on one of Professor Frankfurter's examinations.[172] Also, there was not a little force—and irony— in the majority's observation that one basis expressed in the first of the four cases relied on by the Justice, the doctrine forbidding review of a "negative order," was ". . . wholly abandoned" in one of Frankfurter's first important opinions, Rochester Telephone Corp. v. United States,[173] which had itself overruled supposedly well-established precedents and had silently vaulted over the self-same barrier of congressional re-enactment,[174] even though, as the Justice replied, the *Rochester* opinion had distinguished the reparations cases as resting mainly on other grounds.[175]

The theme that re-enactment, or occasionally even silence, on the part of Congress supports adherence to an established course of decisions construing a statute resounds frequently in the Justice's opinions. Protesting against what he considered abandonment of the established rule that an assignor of a patent may not raise invalidity as a defense against an assignee's claim of infringement, he urged that this doctrine "has never been questioned by Congress in the successive enactments amending the patent law. . . . The place for reconsidering the policy which this Court more than twenty years ago characterized as 'a rule well settled by forty-five years of judicial consideration,' *Westinghouse Co. v. Formica Co.*, 266 U.S. at 349, is the Congress."[176] With great eloquence and persuasiveness,[177] he objected to the complete overruling of May v. Heiner,[178] eighteen years after it had been decided, despite a restricted overruling by Congress,[179] and repeated re-enactment of the prior law which made "the meaning announced in *May v. Heiner* and reaffirmed four times as much a part of the wording of the statute as if it had been written in express terms."[180] Even when a prior opinion had not decided the precise issue of construction later raised and there had been no re-enactment, he believed that a considered relevant statement should continue to be heeded, since "A legal faggot ought not to be broken into verbal sticks."[181] Having joined with the majority in holding that the combined effect of a prior decision and congressional refusal to alter it, in this instance rather clearly deliberate, precluded reading the Sherman Act to include professional baseball,[182] he insisted that *stare decisis* required the same result as to boxing: "If *stare decisis* be one aspect of law . . . to disregard it in identic situations is mere caprice."[183] He has urged also that an act of Congress must be read in the light of decisions as to the constitutional bounds of congressional power accepted at the time of enactment; thus, when Congress passed the Sherman Act, it did not mean to include insurance, which no one would have thought within the commerce power at the time.[184]

Although the Justice thus goes far in relying on *stare decisis* in matters of statutory interpretation, this rule, like all others, has its limits. What is important for him is not any single decision but the principle embodied in a course of decisions. Dealing with a series of estate tax decisions that were barely reconcilable, he said that *stare decisis* is "not a mechanical formula of adherence to the latest decision, however recent and questionable, when such adherence involves collision with a prior doctrine more embracing in its scope, intrinsically sounder, and verified by experience"; he denied that "Congress, under any rational canons of legislative significance, by its compilation of internal revenue laws to form the Internal Revenue Code of 1939 . . . impliedly enacted into law a particular decision which, in the light of later experience, is seen to create confusion and conflict. . . ."[185] Reasonable as this sounds and doubtless was, it opens a considerable hole in the doctrine that an interpretive decision is adopted by silence or, more probably, by re-enactment. Everything depends on the frame of reference. Mr. Justice Black and the other members of the majority in United States v. Interstate Commerce Commission doubtless thought that the decisions against review of a Commission order denying reparations, so strongly relied on in Frankfurter's dissent, collided with "a prior doctrine" of judicial review of administrative orders, including many "negative" orders, "more embracing in its scope, intrinsically sounder, and verified by experience." The hole becomes even larger when we learn that "Loose language and a sporadic, ill-considered decision"—in fact, two Supreme Court decisions —"cannot be held to have imbedded in our law a doctrine which so patently violates the expressed prohibition of Congress" against federal court injunctions of state court proceedings, and that "It is indulging in the merest fiction to suggest that the doctrine which for the first time we are asked to pronounce with our eyes open and in the light of full consideration, was so obviously and firmly part of the texture of our law that Congress in effect enacted it through its silence."[186] Further limitations on the effect to be given prior decisions—even quite recent and consistent ones, followed by amendment of other portions of the statute—are expressed in a dissent challenging the reaffirmation that acts by state officials forbidden by the state may nevertheless be "under color" of state law for purposes of the Civil Rights Act:

> While we may well decline to re-examine recent cases which derive from the judicial process exercised under its adequate safeguards—documenting briefs and adequate arguments on both sides as foundation for due deliberation—the relevant demands of *stare decisis* do not preclude considering, for the first time

thoroughly and in the light of the best available evidence of congressional purpose, a statutory interpretation which started as an unexamined assumption on the basis of inapplicable citations and has the claim of a dogma solely through reiteration.[187]

Again, in one of his latest opinions,[188] dealing with 28 U.S.C. Section 2281, which bars a suit for an injunction "upon the ground of the unconstitutionality" of a state statute "unless the application therefor is heard and determined by a district court of three judges," the Justice distinguished many cases generally thought to mean that this requirement attached only when the unconstitutionality of the state statute was claimed to arise from a collision with the federal Constitution as opposed to one with a federal statute.[189] All that these cases held, he tells us, was that the three-judge requirement does not exist "if in immediate controversy is not the unconstitutionality of a state law but merely the construction of a state law or the federal law," although the construction of the federal law was important only because, if construed as the plaintiff contended, the state law would conflict with it and thus be unconstitutional; a case presenting "a sole, immediate constitutional question" of conflict between a state and a federal statute requires three judges.[190]

One of the Justice's most illuminating analyses of the significance of re-enactment relates to administrative construction. In N.L.R.B. v. Seven-Up Bottling Co.,[191] the issue was the power of the Labor Board to alter the formula for calculating the back pay of employees ordered to be reinstated which it had used for many years prior to the Taft-Hartley Act. The question, not on its face a hard one, was somewhat complicated by an opinion two years earlier, which, in sustaining the Board's continued practice of not deducting unemployment compensation from back pay, had relied on the comprehensive consideration given by Congress "in the course of adopting the 1947 amendments" to "the provisions of the earlier legislation as they had been applied by the Board." From this it had been deemed to be "a fair assumption that by reenacting without pertinent modification the provision with which we here deal, Congress accepted the construction placed thereon by the Board and approved by the courts."[192] Over a strongly worded dissent by Mr. Justice Minton, the writer of the earlier opinion, Frankfurter neatly clipped this broad and conventional language:

> Assuming Congress was aware of the Board's . . . practice of calculating back pay on the basis of the entire period from discharge to offer of reinstatement, we could say here, as we did in Gullett Gin, that Congress by its reenactment indicated its agreement that the Board's practice was authorized. That leads us nowhere on the present issue, though it is only this far that what we have said in *Gullett Gin* can lead us. . . . If Congress had been more than satisfied with the Board's practice, if it had wanted to be certain that the Board would not in future profit by its experience, it would have had to do more than it did; it would have had to change the language of the statute so as to take from the Board the discretionary power to mould remedies suited to practical needs which we had declared the Board to have and which the Board was asserting and exercising.[193]

Indeed, this reasoning is so forceful as to raise serious question as to the weight to be given to re-enactment after judicial construction in cases where there is no legislative history to show that Congress meant to perpetuate what the courts had said. A distinction on the basis that Congress assumes that administrative agencies will learn from experience, but that courts bound by *stare decisis* cannot, not only is rather unflattering but seems factually dubious in these days when overruling of judicial precedents is quite commonplace. We ought not get into the position where Congress re-enacts a statute in the expectation that the courts will retain freedom to interpret it but the courts deny themselves that freedom because of a supposition that Congress meant them not to have it.

When the Justice's various opinions are thus assembled, his position as to *stare decisis* in the construction of statutes appears much less rigid than has often been supposed. Despite some expressions giving color to an absolutist view, his general approach has been the realistic one of seeking to divine whether the judicial construction was of such a nature and on such a subject that silence or, much more significantly, re-enactment by Congress gives rise to a reasonable inference that the construction had entered the congressional mind—or at least some important congressional minds—and thereby "infiltrated" the text. In taking this more limited position he is surely right. It is highly doubtful whether, in the absence of pertinent legislative history, weight should ever be given to silence or even re-enactment after decisions of "inferior" courts.[194] Even as to decisions of the highest court, the "silence" principle should be limited to the rather rare case where the history fairly supports the inference of legislative rejection of a proposal for change[195] rather than more likely inferences of ignorance, indifference or inertia,[196] and the re-enactment principle should be applied with discrimination.

Mr. Justice Frankfurter has fashioned a corpus of opinions on the reading of statutes that has not been matched in our time and does not seem likely to be in the future. His approach to statutory construction has been an expansive one; his opinions exemplify the wisdom of the great Chief Justice that he is so fond of quoting, "Where the mind labors to discover the design of the legislature, it seizes everything from which aid can be derived."[197] As has been well said:

He looks to the historical line of development, the needs out of which the statute grew and even to subsequent events and present practical needs—in short, to the whole legal and social environment of a statute. . . . Clearly, he goes beyond the minds of the men who drafted or enacted the statute. He patches, enlarges and fulfills their awkward product."[198]

He has outstandingly performed the judge's task, as Learned Hand defined it, to "try as best he can to put into concrete form what [the common] will is, not by slavishly following the words, but by trying honestly to say what was the underlying purpose expressed,"[199]—within his own credo that for a judge to go altogether beyond the words "is to usurp a power which our democracy has lodged in its elected legislature."[200]

Only a man with Olympian pretensions, from which Mr. Justice Frankfurter is happily free, would claim to have done this "exactly right" in every decision over a quarter of a century. But his place in the front rank of those "great [judges] who do it better than the rest of us"[201] is altogether secure. That is enough for a man whose intensely human qualities have ever sealed off the temptation of allowing his long held post of finality to engender an illusion of infallibility.[202]

# Voice of a Modern Federalism

Louis Henkin, *Professor,*
*Columbia University Law School*

The "more perfect union" formed by the Constitution of the United States was a "confederate republic," the ideal of Montesquieu. The details of this first modern federalism have been long and widely studied, and the success of our "sovereign nation of many sovereign states" continues to inspire emulation by nations old and new. Yet the nature of that federal system has never been wholly agreed, and has raised divisive issues in American constitutional law and in American politics since this country was born. Questions of federalism, of course, lay at the heart of American law and politics when political parties spoke of themselves as federalist or anti-federalist; they were the focus of our terrible Civil War; they attended Reconstruction, the race across the continent and across the seas, the growth of the United States, through depressions and world wars, into the age of the new science and the reach into space. American federal government today is not that which came out of the Constitutional Convention, but issues of federalism continue to permeate

68

the daily press as well as the reports of the Supreme Court of the United States.

No Justice of the Supreme Court in this century, perhaps no student of its work or of the workings of the American government, has been more aware of the federal character of American government than has Felix Frankfurter, as citizen, as lawyer, as professor, as Justice. In no one else today is this awareness combined with so deep an appreciation of what federalism has meant in the life of this country. Surely, federalism is a major key to the judicial philosophy of Mr. Justice Frankfurter.

So much can be said easily, and with confidence. To attempt more, to articulate, however generally, exactly what is the Justice's federalism and how it is reflected in his many hundreds of opinions, would be a formidable and perhaps foolhardy task. It is not only that it is, happily, much too soon to praise or appraise the judicial career of Justice Frankfurter, that the Justice, happily, is very much here to say, "It was not that way at all." There is, too, the different difficulty, that federalism, in some form and degree, is involved in every case, in every opinion, in every issue. For Justice Frankfurter federalism has permeated—and has in turn been shaped by—his philosophy of government, particularly of the American government, his readings of the Constitution and of federal statutes, his convictions about the role and function of the Supreme Court of the United States, his views of proper judicial process.

Of Justice Frankfurter's federalism, then, I can only hope to suggest, with broad brush, the dominant motifs. I think they are these: that federalism remains a fundamental and important principle in a living Constitution; that American federalism does not frustrate government, but rather promotes co-operative, interlocking government by both nation and states; that the Supreme Court has an important, secondary role in monitoring the federal system, particularly against state interference with interstate commerce; that, otherwise, federalism suggests that Supreme Court review of the action of the states is and ought to be minimal; that, finally, federalism has a price which must be paid.

## THAT FEDERALISM MATTERS

For Justice Frankfurter, federalism is not a relic, a reluctant compromise with history and politics; it remains a profound reality of American life, American government, American law— a balanced system, profoundly to be wished, contributing to democracy and freedom.

To many, federal government in the United States has appeared as an eighteenth-century survival, redolent of archaic notions of state sovereignty and "states' rights," an obstacle to progress in national welfare and individual liberty. If states' rights survived the Civil War, they were left behind as this country raced across a continent and beyond to develop national needs of a complex interdependent society. Surely, it is said, the confining attitudes of federalism are irrelevant and unacceptable to the greatest nation on a diminishing earth reaching for the moon. It is time to recognize that we can no longer be a federal union but must be a nation, that local interests are incidental, that power and decision must be concentrated in the nation and delegated from the center.[1]

Not so to Justice Frankfurter. It is not only that federal government is the framework of the Constitution; after all, "the Constitution is not primarily a text for interpretation but the means of ordering the life of a progressive people."[2] If federalism matters, it is not because of the accidents and compromises of 1787; it is because the history of this country has proved its validity as a principle of progressive government.

More than most, Mr. Frankfurter has been aware, and maintained awareness, of the history of his country, and of the role that federalism has played in it. He is aware how different is today's federalism, and how and why the changes happened. "For judges at least it is important to remember that continuity with the past is not only a necessity but even a duty."[3] History, of course, is not for dwelling in the past; the uses of history are "for the light it throws upon the present."[4] The history of a constitution takes account not only of what was but what has become, and of how it got here and where it is going. But, being acutely aware of this history, he could not—had he wished—lightly leap to easy conclusions that the national element in our society is all, the federal element nothing. At no time—not at the height of national supremacy under the New Deal or in the atomic-space age, perhaps not even during world wars—has federalism been less than a vital actuality in American political life. That the powers of the nation have grown with its needs has not made it less important to render unto the states the respect and responsibility that can and ought to remain theirs.

To Justice Frankfurter, in fact, federalism in the United States has been a guarantee of freedom. Like the horizontal separation of powers, the vertical distribution between state and nation was designed, and has served, to frustrate possible tyrannies of centralization. "Time has not lessened the concern of the Founders in devising a federal system which would likewise be a safeguard against arbitrary government."[5] He invokes "the principle of diffusion of power not as a matter of doctrinaire localism but as a promoter of democracy."[6] Even the Justice's known insistence on judicial self-limitation includes an element of resistance to the Court's unreviewable centralizing power.

Federalism has also been a condition of progress. The history to which the Justice attends includes the long turbulent years he has lived. It includes, of course, the years when the United

States became the greatest nation and sought national solutions to economic and social necessities. It includes, too, the years when progressivism burgeoned locally in the face of centralized apathy or impotence or hostility, when new ideas born in Wisconsin or Oregon or New York struggled to survive reaction ensconced on the Bench of a national Supreme Court. He has remembered, as Tocqueville early observed, that in America "the township was organized before the county, the county before the state, the state before the union."[7] It was in the townships and the states that, in the Justice's own experience, progress and good government—even the ideas that fertilized the national New Deal—were born.

Federalism reflects also democracy and representative government. Living and working and judging in metropolitan centers and the national capital, Mr. Frankfurter has, nonetheless, been aware that the urban centers are not all of the United States, and indeed are not representative of the most of it. He knows that even in the middle of the twentieth century, even after the New Deal and the recognition of vast powers in the national government, the citizen of the United States lives in his township and state, is concerned with local matters, cares for local interests, is reluctant to leave everything to be done by Washington, from Washington, as Washington thinks best. Often, the state and the township have been more responsive to the will and the interests of the people. Often local government has been better government, sometimes more expert government. Even the Congress of the United States, the principal repository of national power, is acutely aware of local interests, seeks to promote and foster them, often, unfortunately, at the expense of the national interest. Time and again, on a court engaged in interpreting the wishes of Congress, the Justice has recognized—as some of his brethren have not or would not—the localism of Congress and how much Congress wished to leave to the states.

Professor Frankfurter was speaking not only for Justice Brandeis when he wrote:

> [His] regard for the States is no mere lip service. He is greatly tolerant of their powers because he believes intensely in the opportunities which they afford for decentralization. And he believes in decentralization not because of any persisting habit of political allegiance or through loyalty to an anachronistic theory of states' rights. His views are founded on deep convictions regarding the manageable size for the effective conduct of human affairs and the most favorable conditions for the exercise of wise judgment.
>
> In the practical adjustments between national rule and local diversities, he is keenly mindful that the Nation spans a continent and that, despite the unifying forces of technology, the States for many purposes remain distinctive communities. As to matters not obviously of common national concern, thereby calling for a centralized system of control, the States have a localized knowledge of details, a concreteness of interest and varieties of social policy, which ought to be allowed tolerant scope.
>
> ... The ultimate organic nature of society is not a decree of constitutional centralization. Just because the national government will necessarily absorb more and more power, the States ought to be allowed to manage those activities which bear an essential state emphasis.[8]

## FEDERALISM FOR EFFECTIVE GOVERNMENT

The federalism of the Constitution does not require laissez-faire, does not prevent government, either federal or state. Rather it provides for most effective government by both nation and state.

The charter of American federalism is, of course, the Constitution, as read by the Supreme Court. A federal system, Mr.

Frankfurter noted long ago, must have a written Constitution. And it must have an authoritative body to monitor the play between whole and part. Under the American Constitution, the Supreme Court, itself a branch of the federal government, is also the arbiter of the American federalism. The Supreme Court's reading of the Constitution determines ultimately the character and content of American federalism, the distribution between nation and state, as well as the Court's own role in the process of government.[9]

> Of all the means for ordering the political life of a nation, a federal system is the most complicated and subtle; it demands the most flexible and imaginative adjustments for harmonizing national and local interests. The Constitution of the United States is not a printed finality but a dynamic process; its application to the actualities of government is not a mechanical exercise but a function of statecraft.[10]

> From the beginning, the Court had to resolve what were essentially political issues—the proper accommodation between the States and the central government. These political problems will persist as long as our federalism endures; and the Supreme Court will remain the ultimate arbitrator between Nation and States.[11]

This is "the most exacting demand that is made upon judges —to compose clashing interests of an empire by appeal to law."[12] The Court must protect the states against encroachment by the nation, lest we cease to be a federalism. It must protect the national interest against encroachment by the states, lest we cease to be a nation. The Union, in Holmes's oft-quoted dictum, could probably not survive if the Supreme Court did not have the authority to identify and prevent state disruptions and violations of the federal union.[13]

To arbitrate between nation and states, or between states, requires, of course, a determination of their respective domains under the Constitution. The federalism which the Court will apply will depend, then, on its reading of the Constitution, on the philosophy of government it finds in, or brings to, that reading.

Mr. Justice Frankfurter believes in government.[14] Democratic government is not some hostile "they"; it is "we" organized the better to promote the common weal. He does not fear to grant power to government, lest government govern unwisely. Against the danger of bad government the remedy is not to deny power but to promote its wise exercise.

> To whatever extent history may confirm Lord Acton's dictum that power tends to corrupt, such a doctrine of fear can hardly serve as a test . . . of a particular exercise of a State's legislative power. And so, the constitutionality of a particular statute . . . cannot be determined by deriving a troupe of hobgoblins from the assumption that such a particularized exercise of power would justify an unlimited, abusive exercise of power. . . . [W]e are admonished from time to time not to adjudicate on the basis of fear of foreign totalitarianism. Equally so should we not be guided in the exercise of our reviewing power over legislation by fear of totalitarianism in our own country.[15]

Through such eyes Justice Frankfurter reads the Constitution and the federal union which it established. "[T]here emerges from the Constitution the conception of a nation adequate to its national and international duties, consisting of federated states possessed of ample power for the diverse uses of a civilized people."[16] Federalism, then, is not a conceptual formula to assure that government will govern little. It is a pragmatic allocation and distribution of the powers of government. Together, the nation and the states have all the powers of government; nothing falls between them. What the states cannot do is not likely to be denied by the Constitution to the federal government.[17] In modern federalism the keynote is no longer limitation on national government. The Justice's federalism has nothing to do with archaic cries of "states' rights" designed to thwart and flout national government and national law, to frustrate necessary national solutions, in order to roll back the pages of the Constitution and its history, to perpetuate social or racial inequalities.[18] The Civil War and the Civil War Amendments radically changed the original federalism, surely to empower a national Congress and a national Supreme Court to protect the Negro against state discriminations and deprivations. The history of the New Deal established finally that the powers given to the federal government are sufficient to the needs of modern government.

Of course, federalism implies some reciprocal limitations corresponding to the distribution between nation and states. A central government of enumerated powers is subject to the limitations of the enumeration, and the implied limitations of non-enumeration, underscored by the explicit reservations of the Tenth Amendment. (The Constitution contains, too, of course, the limitations that inhere in the express prohibitions, on the federal government, on the states, or both.) The Justice, fertile of mind, is honest of mind and recognizes that the ambiguities and flexibilities of language are yet not without limits. For him, Congress cannot, say, regulate by a sham tax what it could not reach under its regulatory powers.[19] He is particularly reluctant to find in the Constitution authority for Congress to replace state institutions, as by extending the jurisdiction of federal courts, or requiring the application of new federal law, at the expense of state courts and state law.[20] But subject to these inescapable and limited limitations in the Constitution, the Justice's philosophy of government and of the American Constitution is not one of denying power to the federal government.

The Constitution has been sufficient to the national needs ever since McCulloch v. Maryland, "Marshall's greatest single judicial performance."[21] The Constitution proved adequate even when the conception of government changed from the "watchdog government" of the eighteenth century to today's "service state."[22] A living federalism entails no obstacles to the full exercise of delegated powers when the national Congress seeks to meet national problems of a new day, through the commerce power, or the spending power, or the war powers, or the foreign affairs power.[23] Congress will be alert to the political limits on national action, and to the local interests that will be affected. Surely, it is not for the courts to tell Congress nay, except where the written Constitution entrusted to the Court's care leaves no doubt that Congress has transgressed.

The interpenetrations of modern society have not wiped out state lines. It is not for us to make inroads upon our federal system either by indifference to its maintenance or excessive regard for the unifying forces of modern technology. Scholastic reasoning may prove that no activity is isolated within the boundaries of a single State, but that cannot justify absorption of legislative power by the United States over every activity. On the other hand, the old admonition never becomes stale that this Court is concerned with the bounds of legal power and not with the bounds of wisdom in its exercise by Congress. When the conduct of an enterprise affects commerce among the States is a matter of practical judgment, not to be determined by abstract notions. The exercise of this practical judgment the Constitution entrusts primarily and very largely to the Congress, subject to the latter's control by the electorate. Great power was thus given to the Congress: the power of legislation and thereby the power of passing judgment upon the needs of a complex society. Strictly confined though far-reaching power was given to this Court: that of determining whether the Congress has exceeded limits allowable in reason for the judgment which it has exercised. To hold that Congress could not deem the activities here in question to affect what men of practical affairs would call commerce, and to deem them related to such commerce merely by gossamer threads and not by solid ties, would be to disrespect the judgment that is open to men who have the constitutional power and responsibility to legislate for the Nation.[24]

Federalism means that the nation is largely free to act. Inevitably, it means too that when the nation has acted the states cannot frustrate or hamper the national action. There is no tolerance for state lawlessness however polite and old the label it may wear.[25] But federalism, to Justice Frankfurter, means too that the states have power to govern. The states do not derive their power from any enumerations in the United States Constitution. They have the independent authority, the competence, and the responsibility to govern, except insofar as the federal Constitution, directly or through supreme federal legislation, clearly forbids them. Constitutional prohibitions on state government, being practically irreversible, ought not to be found, except where explicit language leaves little doubt. Congressional prohibitions, limitations, exclusions of state authority ought not to be found, except where Congress has left little doubt. Federalism surely does not mean that neither nation nor state can act. Nor does federalism mean either federal government or state. Federalism means the best conjunction, interaction, balance between nation and state.

If constitutional federalism means the maximum freedom for effective government, the Court should not lightly find limitations and prohibitions on government, either federal or state. The constitutional prohibitions, applicable for the most part to both federal and state governments, should be narrowly viewed since, in effect, they close off areas to all government.[26] Early, too, Justice Frankfurter insisted that the Court ought not to build up unnecessary limits on the governments in their relation with each other, deriving from conceptual and mistaken notions of "sovereignty" under federalism. Immunity of state or federal government to regulation or taxation by the other is not written into the Constitution. It can only be derived from necessity inherent in the fact that there are two governments overlapping and affecting each other. But "pernicious abstractions," even hallowed and "seductive clichés"—"the power to tax involves the power to destroy"—cannot be allowed to support unnecessary frustrations of important powers of government.[27] Of course, it is inherent in federal supremacy that the state cannot by regulation or by tax frustrate or hamper the nation or any national program. As a simple safeguard to this end, the Justice thought in dissent, there had been established a rule of thumb that property owned by the United States Government itself shall be automatically immune to state taxation unless Congress says it should not be.[28] For related reasons, perhaps, the state *qua* state, and the property and operations unique to it as a state, are constitutionally immune to federal disruption or tax. But for the largest part the test is practical, not doctrinaire; government—neither state nor federal—is not limited where there are no reasons in practical need for limiting it. It is a question of policy, not of power; Congress can decide whether federal immunity is necessary, or whether states shall be excluded from federal tax or regulation. There is nothing in the Constitution that requires that the salaries of employees of either government, state or federal, be immune from tax by the other; that exempts contractors of the United States from non-discriminatory taxes, although the cost of these taxes is ultimately borne by the United States; that exempts federal operations, needlessly, from state regulations that Congress did not see fit clearly to outlaw; that exempts state mineral water from a non-discriminatory federal tax.[29]

## CO-OPERATIVE FEDERALISM

Federalism does not inevitably suggest exclusion or supersession; it suggests rather the need for co-operation, between nation and state, between state and state.

Federalism implies national supremacy within its domain. But supremacy does not imply conflict or exclusiveness. The forms of co-operation under federalism are manifold and increasing.[30] Congress has long ago developed grants-in-aid, tax credits, and similar bases for federal-state co-operation.[31] The Constitution does not even bar Congress from supporting state programs by authorizing burdens on interstate commerce.[32] Co-operation may also consist of permitting the states to operate where Congress could take over. The states should be allowed to govern, so far as national interest will permit. Even where the Constitution grants Congress authority to exercise "exclusive legislation," as in federal enclaves, it is not to be interpreted to bar the application of some local laws where Congress has said nothing.[33] Where Congress has legislated, the problems of supremacy are not resolved: some of them only begin. As a national legislator, one might guess, the Justice would have been careful to assure that legislation gave maximum regard and scope to local interests consistent with the national purpose. As a judge he has to take what Congress did as he finds it. But he will not lightly assume a purpose on the part of Congress to prohibit or impinge unnecessarily on the freedom of the states to govern, or to modify the accepted distribution of authority between state and nation. Although for him the traditional canons of construction are only "axioms of experience" and cannot "save us from the anguish of judgment,"[34] federalism is for Justice Frankfurter a special kind of principle of construction for congressional legislation.

More frequently still, in the interpretation of recent regulatory statutes, it becomes important to remember that the judicial task in marking out the extent to which Congress has exercised its constitutional power over commerce, is not that of devising an abstract formula. The task is one of accommodation as between assertions of new federal authority and historic functions of the individual states. Federal legislation of this character cannot therefore be construed without regard to the implications of our dual system of government. In such cases, for example, it is not to be assumed as a matter of course that when Congress adopts a new scheme for federal industrial regulation, it deals with all situations falling within the general mischief which gave rise to the legislation. The underlying assumptions of our dual form of government, and the consequent presuppositions of legislative draftsmanship which are expressive of our history and habits, cut across what might otherwise be the implied range of legislation. The history of congressional legislation regulating not only interstate commerce as such but also activities intertwined with it, justifies the generalization that, when the Federal Government takes over such local radiations in the vast network of our national economic enterprise and thereby radically readjusts the balance of state and national authority, those charged with the duty of legislating are reasonably explicit and do not entrust its attainment to that retrospective expansion of meaning which properly deserves the stigma of judicial legislation.[35]

In "ascertaining the scope of congressional legislation a due regard for a proper adjustment of the local and national interests in our federal scheme must always be in the background."[36] Except where Congress has left no doubt of a contrary purpose, every federal statute should be construed so as to disturb as little as possible the traditional domains of nation and state, the "delicate"[37]—the Justice's frequent warning—balance of the federal system. Since, generally, federal regulation increases the federal domain and takes from the states, federal regulation should not be construed to extend to the limits of the powers of Congress unless Congress has clearly indicated it. If Congress authorized the regulation of trade practices "in interstate commerce," it has not indicated any purpose to include also practices that merely affect interstate commerce.[38] And Justice Frankfurter has even rejected the interpretation of a statute by the administrative body in charge of its implementation when he thought that Congress had not wished to subject to federal regulation towing operations between points in New York State that were technically in interstate commerce.[39]

In construing federal statutes, Justice Frankfurter is, again, particularly jealous for state law and state courts. "The happy relation of States to Nation—constituting as it does our central political problem—is to no small extent dependent upon the wisdom with which the scope and limits of the federal courts are determined."[40] He sees the federal judiciary as a happy and select few and does not look with favor on increases in their jurisdiction which take from the states and also cause "depreciation of the judicial currency and the consequent impairment of the prestige and of the efficacy of the federal courts."[41] Long ago he saw the answer to the growing burdens of the federal courts in leaving much, including some vindication of federal rights, to the state courts—as was done when the country was younger.[42] He has long favored the abolition or at least further curtailment of diversity jurisdiction—a no longer necessary manifestation of distrust of the state courts to treat non-residents fairly.[43] Surely, the statutes conferring diversity jurisdiction should be strictly construed. "The dominant note in the successive enactments of Congress relating to diversity jurisdiction, is one of jealous restriction, of avoiding offense to state sensitiveness, and of relieving the federal courts of the overwhelming burden of business that intrinsically belongs to the state courts, in order to keep them free for their distinctive federal business."[44] Similarly, the Court should not, with little warrant, construe statutes to extend the jurisdiction of federal courts in other cases, for example, bankruptcy; or to terminate traditional jurisdiction of state courts, for example, in some maritime suits;

or to limit traditional powers of state courts to enjoin inconvenient actions in federal or other state courts; or to compel
state courts to vary their procedures where a federal interest
is involved.[45] Nor should the Court read broadly the authority
which Congress gave to three-judge federal courts to enjoin
state action.[46] And Justice Frankfurter has refused to find an
intent by Congress to create new areas of federal authority,
applying to labor relations new federal law instead of the law
of the states.[47]

Some of the Justice's sharpest dissents reflect his view that
the Court was putting into federal statutes federal authority in
traditional state areas, which Congress never intended. Perhaps
Congress should help enforce civil rights even where the states
could do so, because they are not doing it. But Congress, he is
satisfied, never intended to impinge on traditional domains of the
states and provide federal enforcement, by criminal or civil
action, against violations of civil rights by state officials where
the actions are also violations of state law which the states can
enforce.[48] Mr. Justice Frankfurter will not be a judicial libertarian by being a judicial libertine[49]; he will not read in the Act
what he might wish to see there instead of what Congress put
there. Congress—and here, one suspects, Justice Frankfurter also
—has confidence in the states, in the large and in the long run.[50]
And taking authority from government, even from state government, is debilitating to good government and atrophies the
muscles of responsibility. In sharp dissents, the Justice has criticized the Court in phrases ringing with his federalism.

> . . . the always relevant implications of our federal system espe-
> cially in the distribution of power and responsibility for the en-
> forcement of the criminal law as between the States and the Na-
> tional Government. . . . It fails not merely to leave to the States
> the province of local crime enforcement, that the proper bal-
> ance of political forces in our federalism requires. . . . But to at-

tribute to Congress the making overnight of a revolutionary change in the balance of political relations between the National Government and the States without reason . . . Regard for maintaining the delicate balance "between the judicial tribunals of the Union and of the States" in the enforcement of the criminal law . . . needless extension of federal criminal authority into matters that normally are of State concern and for which the States had best be charged with responsibility.[51]

The issue in the present case concerns directly a basic problem of American federalism: the relation of the Nation to the States in the critically important sphere of municipal law administration. In this aspect, it has significance approximating constitutional dimension. Necessarily, the construction of the Civil Rights Act raises issues fundamental to our institutions. This imposes on this Court a corresponding obligation to exercise its power within the fair limits of its judicial discretion.[52]

Every assertion of federal power asserts also its constitutional supremacy excluding any inconsistent state law and authority. The difficult question often is whether Congress also sought to exclude state law which is not in direct conflict—whether Congress pre-empted the field of regulation, or whether, on the other hand, Congress wished or accepted coexistence between federal and state regulation. Especially since in many instances Congress did not think of the question, Justice Frankfurter has generally insisted that the federal statute be construed to permit co-operation, particularly where the federal regulation operated in the area of local interests and traditional state authority. Exclusion of the states has constitutional overtones and courts should exercise restraint in finding it, akin to that required of them when asked to hold acts of the state unconstitutional.[53] Displacement of the states "does not present a problem in physics,"[54] but a pragmatic determination reflecting the assumptions of our federal government.[55] In particular, the states should not be excluded where the federal government is not in fact regulating what the states seek to reach.[56]

> When construing federal legislation that deals with matters that also lie within the authority, because within the proper interests, of the States, we must be mindful that we are part of the delicate process of adjusting the interacting areas of National and State authority over commerce. . . . Federal legislation of this character must be construed with due regard to accommodation between the assertions of new federal authority and the functions of the individual States, as reflecting the historic and persistent concerns of our dual system of government. . . . To construe federal legislation so as not needlessly to forbid preexisting State authority is to respect our federal system. Any indulgence in construction should be in favor of the States, because Congress can speak with drastic clarity whenever it chooses to assure full federal authority, completely displacing the States.[57]

Justice Frankfurter recognizes that when judges come to construe statutes to determine whether the states have been preempted, it "may make a decisive difference what view judges have of the place of the States in our national life."[58] He is, of course, reflecting his own view of federalism. And he knows that if he is mistaken as to the wishes of Congress, Congress can come back and tell him so "with drastic clarity." But, in fact, he has sensed too the temper of Congress, recognizing that it is a localist Congress that was legislating, not a nationalist Court. And time and again Congress has proceeded to vindicate Justice Frankfurter's insights and make clear its intention not to exclude the states.[59]

Federalism to the Justice does not mean conflict between nation and state. The most common words in the Justice's federalism—repeated hundreds of times—are "harmony," "balance," "adjustment," "accommodation." The answer to the dilemmas of federalism, said Mr. Justice Johnson, "one of the greatest of the Justices,"[60] is "a frank and candid co-operation for the general good."[61]

Co-operation and accommodation are also the answers to that other problem of federalism, the independence of the respective states vis-à-vis each other. For all the states are free to govern and they are free to govern in their own ways. In regard to each other, too, apart from the implied immunities of interstate commerce to state encroachments, the limitations of the Constitution are few and, generally, they are not to be liberally regarded. Discrimination against residents of other states is, of course, expressly forbidden in the Constitution, although in some respects "the State may care for its own."[62] Even the explicit requirement to give full faith and credit to the "Acts, Records and Judicial Proceedings" of other states is not to be literally and broadly interpreted, since it is a limitation on the freedom of the states to govern within their borders as they see fit.[63] For the ensuing problems the answer is in co-operation. State compacts, subject to approval by Congress which can protect the national interest, were expressly contemplated by the Constitution and are to be encouraged and enforced; to do so, Justice Frankfurter was prepared, once only, to read a state's constitution differently from the way it was read by the state's own highest court.[64] And even without a compact, the Justice is quick to recognize the rights of states which can govern separately to co-operate for uniform or reciprocal action.

Unless there is some provision in the United States Constitution which clearly prevents States from accomplishing this end by the means chosen, this Court must sustain the Uniform Act. . . . In adjudging the validity of a statute effecting a new form of relationship between States, the search is not for a specific constitutional authorization for it. Rather, according the statute the full benefit of the presumption of constitutionality which is the postulate of constitutional adjudication, we must find clear incompatibility with the United States Constitution. The range of state power is not defined and delimited by an enumeration of legislative subject-matter. The Constitution did not purport to exhaust imagination and resourcefulness in devising fruitful interstate relationships. It is not to be construed to limit the variety of arrangements which are possible through the voluntary and cooperative actions of individual States with a view to increasing harmony within the federalism created by the Constitution. Far from being divisive, this legislation is a catalyst of cohesion. It is within the unrestricted area of action left to the States by the Constitution.

In any event, to yield to an argument that benefiting other States is beyond the power of a State would completely disregard the inherent implications of our federalism within whose framework our organic society lives and moves and has its being —the abundant and complicated interrelationship between national authority and the States . . . and between the States *inter sese*. To yield to this argument would foreclose to the States virtually all arrangements which increase comity among the States. These extra-constitutional arrangements are designed to solve "problems created by a constitutional division of powers without disturbance of the federal nature of our government."

To hold that these and other arrangements are beyond the power of the States and Federal Government because there is no specific empowering provision in the United States Constitution would be to take an unwarrantedly constricted view of state and national powers and would hobble the effective functioning of our federalism. Diffusion of power has its corollary of diffusion of responsibilities, with its stimulus to cooperative effort in devising ways and means for making the federal system work. That is not a mechanical structure. It is an interplay of living forces of government to meet the evolving needs of a complex society.

The Constitution of the United States does not preclude resourcefulness of relationships between States on matters as to which there is no grant of power to Congress and as to which the range of authority restricted within an individual State is inadequate. . . . Comity among States, an end particularly to be cherished when the object is enforcement of internal criminal laws, is not to be defeated by an *a priori* restrictive view of state power.[65]

## THE SUPREME COURT
## MONITORS INTERSTATE COMMERCE

The growth of supreme, national power to meet new national need means that Congress can ultimately determine, within large limits, the distribution of authority in our federal system. But Congress has, in effect, left to the Supreme Court an important task: to monitor the impacts of the states on interstate commerce.

Perhaps the most difficult cases for Justice Frankfurter's philosophy of the Constitution and of judicial review involve the impact of the states on interstate commerce. Devotion to letting the political organs govern, and to co-operative federalism, might suggest that the Court should not bar state regulation unless the Constitution or Congress clearly forbids it. In regard to interstate and foreign commerce the Constitution gives power to Congress to regulate: it does not deny a concurrent power to the states. It is "an excluding, not an exclusive, power."[66] Although the Court settled, more than a hundred years ago, that even in the absence of congressional action the Constitution itself bars some regulation of interstate commerce by the states, one might have expected Justice Frankfurter to view grudgingly the asserted power of the Court to invalidate state laws as contrary to the commerce clause itself. And indeed, early dissenting from invalidation of a state tax, the Justice agreed that "it becomes more and more important that potential conflicts between state and national powers should not be found where Congress has not found them, unless conflict is established by demonstrable concreteness."[67] It is for Congress to use its power to regulate possible conflict—to determine what the states might do in relation to interstate commerce, or to specific programs of federal regulation under the commerce power. The Court cannot write legislation for Congress. It cannot, for Congress, determine the proper apportionment of state taxes on the instrumentalities of interstate commerce. If Congress does not act, the Court can, in large measure, only let the states do as they like.

> The Commerce Clause does not deprive Minnesota of the power to protect the special interest that has been brought into play by Union's localized pursuit of its share in the comprehensive process of foreign commerce. To deny the states the power to protect such special interests when the Congress has not seen fit to exert its own legislative power would be to give an immunity to detached aspects of commerce unrelated to the objectives of the Commerce Clause. By its own force that Clause does not imply relief to those engaged in interstate commerce or foreign commerce from the duty of paying an appropriate share for the maintenance of the various state governments. Nor does it preclude a State from giving needful protection to its citizens in the course of their contacts with businesses conducted by outsiders when the legislation by which this is accomplished is general in its scope, is not aimed at interstate or foreign commerce, and involves merely burdens incident to effective administration.[68]

Increasingly, however, the Justice has found himself among those on the Court who would strike down state legislation under the commerce clause itself. Perhaps he has been reluctant to break sharply with "the historic duty of the Court."[69] Perhaps, disposed though he be to let the states govern, the Justice yet has to recognize that the states do not always govern wisely;

that they are likely to be less wise when tempted to favor local interests against foreign and interstate interests; that the dangers to the nation and the national interests from fragmentation and balkanization are too great pending the slow, sometimes hopeless, path of federal legislation. And some isolated areas of impact between local regulation and interstate commerce are hardly likely to move the national legislature to act, or even the federal administrative agencies to whom Congress has delegated the care of interstate commerce. The inertia of government, he may have become persuaded, bears on the side of restraint of commerce enhancing the dangers of fragmentation.[70] Perhaps, too, he has felt that Congress had accepted and was content to let the Court act as a kind of *ad hoc* commerce commission, confident that the Court was, generally, alert to the nation's needs and would read accurately the unexpressed wishes of Congress. Most important, perhaps, although its judgments appear as constitutional invalidations the Court is not in fact prohibiting state action finally. It is merely allocating tentatively responsibility between Congress and the states. Congress can always enter to reallocate, to permit what the Court has forbidden, or to forbid what it has permitted.

And so, although Congress has not acted, and has indicated nothing about its desires in regard to state action, the Justice has followed the established view. The states may not discriminate against interstate commerce. They may not interfere with commerce "unduly." The standard is vague, and depends on measures and degrees. But "the whole law does so," said Holmes, "as soon as it is civilized."[71] Government implies judgment, and constitutions impose not absolutes but tendencies. Justice Frankfurter is prepared to invalidate state laws when the state's interest in a regulation affecting interstate commerce seems less important than the burdens on that commerce.[72] He might prefer that the balancing be done by Congress, or by an administrative body authorized by Congress, but Congress has been content to leave it to the courts.

> Practical necessities and shrewd judgments about practical matters decide the fate of state legislation when challenged by the power or the action of Congress. State necessities, the fitness of state relief as against nation-wide action, the limited manifestation of a given evil or the limited benefits of its correction, the actual interest of the whole country in a phenomenon especially virulent in a particular state, the advantage of local regulation balanced against the cost or inconvenience to interests outside the state—these and like questions are involved in the process by which the Supreme Court in concrete cases has held for or against state and national action in the interacting areas of state and national interests.[73]

In regard to taxation of interstate commerce, the Justice found a confused pattern of cases and doctrines, forbidding some taxes, permitting others, with little basis in logic, or politics, or economics. The need cried for Congress to establish some pattern of taxation for the interstate economy, but the difficulties and complexities of the task have rendered Congress unwilling, or unable, to attempt major "solutions."[74] Sometimes it appears that the Justice was tempted to "clear up the mess" but it has proved not to be a task for judges.[75] How to give the states proper shares of revenue from a complex economy involves difficult determinations of policy in which logical categories derived from the commerce clause would help little. The Court cannot "devise appropriate standards for dividing up national revenue on the basis of more or less abstract principles of Constitutional law, which cannot be responsive to the subtleties of the interrelated economies of the Nation and State."[76] Sometimes his best hopes and efforts to clarify and systematize have led him— perhaps in despair—to accept less than logical categories, as when the states are forbidden "direct interference," to tax the interstate "sale itself," "the very freedom of commercial flow."[77] The Justice agrees that the states have power to tax and that interstate commerce "must pay its way." But the "diverse and fluctuating exercise of power by the various States . . . imposes an undue burden on interstate commerce."[78] Some principles seem obviously in the spirit of federalism: the need for an open economy suggests invalidation of taxes on interstate transactions that have the effect of tariffs. "The very purpose of the Commerce Clause was to create an area of free trade among the several States."[79] And the state does not need a particular tax, for there are enough sources of taxation that in impact as in principle do not strike too heavily at interstate commerce.[80] For the rest, artificial distinctions of the past have authority, and if they seem to have little rational basis, there is as little for rejecting them. And Congress, the states, as well as taxpayers may have come to count on them. Here again, the Justice recently anticipated the mood of Congress, this time to have the states leave alone what the Court had long said it must.[81]

In these commerce cases, co-operative federalism does not work without the Court to umpire and maintain the balance. The states cannot be allowed to govern as they will. The Congress ought to set the limits, but it has not effectively done so. The Justice has found himself the unwilling inheritor of congressional inadequacies in an area where the states quite clearly could not be counted on to forgo immediate local advantage in the national interest. He has accepted for the Court an unaccustomed and unwanted role, as a surrogate of Congress, trying to guess at what Congress would or should do, hoping that Congress can be moved to remedy the Court's mistakes at least when they are egregious.

# LIMITS OF A FEDERAL SUPREME COURT

Interstate commerce apart, federalism—among other considerations—requires that a federal Supreme Court exercise sparingly its power to invalidate state laws and state actions.

The Court must scrutinize state impingements on interstate commerce, and perhaps also express constitutional prohibitions federalistic in spirit—like those forbidding a state to enter into a treaty, or to coin money. Of very different significance is the role of the Court in applying those other prohibitions of the Constitution which seek not accommodation of competing needs of two governments but limitation on government on behalf of the individual, often expressed in terms of some ideal not clearly stated or conceived in the Constitution. When such prohibitions are invoked in the courts against the action of a state there is also—as part of the Justice's known philosophy of judicial self-restraint—a dimension of federalism to govern the role of the Supreme Court. That legislators are ultimate guardians of the liberties of the people quite as much as the courts applies equally, or perhaps more, to the states.[82] The Court must trust the states because the Constitution does; must have confidence that state officials will not lightly disregard their oath to support the United States Constitution.[83] It is a confidence not of naïveté, perhaps of politesse, or noblesse oblige; even more it reflects the conviction that under the Constitution it is the state's duty and responsibility to govern. Justice Frankfurter's famous statements on judicial review deal with Supreme Court scrutiny of state legislation and their undertones sound the Justice's federalism.

> Even where the social undesirability of a law may be convincingly urged, invalidation of the law by a court debilitates popular democratic government. Most laws dealing with economic and social problems are matters of trial and error. That which

before trial appears to be demonstrably bad may belie prophecy in actual operation. It may not prove good, but it may prove innocuous. But even if a law is found wanting on trial, it is better that its defects should be demonstrated and removed than that the law should be aborted by judicial fiat. Such an assertion of judicial power deflects responsibility from those on whom in a democratic society it ultimately rests—the people. If the proponents of union-security agreements have confidence in the arguments addressed to the Court in their "economic brief," they should address those arguments to the electorate. Its endorsement would be a vindication that the mandate of this Court could never give. That such vindication is not a vain hope has been recently demonstrated by the voters of Maine, Massachusetts, and New Mexico. And although several States in addition to those at bar now have such laws, the legislatures of as many other States have, sometimes repeatedly, rejected them. What one State can refuse to do, another can undo.

But there is reason for judicial restraint in matters of policy deeper than the value of experiment: it is founded on a recognition of the gulf of difference between sustaining and nullifying legislation. This difference is theoretical in that the function of legislating is for legislatures who have also taken oaths to support the Constitution, while the function of courts, when legislation is challenged, is merely to make sure that the legislature has exercised an allowable judgment, and not to exercise their own judgment, whether a policy is within or without "the vague contours" of due process. Theory is reinforced by the notorious fact that lawyers predominate in American legislatures. In practice also the difference is wide. In the day-to-day working of our democracy it is vital that the power of the non-democratic organ of our Government be exercised with rigorous self-restraint. Because the powers exercised by this Court are inherently oligarchic, Jefferson all of his life thought of the Court as "an irresponsible body" and "independent of the nation itself." The Court is not saved from being oligarchic because it professes to act in the service of humane ends. As history amply proves, the judiciary is prone to misconceive the public good by confounding private notions with constitutional requirements, and such misconceptions are not subject to legitimate displacement by the will of the people except at too slow a pace. Judges appointed for life whose decisions run counter to prevailing opinion cannot be voted out of office and supplanted by men of views more consonant with it. They are even farther removed from democratic pressures by the fact that their deliberations are in secret and remain beyond disclosure either by periodic reports or by such a modern device for securing responsibility to the electorate as the "press conference." But a democracy need not rely on the courts to save it from its own unwisdom. If it is alert—and without alertness by the people there can be no enduring democracy—unwise or unfair legislation can readily be removed from the statute books. It is by such vigilance over its representatives that democracy proves itself.

Our right to pass on the validity of legislation is now too much part of our constitutional system to be brought into question. But the implications of that right and the conditions for its exercise must constantly be kept in mind and vigorously observed. Because the Court is without power to shape measures for dealing with the problems of society but has merely the power of negation over measures shaped by others, the indispensable judicial requisite is intellectual humility, and such humility presupposes complete disinterestedness. And so, in the end, it is right that the Court should be indifferent to public temper and popular wishes. Mr. Dooley's "th' Supreme Coort follows th' iliction returns" expressed the wit of cynicism, not the demand of principle. A court which yields to the popular will thereby licenses itself to practice despotism, for there can be no assurance that it will not on another occasion indulge its own will. Courts can fulfill their responsibility in a democratic society only to the extent that they succeed in shaping their judgments by rational standards, and rational standards are both impersonal and communicable. Matters of policy, however, are by definition matters which demand the resolution of conflicts of value, and the elements of conflicting values are largely imponderable. Assessment of their competing worth involves differences of feeling; it is also an exercise in prophecy. Obviously the proper forum for mediating a clash of feelings and rendering a prophetic judgment is the body chosen for those purposes by the people. Its functions can be assumed by this Court only in disregard of the historic limits of the Constitution.[84]

To Justice Frankfurter judicial review may be of questionable wisdom, but it is here. "There is a gulf, however narrow, between deference to local legislation and complete disregard of the duty of judicial review. . . . This duty is not to be escaped, whatever I may think of investing judges with the power."[85] Prohibitions of the Constitution, however, are limitations on the freedom to govern. They are therefore to be narrowly construed, and hardly as absolute prohibitions. Many of them apply, in fact, to both the federal government and the state, so that a finding of a prohibition often means that action is forbidden to all government.[86] As concerns the states, in particular, the Constitution leaves them large freedom to do what they like —and what the Justices may not like—subject only to the clearest and narrowest limitations. Even the Fourteenth Amendment was not intended to deprive states of the freedom to govern, to take away the states' traditional responsibilities—say for administering the traditional criminal law[87]; only in regard to the Negro did that Amendment sharply curtail the states and subject them to the sharpest federal scrutiny. Again, Justice Frankfurter has been mindful too that the Supreme Court is a federal agency, and that its power is itself "an aspect of centralization too often overlooked."[88]

No discussion of the Justice's federalism can fairly avoid mention of due process. Long before he came to the Court he urged the abolition of the due process clauses, or their abandonment as a source of judicial limitation on government.[89] He was mindful of the sad history of the Court's efforts to read into these generalities economic theories of laissez-faire to frustrate state experiment in social and economic legislation. (The science of government, the Justice likes to quote Mr. Justice Johnson, is "the science of experiment."[90]) Against these judicial usurpations, Professor Frankfurter helped to develop and propagate the constitutional and political philosophy which recognized as paramount the authority to govern and sharply curtailed the authority of the Court to interfere with government. "The Supreme Court has interposed its veto against state action in matters confessedly of local concern, dealing solely with local situations, and expressing remedies derived from local experience."[91] The questions which the Court was deciding under "due process" were political, akin to other "political questions" that the Court has recognized as beyond its ken under the Constitution.[92] He was particularly reluctant to find reason for limiting free government in words of "convenient vagueness" like due process which derive their content not from the Constitution but from the disposition of the Justices, a phrase which "shelters the fallible judgment of individual Justices, in matters of fact and opinion not peculiarly within the special competence of judges, behind the impersonal authority of the Constitution."[93] "[No] nine men are wise enough and good enough to be entrusted with the power which the unlimited provisions of the due process clauses confer. . . . [The] centralizing authority lodged with the Supreme Court over the domestic affairs of forty-eight widely different states is an authority which it simply cannot discharge with safety either to itself or to the states. The due process clauses ought to go."[94]

Due process did not go. But Justice Frankfurter has judged by the philosophy which Professor Frankfurter professed. By 1939 when he came to the Court, due process had been reduced, in regard to the economic and social regulations that had fallen afoul of it earlier, to a requirement that state legislation have reasonable ends and that it pursue them by reasonable means. In no case during the Justice's twenty-three years on the bench did the Court find that an economic regulation violated due process.[95] But even as economic due process virtually disappeared, libertarian due process came of age. Here Justice Frankfurter has recognized substantive due process as a limitation on the freedom of the states to govern.[96] In part, he has accepted the compulsions of the Court's jurisprudence. In part, too, he has strong views that some areas of individual liberty and privacy are not lightly to be disturbed by government. Although he has resisted some connotations of "preferred freedoms," he recognizes that freedom of speech and press come to the Court "with a momentum for respect lacking when appeal is made to liberties which derive merely from shifting economic arrangements."[97] He has been particularly alert to interference by government, state or federal, with the privacy of the individual and his home, or with academic freedom.[98] But even here the due process clause "expressed a mood rather than a command."[99] Long ago he had affirmed "the conviction that our constitutional system rests upon tolerance and that its greatest enemy is the Absolute."[100] Due process imposes no absolute bars to government even where these fundamental liberties are involved. Order has its claims as does liberty, and order is itself a condition of liberty. The Court must, as best it can, judge the action of the states by balancing the asserted needs of government against the individual's freedom, giving respect to the judgment of those who primarily govern. He has been alert too to recognize competing liberties, competing fundamentals in a good society—allowing the state to safeguard the right of an individual to an impartial trial, or the integrity of the judicial process, against the freedom of others to express themselves.[101] In one area perhaps he has carried the limitations on government further than most—"matters, like censorship of the press or separation of Church and State, on which history, through the Constitution, speaks so decisively as to forbid legislative experimentation."[102] But even separation of Church and State does not prevent government from impinging on an individual's freedom of religion in its quest for some secular purpose it deemed superior—witness his famous dissent in the flag salute case.[103]

There are also elements of federalism, as of his views of government and of constitutions, in the Justice's application of procedural due process. He has been the chief spokesman against the view that the Fourteenth Amendment incorporated the whole Bill of Rights, the chief exponent of Cardozo's "ordered liberty" as the test of the process due from the states.[104] And he is led there not only by the history and language of the Amendment, or the unbroken jurisprudence of the Court, or the conviction that the states, essential participants in the ratification of the Amendment, had not bowed so low to national control. His views of American federalism resist the thought that the Fourteenth Amendment sought to tie the states to what the states had required of the federal government a century before. They resist the attempt to make specific what had better be general so as to lend itself more readily to progressive development in the light of growing enlightenment. They resist too the attempt to make uniform what had better be left open to diversity, to the experience and values of particular states and localities—so long as contemporary standards of fundamental justice are not at stake. The states accepted "not a stagnant formulation of what has been achieved in the past but a standard for judgment in the progressive evolution of the institutions of a free society."[105] The Amendment did not redistribute power as between the states and the national government, did not withdraw from the states the principal administration of criminal jusice. And so the Justices must "exercise with due humility our merely negative function in subjecting convictions from state courts to the very narrow scrutiny which the Due Process Clause of the Fourteenth Amendment authorizes."[106] The states are free to follow any procedures they like so long as they do

not shock the conscience. They may even admit evidence un-
lawfully obtained, although the methods for obtaining it violated fundamental privacies protected by the Constitution.[107]
He can invite executive clemency for Willie Francis; he cannot
find in due process authority to compel Louisiana to forgo the
penalty.[108] But the states cannot violate contemporary standards
of fairness, and the Justice is particularly sensitive to violations
of the dignity of the individual by coerced confessions or the
forced stomach pump, or inadequate attention to claims of in-
sanity.[109]

> In the illuminating phrase of Judge Learned Hand, due proc-
> ess "represents a mood rather than a command." The mood of
> the Supreme Court in subjecting the conduct of State criminal
> trials to the measure of the Fourteenth Amendment has been
> insistently cautious. Properly so, for the Amendment is not the
> basis of a uniform code of criminal procedure federally im-
> posed. Alternative modes of arriving at truth are not—they
> must not be—forever frozen. There is room for growth and
> vitality, for adaptation to shifting necessities, for wide differ-
> ences of reasonable convenience in method. . . .
> . . . In no sense is the Supreme Court a general tribunal for
> the correction of criminal errors, such as the Court of Criminal
> Appeal in England. On a continent peopled by 120,000,000 that
> would be an impossible task; in a federal system it would be a
> function debilitating to the responsibility of state and local
> agencies. But the Court, though it will continue to act with
> hesitation, will not suffer, in its own scathing phrase, "judicial
> murder."[110]

Due process, procedural and frequently even substantive due
process, bring to the Supreme Court for review what state courts
have done. In these and in other cases the Justice has revealed
what he thinks federalism requires of a federal Supreme Court
reviewing the judgment of the highest court of a state. Long

ago he remarked that "*Marbury* v. *Madison* has unduly over-shadowed *Cohens* v. *Virginia*,"[111] and repeatedly the Justice has referred to the delicacy of the Court's role in reviewing state cases.[112] Under the Constitution there is, in effect, a "distribution of judicial power between this Court and the highest courts of the States,"[113] but it is the Supreme Court that monitors the distribution. When the Court reviews a state court decision, the state itself is being reviewed, and that must be done sparingly, with deference, and only in accordance with the rules of review. In his first judicial opinion, invalidating a state discrimination against foreign commerce, he said: "it can never be pleasant to invalidate the enactment of a state, particularly when it bears the imprimatur of constitutionality by the highest state court."[114] An "alert deference to the judgment of the State court under review" is also an important safeguard against judicial whimsicality, against judges writing their personal preferences into law.[115]

The Justice's federalism permeates all his positions on review of state courts. Federalism, in part, underlies his desires to limit the interferences of the Supreme Court by a sparing exercise of an optional review. And nowhere has Justice Frankfurter been so meticulous as in his concern for the rules and procedures of review which often rise to constitutional importance because they reflect fundamentals of federalism. "We do not sit like a kadi under a tree dispensing justice according to considerations of individual expediency."[116] "A finding that a State court disregarded the Constitution of the United States should not be like a game of blind man's buff."[117] The states are entitled to insist on respect for their own procedures, though they may not exploit procedures to defeat federal interests.[118] They may insist on their own rules of evidence and their own findings of fact, except to the narrow extent that a federal question might be involved.[119] They are, we have seen, entitled to their own way of doing things unless that way denies due process because it shocks the conscience of mankind. Justice Frankfurter has paid close attention to the Court's doctrines for not reviewing acts of states and state courts, or for not reviewing them too soon—for requirements of standing, ripeness, case or controversy.[120] Justice Frankfurter is largely responsible for other doctrines now deep in the Court's jurisprudence, for example that federal courts should refrain from decision of local questions until the state courts have had the opportunity—to determine local law; to interpret a local statute, and to consider its constitutionality; to hear a claim that federal rights were violated; to clarify whether it decided a federal question or rested on an adequate state ground; even to rectify its own errors.[121] The additional time consumed in litigation is small price for the needs of federalism.[122]

Most important, perhaps, federalism requires the Supreme Court to dismiss a case which was—or might have been—decided on an adequate state ground, rather than one involving a federal interest.

These sound like dry rules of technical jurisdiction. In fact they express an important phase of due regard for our federal constitutional system. State Courts are no less under duty to observe the United States Constitution than this Court. To be sure, authority is vested in this Court to see to it that that duty is observed. But to assume disobedience instead of obedience to the Law of the Land by the highest courts of the States is to engender friction between the federal and state judicial systems, to weaken the authority of state courts and the administration of state laws by encouraging unmeritorious resorts to this Court, and wastefully to swell the dockets of this Court.[123]

Such reasoning is not what is invidiously called legalistic. Law is essentially legalistic in the sense that observance of well-recognized procedure is, on balance, socially desirable. In the well-being of a federalism like ours observance of what on casual view may appear as a sterile technicality is important whenever this Court is brought in potential conflict with State courts. Especially is it important as to those vast reaches of the criminal law which are exclusively within State domain, and which are therefore not subject to the supervision which this Court may exercise over the lower federal courts. Of course this Court has the duty of alertness in safeguarding rights guaranteed by the Constitution of the United States against infringement by the States even in their difficult task of repressing crime and dealing with transgressors. At best, however, intervention by this Court in the criminal process of States is delicate business. It should not be indulged in unless no reasonable doubt is left that a State denies, or has refused to exercise, means of correcting a claimed infraction of the United States Constitution.

Intervention by this Court in the administration of the criminal justice of a State has all the disadvantages of interference from without. Whatever short-cut to relief may be had in a particular case, it is calculated to beget misunderstanding and friction and to that extent detracts from those imponderables which are the ultimate reliance of a civilized system of law. After all, this is the Nation's ultimate judicial tribunal, not a super-legal-aid bureau. If the same relief, although by a more tedious process, is available through a State's self-corrective process, it enlists the understanding and support of the community. Considerations rooted in psychological and sociological reason underlie the duty of abstention by this Court from upsetting convictions by State courts or their refusal to grant writs of *habeas corpus* to those under State sentences, where state action may fairly be attributed to a rule of local procedure and is not exclusively founded on denial of a federal claim. When a State court explicitly rests its decision on a State ground it is easy sailing. But even when a State court summarily disposes of a case without spelling out its ground, led to do so, as is this Court in many cases, by the burden of its docket, it is our duty not to attribute to the State court flouting of the United States Constitution but to infer regard for its own law, if to that law may reasonably be attributed a finding of inadequacy in the mode of presenting the constitutional claim for which relief is here sought on the merits.[124]

## FEDERALISM HAS ITS PRICE

Federalism has its price and it must be paid—in state differences, in lacks of uniformity, in inadequacies of order or of liberty which are not given to the nation and its Supreme Court to remedy.

"We must pay a price for federalism—at one time the impotence of the federal government to correct glaring evils unheeded by some of the states, at other times the impotence of states to correct glaring evils unheeded by the federal government."[125] If it is for Congress largely to distribute the roles of nation and state, Congress may make mistakes, or do nothing or not enough—as, for example, about state taxation of interstate commerce, or even the rights of the Negro. If the states are free to govern, they may govern unwisely. If some states use their freedom to be progressive others may take the road of reaction. Unless they transgress the will of Congress, or one of the explicit prohibitions in the Constitution, or the moods of equality, of reasonableness, of "ordered liberty" in the Fourteenth Amendment, the states can be as foolish as they will and there is none—not even the Supreme Court—to say them nay. The Court can help make federalism work; it cannot supply those inadequacies inherent in federalism.

Federalism means that the federal and state governments, too, are largely independent, permitting consequences that could not be in a unitary government. So, both governments might punish separately for the same act.[126] So, despite the privilege against self-incrimination in federal proceedings, the state may compel testimony which "may facilitate to some extent his amenability to federal process."[127]

[The] bulk of authority to legislate on what may be compendiously described as criminal justice . . . is under our system the responsibility of the individual States. . . . The choice of this form of federal arrangement was the product of a jealous concern lest federal power encroach upon the proper domain of the States and upon the rights of the people. It was the same jealous concern that led to the restrictions on the National Government expressed by the . . . Bill of Rights. . . . [The] adoption of the Fourteenth Amendment in 1868 did not change the distribution of powers between the States and the Federal Government so as to withdraw the basic interests of criminal justice from the exclusive control of the States. . . . [Due process] does not blur the great division of powers between the Federal Government and the individual States in the enforcement of the criminal law. . . . [W]hatever inconveniences and embarrassments may be involved, they are the price we pay for our federalism.[128]

There is also the price of fifty different states pursuing their own way, unwilling or unable to find the path of co-operation. States may not act outside their own territory, but subject to general constitutional limitation they can act within regardless of consequences elsewhere.[129] Several states may impose several taxes, often on aspects of a single enterprise.[130] The states can impose burdens on foreign corporations as a condition of coming in to do local business.[131] They can force foreign creditors to come into the state, according to its procedures, for their share in a local corporation's assets.[132] Congress (and sometimes the Supreme Court) can keep the states from going their own ways to the detriment of interstate commerce. But neither the Court nor perhaps even Congress could forbid, say, one state from offering easy divorces to the residents of other states. Here again, State A, free to govern as it will, is free to grant easy divorces. And the Constitution requires State B to give full faith and credit to State A's judgments. But this is a provision in derogation of State B's freedom to govern, and need not be literally and liberally construed.[133] That state may also have legitimate interests and should be able to scrutinize whether State A had the necessary jurisdiction for its judgment.[134] Surely the state offering the "cheapest" divorce should not, without the necessary jurisdiction, be able to impose its lowest standard on all the states.[135] If this independence of states may breed small chaos, it is the small price of federalism. The answer we have seen is co-operation— by compact, by uniform act, by settling their differences through negotiation, sometimes in original suit in the Supreme Court.[136] If the states will not co-operate, the price of federalism is higher than it need be.

Such appear, to me, to be the principal outlines of the federalism of Mr. Justice Frankfurter. (Federal jurisdiction, a major element only glanced at here, is discussed elsewhere in this volume.) There are other pieces which might be added, for federalism permeates the Justice's views of the Constitution and of the role of the Supreme Court. That it is a federal Supreme Court, applying a federalist Constitution, is surely an element in virtually every constitutional question—even, say, his strong views that the inadequacies of districting or apportionment for voting are political questions not given to the federal courts to rectify.[137] Inevitably this picture of the Justice's federalism suffers the distortion of selection, of omitting the variations, the modifications, even the seeming inconformities. It is incomplete, too, in so far as it derives mainly from Justice Frankfurter's own opinions and writings. (And what he quotes of others. A man, it sometimes seems, might be known by what he quotes.) Obviously, his views are reflected also in the opinions of others which he saw fit to join; there are reflections too in opinions which cried to be written, and were not. Obviously, too, his own opinions are not always all his. Many a Supreme Court opinion is "an orchestral and not a solo performance."[138] But perhaps more than most he has played his own piece,[139] and issues of federalism evoked his most sensitive performance.

In regard to federalism, too, the Justice has practiced with remarkable fidelity what the professor had taught. And the portrait of his federalism has been remarkably whole, although Justice Frankfurter's mind—as fine a mind perhaps as any the Court has known—is too big to be plagued by hobgoblins of inconsistency. Some may find more inconsistencies than are indeed necessary. In fact, of course, to one whose philosophy is that government should be allowed to govern, only those cases which deny authority to government, federal or state, need to be justified and explained. And to one whose hallmark is the balancing of interests and the drawing of lines, one can hardly talk of consistency, although some might differ with him as to the weight to be given to a factor, how the balance reads, where a line should be drawn. Some may differ with the Justice about the continuing importance of federalism, or what indeed federalism requires in a given case. Some may think it abdication and even demeaning that the Justice sees the Court's role as only to smooth the workings of constitutional federalism so others can govern wisely. Some, admitting that the freedom to govern had to be asserted when the spirit of laissez-faire threatened, may wish for less concern now to assure the freedom to govern, more active intervention by the Court on behalf of individual against government—even state government. None can ask for greater sensitiveness to the competing interests or greater awareness of the role of the Supreme Court in our federal system. None can wish for more meticulous and dedicated effort to carry out that role as he has seen it.

His own constitutional outlook was, throughout a long life, free from fluctuations. This was so because it was born of a deeply rooted and coherent philosophy concerning the dynamic character of the American Constitution and of a judge's function in construing it. If he threw the weight of his authority on the side of social readjustments through legislation it was not because of any faith in panaceas in general or in measures of social amelioration in particular. . . . But his skepticism and even hostility, as a matter of private judgment, toward legislation which he was ready to sustain as a judge only serve to add cubits to his judicial stature. For he thereby transcended personal predilections and private notions of social policy and became truly the impersonal voice of the Constitution.[140]

This was said of Mr. Justice Holmes, in 1938, by Professor Felix Frankfurter. It would have pleased the professor, as it will please the Justice, that it is not far from what might be said today about the federalism of Mr. Justice Frankfurter.

# All Sides of the Question
# Felix Frankfurter and Personal Freedom

Archer E. Sutherland

*Bussey Professor of Law,*
*Harvard Law School*

This brief essay concerns the nature of the Supreme Court's work in cases touching personal liberty; in particular it treats of Justice Frankfurter's part in such cases during his twenty-three years on that Court. At the outset an academician is beset by a somewhat guilty sense of his own effrontery in attempting any such estimate in a few pages. Indeed a onetime pupil, still filled with a certain affectionate awe, hesitates, has doubts about attempting it at all, when four decades have increasingly convinced the observer that no part of adjudication is plain or easy and that time, upsetting many faiths once confidently fought for, should give the critic some share of Felix Frankfurter's own doubt at the hasty acceptance of jurisdiction.

---

* To Miss Susan Schapiro I owe much gratitude for generous and scholarly aid in the preparation of this paper.

Perhaps the greatest difficulty in the judge's work arises because of its normative function—its lawmaking. Little novelty remains in the statement that policy making is part of the judge's daily task, though even today the conventions of discussion still treat this function a trifle delicately. Holmes made the classic statement of an evident truth in 1881:

> . . . In substance the growth of the law is legislative. . . . The very considerations which judges most rarely mention, and always with an apology, are the secret roots from which the law draws all the juices of life. I mean, of course, considerations of what is expedient for the community concerned.[1]

What is perhaps a little less evident is the ubiquitous pervasiveness of these policy aspects of appellate judges' work.

Policy considerations arise even in the decision of questions of fact—not, one hopes, in such a way as to control fact finding by the result it will produce, but quite properly in considering how far, in a federal nation having both state and national courts, the federal courts will reconsider state-court determinations of fact.[2] The Supreme Court at its October 1963 term will consider the amount of damages properly awarded by a state court in a civil libel suit. Instead of presenting a simple "question of fact," this litigation involves intricate problems of federal-state relations, and the extent to which the Fourteenth Amendment should prevent a state from regulating criticism of its officials by awards of libel damages immune from Supreme Court supervision.[3]

Policy questions clearly arise in the decision of such complex constitutional questions as Justice Brandeis described in his 1932 Burnet v. Coronado dissent:

> In the cases which now come before us there is seldom any dispute as to the interpretation of any provision. The controversy is usually over the application to existing conditions of some

well-recognized constitutional limitation. This is strikingly true of cases under the due process clause when the question is whether a statute is unreasonable, arbitrary or capricious; of cases under the equal protection clause when the question is whether there is any reasonable basis for the classification made by a statute; and of cases under the commerce clause when the question is whether an admitted burden laid by a statute upon interstate commerce is so substantial as to be deemed direct. These issues resemble, fundamentally, that of reasonable care in negligence cases, the determination of which is ordinarily left to the verdict of the jury. In every such case the decision, in the first instance, is dependent upon the determination of what in legal parlance is called a fact, as distinguished from the declaration of a rule of law. When the underlying fact has been found, the legal result follows inevitably. The circumstance that the decision of that fact is made by a court, instead of by a jury, should not be allowed to obscure its real character.[4]

As soon as a judge has to construe a statute or attribute specific meaning to one of the "broad inexplicit clauses of the Constitution"[5] he clearly engages in a normative process, and must consider the effect of his choices on individual men and on the structure and well-being of government. Still more obvious lawmaking occurs when the judge selects one of two, or perhaps more, lines of precedent to be his justification for deciding a lawsuit. Such opinions at their best are frankly creative, canvassing the social or economic effects of the proposed judicial rule just as a legislative committee does, or should do, in considering the effect of a proposed statute.[6] But perhaps the critic's convassing of categories of decision, law or fact, his construction or selection of precedent, his making of fine distinctions in "legal concepts around which dialectic conflicts have been fought time out of mind,"[7] is here hardly worth the effort. The Supreme Court is one of the nation's lawmaking organs; the only question is how well it has done this work and how well it will continue.

Ideally the judge is sensitive to all this, conscious of the multiple relevances bearing on his decision. One of the greatest of our judges has told us of the dangers of judicial simplicity, of the need for a sophisticated sense of the complications of life.[8] Judging is a difficult discipline, involving much renunciation of the luxury of certitude, of firm conviction. Various callings in life are inconsistent with simplistic and assured zeal for causes. A military officer evaluating intelligence will be a dangerous reliance if he permits his wish for victory to occlude judgment of inconveniently strong enemy capabilities. A diplomat under a duty to report to his government the state of opinion in the nation to which he is accredited will lose his value if his hopes for success of his own country's policy come to conceal from him adverse trends abroad. A social scientist who permits political or social sympathies to minimize indications tending toward unwelcome conclusions impairs the integrity of his science. Indeed the same is true of many other scholarly fields, in which zeal for a cause can affect what the scholar concludes from evidence. The essential maladjustment in all these situations is unilateralism; one factor comes to preponderate in thinking, until judgment is distorted. Talleyrand's classic caution against zeal has for nearly two centuries been quoted to demonstrate the utter cynicism of that worldly but highly intelligent statesman. This estimate may be unjust; he may, for once, have been stating a genuine conviction about essential detachment in the weighing of conflicting policies.

Except when a decision is adverse to their wishes, most men recognize the necessity that the judge see all sides of policy questions—which are generally polyhedral. No event in American history points up the widespread expectation of judicial detachment (that is, the ability to see more than one aspect) so dramatically as the reaction to President Roosevelt's plan for change in the composition of the Supreme Court, announced in his message to Congress on February 5, 1937. Men who had been, and who continued to be, sympathetic with the social and economic aspirations of the New Deal were shocked by what seemed a proposal to appoint judges committed in advance to deciding certain issues in a certain way. In this episode clearly appears the difference between well-intended zeal for a cause, which men quite properly expect to animate the popular politician, and the reserved opinion which the wise expect of a judge.

Of course complete severance from all human predisposition is as impossible for a judge as for anyone else. If he has had an active career at the bar he will have worked his heart out in some hopeless causes, and he will take with him to the bench an urge to decide the other way when chance offers. If he has been active in a political party he may sense some clinging loyalties—though the fortunate absence of doctrinal content in most American party organization makes severance easier. But if even judges cannot be depersonalized spirits, they can still be conscious of their own predispositions, and in setting a course can allow for them, as a small-boat sailor, knowing his craft's cranky tendency to head off, can keep a little corrective pressure on the tiller.

These observations on judicial detachment and bias are relevant to an estimate frequently made of Felix Frankfurter, that (for no perceivable reason) he underwent a sudden change of character on changing one sort of gown for another; that, from being a bold and zealous liberal professor, he suddenly became a timid and legalistically conservative judge. No abstracter of quintessences could hope to condense in a few pages of print the complex intellect, the wide, swift perceptions of such a man. But here I shall set out briefly the reasons which convince me that precisely Frankfurter's sensitivity to all sides of a question, sensitivity to the displeasing as well as the welcome argument, has made certain of the Justice's critics, whose eyes are single to one set of considerations, judge him some sort of intellectual turn-coat. And because this cannot usefully be discussed in the abstract, I shall consider the matter in relation to four problems which have much troubled thoughtful Americans during the last quarter-century—the perennial question of Church and State; the antithesis between personal freedom and national integrity presented by Communist cases; the pull-and-haul between semi-independence of the states and aspiration of the American Negro to equality; and finally the function of the Supreme Court in requiring fair standards in state administration of criminal justice. All four can develop high emotional pressures, and with them can arouse the sense of mission which often commits men to a single point of view. All four can serve to aid in estimating the quality of Frankfurter's judicature.

## I.

Justice Frankfurter's first full term on the Court[9] brought him the duty of writing the prevailing opinion in Minersville School District v. Gobitis.[10] On June 3, 1940, he and all the rest of the Justices except Stone voted in that case to reverse a decree of the Court of Appeals for the Third Circuit, and to uphold the right of a Pennsylvania school district to expel two children, then ten and twelve years old,[11] for refusing to salute the flag as a daily school exercise. The Gobitis family were Jehovah's Witnesses, and for them this salute was a sin. Liberal ranks joined in opposing the compulsory salute. The Justice's Harvard colleague of the preceding year, Professor George K. Gardner, argued the case for the children. Another erstwhile Harvard colleague, Zechariah Chafee, Jr., joined the rest of the American Bar Association's Committee on the Bill of Rights in a brief in favor of enjoining the School Board. The Civil Liberties Union filed an-

ARCHER E. SUTHERLAND

other brief on the same side.[12] One asks how Felix Frankfurter
came to the conclusion he did. He poses the problem:

[T]he manifold character of man's relations may bring his
conception of religious duty into conflict with the secular interests of his fellow-men. When does the constitutional guarantee compel exemption from doing what society thinks necessary
for the promotion of some great common end, or from a
penalty for conduct which appears dangerous to the general
good? To state the problem is to recall the truth that no single
principle can answer all of life's complexities. The right to
freedom of religious belief, however dissident and however ob-
noxious to the cherished beliefs of others—even of a majority
—is itself the denial of an absolute. But to affirm that the freedom to follow conscience has itself no limits in the life of a
society would deny that very plurality of principles which, as
a matter of history, underlies the protection of religious tolera-
tion. Compare Mr. Justice Holmes in Hudson County Water
Co. v. McCarter, 209 U.S. 349, 355. Our present task then, as
so often the case with courts, is to reconcile two rights in
order to prevent either from destroying the other. But, because
in safeguarding conscience we are dealing with interests so
subtle and so dear, every possible leeway should be given to the
claims of religious faith.
. . . The preciousness of the family relation, the authority and
independence which give dignity to parenthood, indeed the
enjoyment of all freedom, presuppose the kind of ordered
society which is summarized by our flag. A society which is
dedicated to the preservation of these ultimate values of civilization may in self-protection ultilize the educational process for inculcating those almost unconscious feelings which
bind men together in a comprehending loyalty, whatever
may be their lesser differences and difficulties. That is to say,
the process may be utilized so long as men's right to believe as
they please, to win others to their way of belief, and their right
to assemble in their chosen places of worship for the devotional
ceremonies of their faith, are all fully respected.
Judicial review, itself a limitation on popular government, is

115

a fundamental part of our constitutional scheme. But to the legislature no less than to courts is committed the guardianship of deeply cherished liberties. See Missouri, K. & T.R. Co. v. May, 194 U.S. 267, 270. Where all the effective means of inducing political changes are left free from interference, education in the abandonment of foolish legislation is itself a training in liberty. To fight out the wise use of legislative authority in the forum of public opinion and before legislative assemblies rather than to transfer such a contest to the judicial arena, serves to vindicate the self-confidence of a free people.[13]

Here, be it remembered, was an echo of Holmes, who had written in the 1904 Missouri, K.&T. Railway case that Frankfurter cited:

Great constitutional provisions must be administered with caution. Some play must be allowed for the joints of the machine, and it must be remembered that legislatures are ultimate guardians of the liberties and welfare of the people in quite as great a degree as the courts.[14]

Holmes, to be sure, was writing for the Court in upholding a Texas statute which imposed a $25 civil penalty on a railroad for letting weeds go to seed on its right of way. There the issue was property right, not human right; we have become used to the easy distinction. But in Gobitis there was not involved the point Stone had made in part of his prophetic Footnote 4 of 1938,[15] concerning extra judicial scrutiny of ". . . legislation which restricts those political processes which can ordinarily be expected to bring about repeal of undesirable legislation." And even Stone here was voicing a remaining faith in the popular will, a bit of the eighteenth century, bright hope for man if he were only left to govern himself. True it is that Footnote 4 sounded—and was soon to attract much attention by—a new note of doubt concerning the infallibility and the virtuousness of the legislative choice. But pessimism about the legislative process, such a conspicuous strand of thought in American intellectuals in the years after, say, 1947—this by and large had barely begun to stir. The New Deal was recent; some liberals remembered liberal opinion of five years before when the Supreme Court was warned to keep its hands off what the legislatures ordained. The choice of policies in 1941 was not clear and simple: liberal allegiance could divide.

Two years late the Supreme Court overruled Gobitis in West Virginia State Board v. Barnette.[16] Of the old majority of eight, Hughes and McReynolds had retired; Jackson and Rutledge had joined the Court. Stone and the two new Justices voted for the children. The three converts, Black, Douglas, and Murphy, were a bit apologetic; they had felt a reluctance, they explained, to interfere with a state law; but reflection had convinced them that individual freedom had a predominant value. Of the old majority only Roberts, Reed, and Frankfurter remained willing to let the state have its way. Frankfurter's dissent is a touching statement of continuing faith in constitutional values which liberals had embraced a generation earlier. He begins by discounting his own prejudices, and goes on to state limits for judicial competence:

> One who belongs to the most vilified and persecuted minority in history is not likely to be insensible to the freedoms guaranteed by our Constitution. Were my purely personal attitude relevant I should wholeheartedly associate myself with the general libertarian views in the Court's opinion, representing as they do the thought and action of a lifetime. . . . The duty of a judge who must decide which of two claims before the Court shall prevail, that of a State to enact and enforce laws within its general competence or that of an individual to refuse obedience because of the demands of his conscience, is not that of the ordinary person. It can never be emphasized too much that

one's own opinion about the wisdom or evil of a law should be excluded altogether when one is doing one's duty on the bench. The only opinion of our own even looking in that direction that is material is our opinion whether legislators could in reason have enacted such a law. In the light of all the circumstances, including the history of this question in this Court, it would require more daring than I possess to deny that reasonable legislators could have taken the action which is before us for review. Most unwillingly, therefore, I must differ from my brethren with regard to legislation like this. . . .

Not so long ago we were admonished that "the only check upon our own exercise of power is our own sense of self-restraint. For the removal of unwise laws from the statute book appeal lies not to the courts but to the ballot and to the processes of democratic government." United States v. Butler, 297 U.S. 1, 79. . . .

The admonition that judicial self-restraint alone limits arbitrary exercise of our authority is relevant every time we are asked to nullify legislation. The Constitution does not give us greater veto power when dealing with one phase of "liberty" than with another.[17]

Something significant happened in the intellectual life of the Supreme Court between 1938 and 1943, something even now not clearly articulated, perhaps because it concerns a change in our political theory so profound that we hesitate to see it plainly. This doctrinal change becomes apparent, like a dark oracle, half understood, in the change of opinions between Gobitis and Barnette. There was under way in the United States, a revision in thought about majoritarian institutions, and the somewhat tentative, hesitant opinions of Justices Black and Douglas, and of Justice Murphy, show that the change was felt but not yet fully mapped out. Stone had sensed it in 1938 and his Carolene footnote was the earliest hint by any of the Justices that a new doctrine had to be evolved.

War is a great leveler of men's material lives, and modern warfare brings much of this leveling from the field to the factory and the fireside. The passage from Gobitis to Barnette occurred in wartime; and although that fact plays no part in the Justices' expressed reasoning, it must have been conspicuous in their minds. The onetime rich man, who, during the depression, had been ashamed and timid at having conspicuously more abundance than his out-of-work neighbor, was now similarly ashamed to be living in ease and plenty while his son or his neighbor's son was at the front. Rationing; taxation that would once have been thought incredible; governmental recapture of excess profits; national planning of material lives—all went forward as a matter of course, gladly accepted if only the war could be won!

But there must have been doctrinal doubts stirring. On February 1, 1943, Representative Martin Dies had, in a speech on the floor of the House, attacked certain government employees as radical bureaucrats, affiliates of Communist-front organizations, and urged that the Congress take steps to eliminate them from public office. The saboteurs' case[18] in 1942 had troubled the Supreme Court, after most of the petitioners had been hastily executed without its intervention, with the need to explain away the "open court rule" of *Ex parte* Milligan.[19] Martial law continued in Hawaii. Inoffensive citizens of Japanese descent had been rounded up in California and shipped inland to detention centers; unpleasant rumors went round that some of the pressures to get these people out of their homes and businesses did not originate in military fears. The liberal formula of the first four decades of the twentieth century, the theory that our troubles came from small groups of tyrants, monopolists, arms makers, the *Nine Old Men*[20]—the theory that if only oligarchs of every description could be swept away and the general will could be unleashed, then our troubles would be over—this theory in practice began to develop weak spots. Economic leveling we could stand for; we accepted it along with the universe; we'd better! But we began to suspect that we people could be cruel and selfish as readily as those oligarchs. For nearly four decades we had been jesting, around tables at our faculty clubs, at poor old Peckham's agonized cry in his 1905 Lochner opinion,[21] "But are we all, on that account, at the mercy of legislative majorities?" Perhaps we now had to qualify our jokes with an afterword; they had ceased to be entirely droll; perhaps old Peckham had an idea worth dusting off—not, of course, in economic matters, but in—in what? Here one has to pause for definitional troubles. Stone's Footnote 4 of 1938 had suggested the predominance of those constitutional privileges tending to promote the majoritarian political process, and if you read the whole footnote you could find in it further suggestions for the predominance of all First Amendment rights. What was the formula to be for Peckham *redivivus*? "Human Rights but not Property Rights"? This was satisfying if you said it quickly enough and did not stop to think about it.[22] There is, of course, the embarrassing presence of property along with life and liberty in the Fifth and Fourteenth Amendments; there is the lack of any explicit hierarchy of values in the text of the Bill of Rights; there is the uneasy sense that, if a Japanese-American were done out of his curio shop or truck garden by a white neighbor, his property right had become a human right. By the time of Barnette we sensed a need for the restatement of liberal theory. The old one had been too simple.

The constitutional power of a state to override religious scruples had diminished, in Justice Frankfurter's view, by 1947 when he joined Jackson's dissent in Everson v. Board of Education[23] and when he wrote a dissent of his own in 1952 in Zorach v. Clauson.[24] But meantime Frankfurter continued to be skeptical of formulated rules of constitutional law which, he felt, were apt to result in slighting respectable public interests which claimed constitutional standing. In 1948 he dissented from the Court's judgement that Lockport, New York, had improperly limited the Jehovah's Witnesses in their use of a loudspeaker in a park[25]; and two years later he concurred specially in upholding Trenton, New Jersey's regulation of a sound truck commenting, apparently, on a labor dispute.[26] What is particularly striking in the case of the Trenton sound truck is Justice Frankfurter's return to his Barnette theme, that under the Fourteenth mendment there should be no institutionalized upgrading of one freedom at the cost of another. He wrote:

> Wise accommodation between liberty and order always has been, and ever will be, indispensable for a democratic society. Insofar as the Constitution commits the duty of making this accommodation to this Court, it demands vigilant judicial self-restraint. A single decision by a closely divided court, unsupported by the confirmation of time, cannot check the living process of striking a wise balance between liberty and order as new cases come here for adjudication. To dispose of this case on the assumption that the Saia Case, 334 U.S. 558, decided only the other day, was rightly decided, would be for me to start with an unreality. While I am not unaware of the circumstances that differentiate this case from what was ruled in Saia, further reflection has only served to reinforce the dissenting views I expressed in that case. . . .
>
> The opinions in this case prompt me to make some additional observations. My brother Reed speaks of "the preferred position of freedom of speech," though, to be sure, he finds that the Trenton ordinance does not disregard it. This is a phrase that has uncritically crept into some recent opinions of this Court. I deem it a mischievous phrase, if it carries the thought, which it may subtly imply, that any law touching communication is infected with presumptive invalidity. It is not the first time in the history of constitutional adjudication that such a doctrinaire attitude has disregarded the admonition most to be observed in exercising the Court's reviewing power over legislation, "that it is a *constitution* we are expounding," M'Culloch v. Maryland,

4 Wheat (U.S.) 316, 407. I say the phrase is mischievous because it radiates a constitutional doctrine without avowing it. Clarity and candor in these matters, so as to avoid gliding unwittingly into error, make it appropriate to trace the history of the phrase "preferred position."[27]

The Justice discussed a line of cases beginning with Herndon v. Lowry in 1937,[28] running down through Thomas v. Collins in 1945.[29] He found no justification in any majority opinion of the Court for a doctrine of presumptive unconstitutionality where legislation ". . . touches the field of the First Amendment and the Fourteenth Amendment, insofar as the latter's concept of 'liberty' contains what is specifically protected by the First. . . ." He added:

> The objection to summarizing this line of thought by the phrase "the preferred position of freedom of speech" is that it expresses a complicated process of constitutional adjudication by a deceptive formula. And it was Mr. Justice Holmes who admonished us that "To rest upon a formula is a slumber that, prolonged, means death." *Collected Legal Papers*, 306. Such a formula makes for mechanical jurisprudence. . . .
>
> Only a disregard of vital differences between natural speech, even of the loudest spellbinders, and the noise of sound trucks would give sound trucks the constitutional rights accorded to the unaided human voice. Nor is it for this Court to devise the terms on which sound trucks should be allowed to operate, if at all. These are matters for the legislative judgment controlled by public opinion. So long as a legislature does not prescribe what ideas may be noisily expressed and what may not be, nor discriminate among those who would make inroads upon the public peace, it is not for us to supervise the limits the legislature may impose in safeguarding the steadily narrowing opportunities for serenity and reflection. Without such opportunities freedom of thought becomes a mocking phrase and without freedom of thought there can be no free society.[30]

Justice Frankfurter's theory of judicial review is coherent and logical as one would expect from a man of his hard-eyed scholarly tradition. Here is no random deciding, as the winds of sympathy blow. Basically he clings to the classic liberal tradition that popular will, expressed through elected legislative organs, is what ordinarily controls. If, however, that popular will produces some sort of outrage, the Justice wishes to have his judgment guided only by general canons, instead of being tied to a set of specific rules, probably not enacted with the present facts in mind. He remembers Marshall's phrase and emphasis ". . . it is a *constitution* we are expounding"; much of his philosophy stems from his conviction that the judge's guidance must have the general quality of constitutional clauses, not the detail of a municipal traffic ordinance. When Felix Frankfurter delivered the opening address at the Harvard Law School Conference on Government under Law, on the two hundredth anniversary of John Marshall's birth, he said of that phrase of Marshall's:

> "It bears repeating because it is, I believe, the single most important utterance in the literature of constitutional law—most important because most comprehensive and comprehending."[31]

## II.

In 1946 the Supreme Court had to consider the situation of three employees of the executive branch whom the Congress had specified by name in Section 304 of the Urgent Deficiency Appropriation Act of 1943,[32] directing that

> . . . no part of any appropriation . . . shall be used after November 15, 1943, to pay any part of the salary, or other compensation for the personal services, of Goodwin B. Watson, William

E. Dodd, junior, and Robert Morss Lovett, unless prior to such date such person has been appointed by the President by and with the advice and consent of the Senate. . . .

Representative Martin Dies, chairman of the House Committee on Un-American Activities, stimulated this legislation by a speech on the floor of the House in which he named these three, with others, as affiliates of "Communist-front organizations." A subcommittee of the House Appropriations Committee thereupon held hearings about the matter and reported to the full Committee that Watson, Dodd, and Lovett had been engaged in "subversive activity." The House insisted that Section 304 go in the appropriation bill; the Senate gave way; President Roosevelt signed the measure with a statement that he did so only to finance the war; that he considered Section 304 "not only unwise and discriminatory, but unconstitutional." The executive branch kept Watson, Dodd, and Lovett employed after November 15, 1943. The Supreme Court upheld a judgment of the Court of Claims awarding them their pay. Mr. Justice Black wrote the Court's opinion finding Section 304 void as a bill of attainder, forbidden Congress by Article I, Section 9, Clause 3.[33]

Justice Frankfurter concurred in the result, but for himself and Justice Reed he expressed his own reasons. He wrote:

> Not to exercise by indirection authority which the Constitution denied to this Court calls for the severest intellectual detachment and the most alert self-restraint. The scrupulous observance, with some deviations, of the professed limits of this Court's power to strike down legislation has been, perhaps, the one quality the great judges of the Court have had in common. Particularly when congressional legislation is under scrutiny, every rational trail must be pursued to prevent collision between Congress and Court. For Congress can readily mend its way, or the people may express disapproval by choosing dif-

ferent representatives. But a decree of unconstitutionality by this Court is fraught with consequences so enduring and far-reaching as to be avoided unless no choice is left in reason.

The inclusion of Section 304 in the Appropriation Bill undoubtedly raises serious constitutional questions. But the most fundamental principle of constitutional adjudication is not to face constitutional questions but to avoid them, if at all possible. And so the "Court developed for its own governance in the cases confessedly within its jurisdiction, a series of rules under which it has avoided passing upon a large part of all the constitutional questions pressed upon it for decision." Brandeis J., concurring, in Ashwander v. Tennessee Valley Authority, 297 U.S. 288, 341, at 346. That a piece of legislation under scrutiny may be widely unpopular is as irrelevant to the observance of these rules for abstention from avoidable adjudication as that it is widely popular. Some of these rules may well appear over-refined or evasive to the laity. But they have been vindicated, in conspicuous instances of disregard, by the most painful lessons of our constitutional history. . . .[34]

Section 304, the Justice found, was not a bill of attainder within the Constitutional prohibition. He construed the section, instead, to forbid "ordinary disbursal" but not to cancel the obligation to pay for services rendered. Hence the Court of Claims judgment prevailed, and Frankfurter concurred in it.

This, it seems to me, was a *tour de force*, performed for a good reason. Here was a bad law, which the Congress should not have passed. Either it must stand, or somebody had to do something extraordinary with some language. The prevailing opinion somewhat stretched the Constitution's idea of a bill of attainder.[34] Frankfurter gave a somewhat strained construction to an Act of Congress—though he gave it with an unusual knowledge of British and American history and a realization of the irrevocable nature of constitutional invalidation. The Justice is a reverent man, keeping always in mind what is owing to the constitutional system as well as the sad predicament of the individual litigant. The power of the House seems to have been misused in this instance; the courts were in an unpleasant position; who, if he looks at all sides of the question, will be confident that of the possible judicial remedies Frankfurter did not choose the least disadvantageous?

In 1951 the Supreme Court, with no majority opinion, upheld the conviction of Eugene Dennis and others, first-flight leaders of the Communist party of the United States, for conspiring to organize the Communist Party as a group "who teach and advocate the overthrow . . . of the Government of the United States by force and violence. . . ."[35] Justice Frankfurter concurred, but in an elaborate opinion of his own:

> Few questions of comparable import have come before this Court in recent years. The appellants maintain that they have a right to advocate a political theory, so long, at least, as their advocacy does not create an immediate danger of obvious magnitude to the very existence of our present scheme of society. On the other hand, the Government asserts the right to safeguard the security of the Nation by such a measure as the Smith Act. Our judgment is thus solicited on a conflict of interests of the utmost concern to the well-being of the country. This conflict of interests cannot be resolved by a dogmatic preference for one or the other, nor by a sonorous formula which is in fact only a euphemistic disguise for an unresolved conflict. If adjudication is to be a rational process, we cannot escape a candid examination of the conflicting claims with full recognition that both are supported by weighty title-deeds.[36]
>
> The most tragic experience in our history is a poignant reminder that the Nation's continued existence may be threatened from within. To protect itself from such threats, the Federal Government "is invested with all those inherent and implied powers which, at the time of adopting the Constitution, were generally considered to belong to every government as such, and as being essential to the exercise of its functions." Mr. Justice Bradley, concurring in Legal Tender Cases (U.S.) 12 Wall 457, 554, 556; and see Re Debs, 158 U.S. 564, 582.

But even the all-embracing power and duty of self-preservation is not absolute. Like the war power, which is indeed an aspect of the power of self-preservation, it is subject to applicable constitutional limitations. See Hamilton v. Kentucky Distilleries & Warehouse Co., 251 U.S. 146, 156. Our Constitution has no provision lifting restrictions upon governmental authority during periods of emergency, although the scope of a restriction may depend on the circumstances in which it is invoked.

The First Amendment is such a restriction. It exacts obedience even during periods of war; it is applicable when war clouds are not figments of the imagination no less than when they are. The First Amendment categorically demands that "Congress shall make no law respecting an establishment of religion, or prohibiting the free exercise thereof; or abridging the freedom of speech, or of the press; or the right of the people peaceably to assemble, and to petition the Government for a redress of grievances." The right of a man to think as he pleases, to write what he thinks, and to have his thoughts made available for others to hear or read has an engaging ring of universality. The Smith Act and this conviction under it no doubt restricts the exercise of free speech and assembly. Does that, without more, dispose of the matter?

Just as there are those who regard as invulnerable every measure for which the claim of national survival is invoked, there are those who find in the Constitution a wholly unfettered right of expression. Such literalness treats the words of the Constitution as though they were found on a piece of outworn parchment instead of being words that have called into being a nation with a past to be preserved for the future. The soil in which the Bill of Rights grew was not a soil of arid pedantry. The historic antecedents of the First Amendment preclude the notion that its purpose was to give unqualified immunity to every expression that touched on matters within the range of political interest. The Massachusetts Consitution of 1780 guaranteed free speech; yet there are records of at least three convictions for political libels obtained between 1799 and 1803. The Pennsylvania Constitution of 1790 and the Delaware Constitution of 1792 expressly imposed liability for abuse of the right of free speech. Madison's own State put on its books in

1792 a statute confining the abusive exercise of the right of utterance. And it deserves to be noted that in writing to John Adams' wife, Jefferson did not rest his condemnation of the Sedition Act of 1798 on his belief in unrestrained utterance as to political matter. The First Amendment, he argued, reflected a limitation upon Federal power, leaving the right to enforce restrictions on speech to the States.[37]

Justice Frankfurter's opinion is forty-three pages long. He canvasses every aspect of the claim of the defendants to immunity under the political freedoms of the First Amendment, and finds insufficient grounds to vacate their conviction. No one who has followed Frankfurter's intellectual career can suppose him callous to the claims of the radical. By and by the burden of his argument becomes almost monotonous: a judge must weigh all claims, he persistently reminds us, must keep always in mind that courts are not omniscient, must not save himself the worry of weighing all competing claims by adopting a verbal formula and imagining that it is a reasoning process.

In the troubled years that followed the armistice of 1945, the matter of Communism presented itself to the Court again and again: in federal and state requirements of strange oaths[38]; in various types of "investigations" in the course of which some witnesses refused to respond[39]; in litigation concerning statutory disqualification for public employment[40]; in the long-drawn proceedings to require the Communist Party to register under the Subversive Activities Control Act[41]; in a host of other ways. In the opinions Justice Frankfurter wrote, for the Court, or concurring specially, or dissenting, the qualities I have already mentioned are clearly indicated. Conspicuous was his scrupulous attention to the Court's self-imposed restrictions on its functions —for example, the rule that a controversy must reach a stage in which all relevant considerations have clearly emerged before the Court will pass on it, a debatable rule in any instance because reasonable men can differ as to the attainment of that stage.[42] Always he showed patient willingness to examine in detail the complex web of interests involved, interests of individuals and interests of the public not only in the statutory or other public measure at issue but in the maintenance of separate functions of executive, legislator, and judge, and in the preservation of the nation-state allotment of the total of governing power. No paper as brief as this one must be should attempt any exhaustive exposition of all the cases. Samples will have to do.

In 1957 Justice Frankfurter wrote opinions in Watkins v. United States.[43] and in Sweezy v. New Hampshire,[44] in each concurring in the result reached by the Court. In each he agreed that a man, who in the matters under review had been adjudged punishable for refusing to answer questions in an investigation into Communist activities, had been improperly convicted. Two years later in Barenblatt v. United States[45] and in Uphaus v. Wyman[46] he concurred in judgments reaching the opposite result, under circumstances quite similar. Watkins and Barenblatt both involved the House Un-American Activities Committee. Sweezy and Uphaus both concerned investigations conducted by the Attorney General of New Hampshire under a mandate of the state legislature. In each pair of cases the Supreme Court of the United States was asked to invalidate punitive action against non-responsive witnesses. In the 1957 cases Frankfurter voted for invalidation of the punishment and gave his reasons; in the pair decided two years later he voted, without writing an opinion, to uphold the punishment. Some scrutiny of these cases may illustrate the Justice's mode of work.

Watkins[47] was a prosecution under Title 2 United States Code Section 192 for the misdemeanor of "contempt of Congress." This statute penalizes the refusal to answer any question "pertinent to the question under inquiry." Watkins refused to answer certain questions put by a subcommittee of the House Un-American Activities Committee. Counsel for the subcommittee read to him a list of names, and asked if Watkins knew these people to have been members of the Communist Party. Watkins explained to the subcommittee why he refused to answer:

> "I am not going to plead the Fifth Amendment, but I refuse to answer certain questions that I believe are outside the proper scope of your committee's activities. I will answer any questions which this committee puts to me about myself. I will also answer questions about those persons whom I knew to be members of the Communist Party and whom I believe still are. I will not, however, answer any questions with respect to others with whom I associated in the past. I do not believe that any law in this country requires me to testify about persons who may in the past have been Communist Party members or otherwise engaged in Communist Party activity but who to my best knowledge and belief have long since removed themselves from the Communist movement.
>
> "I do not believe that such questions are relevant to the work of this committee nor do I believe that this committee has the right to undertake the public exposure of persons because of their past activities. I may be wrong, and the committee may have this power, but until and unless a court of law so holds and directs me to answer, I most firmly refuse to discuss the political activities of my past associates."

The lower federal courts convicted Watkins under the statute, but the Supreme Court reversed this judgment. Justice Frankfurter gave his reasons succinctly in a separate concurrence:

> By . . . making the federal judiciary the affirmative agency for enforcing the authority that underlies the congressional power to punish for contempt, Congress necessarily brings into play the specific provisions of the Constitution relating to the prosecution of offenses and those implied restrictions under which Courts function.
>
> To turn to the immediate problem before us, the scope of

inquiry that a committee is authorized to pursue must be defined with sufficiently unambiguous clarity to safeguard a witness from the hazards of vagueness in the enforcement of the criminal process against which the Due Process Clause protects. The questions must be put with relevance and definiteness sufficient to enable the witness to know whether his refusal to answer may lead to conviction for criminal contempt and to enable both the trial and the appellate courts readily to determine whether the particular circumstances justify a finding of guilt.

While implied authority for the questioning by the Committee, sweeping as was its inquiry, may be squeezed out of the repeated acquiescence by Congress in the Committee's inquiries, the basis for determining petitioner's guilt is not thereby laid. Prosecution for contempt of Congress presupposes an adequate opportunity for the defendant to have awareness of the pertinency of the information that he has denied to Congress. And the basis of such awareness must be contemporaneous with the witness' refusal to answer and not at the trial for it. Accordingly, the actual scope of the inquiry that the Committee was authorized to conduct and the relevance of the questions to that inquiry must be shown to have been luminous at the time when asked and not left, at best, in cloudiness. The circumstances of this case were wanting in these essentials.

Sweezy[48] presented a more puzzling set of facts. The Attorney General of New Hampshire, pursuing his inquiries under a legislative mandate, had asked Sweezy a long series of questions about his writings, his activities with the Progressive Party, the political activities of his wife, about lectures given by Sweezy at the University of New Hampshire, and about Sweezy's opinions. After the Supreme Court of New Hampshire had found Sweezy guilty of contempt for refusal to answer certain of these questions, the Supreme Court of the Unite States reversed, with dissents written by Justices Clark and Burton. No majority of the Court agreed in the reasons for reversal. Chief Justice

Warren announced the Court's judgment and delivered an opinion in which Justices Black, Douglas, and Brennan joined. Justice Frankfurter agreed that the New Hampshire judgment of contempt must be reversed, but stated his reasons separately in an opinion in which Justice Harlan joined. The opinion is characteristic in its scrupulous regard for federal-state relations, and accordingly in its clear statement of what was not decided. He wrote:

> For me this is a very different case from Watkins v. United States. . . . This case comes to us solely through the limited power to review the action of the States conferred upon the Court by the Fourteenth Amendment. Petitioner claims that respect for liberties guaranteed by the Due Process Clause of that Amendment precludes the State of New Hampshire from compelling him to answer certain questions put to him by the investigating arm of its legislature. Ours is the exceedingly difficult task of making the final judicial accommodation between the competing weighty claims that underlie all such questions of due process. . . .
>
> Whether the state legislature should operate largely by committees, as does the Congress, or whether committees should be the exception, as is true of the House of Commons, whether the legislature should have two chambers or only one, as in Nebraska, whether the State's chief executive should have the pardoning power, whether the State's judicial branch must provide trial by jury, are all matters beyond the reviewing powers of this Court. Similarly, whether the Attorney General of New Hampshire acted within the scope of the authority given him by the state legislature is a matter for the decision of the courts of that State, as it is for the federal courts to determine whether an agency to which Congress has delegated power has acted within the confines of its mandate. See United States v. Rumely, 345 U.S. 41. Sanction of the delegation rests with the New Hampshire Supreme Court, and its validation in Nelson v. Wyman, 99 N.H. 33, 105 A.2d. 756, is binding here.[49]

Turning to the questions asked of and refused by Sweezy, Justice Frankfurter pointed to the narrow issue decided below by the Supreme Court of New Hampshire. Sweezy had been held in contempt for refusal to answer questions as to a lecture he had been invited to give at the University of New Hampshire and certain questions dealing with the activity of Nancy Sweezy, Charles Beebe, and Abraham Walenko in connection with the Progressive Party. Frankfurter wrote:

> The questions that petitioner refused to answer regarding the university lecture, the third given by him in three years at the invitation of the faculty for humanities, were:
> "What was the subject of your lecture?"
> "Didn't you tell the class at the University of New Hampshire on Monday, March 22, 1954, that Socialism was inevitable in this country?"
> "Did you advocate Marxism at that time?"
> "Did you express the opinion, or did you make the statement at that time that Socialism was inevitable in America?"
> "Did you in this last lecture on March 22 or in any of the former lectures espouse the theory of dialectical materialism?"
> "I have in the file here a statement from a person who attended your class, and I will read it in part because I don't want you to think I am just fishing. 'His talk this time was on the inevitability of the Socialist program. It was glossed-over interpretation of the materialist dialectic.' Now, again I ask you the original question."
> In response to the first question of this series, petitioner had said at the hearing:
> "I would like to say one thing in this connection, Mr. Wyman. I stated under oath at my last appearance that, and I now repeat it, that I do not advocate or in any way further the aim of overthrowing constitutional government by force and violence. I did not so advocate in the lecture I gave at the University of New Hampshire. In fact I have never at any time so advocated in a lecture anywhere. Aside from that I have nothing I want to say about the lecture in question."

The New Hampshire Supreme Court, although recognizing that such inquiries "undoubtedly interfered with the defendant's free exercise" of his constitutionally guaranteed right to lecture, justified the interference on the ground that it would occur "in the limited area in which the legislative committee may reasonably believe that the overthrow of existing government by force and violence is being or has been taught, advocated or planned, an area in which the interest of the State justifies this intrusion upon civil liberties." 100 N.H., at 113, 114, 121 A. 2d, at 792. According to the court, the facts that made reasonable the committee's belief that petitioner had taught violent overthrow in his lecture were that he was a Socialist with a record of affiliation with groups cited by the Attorney General of the United States or the House Un-American Activities Committee and that he was co-editor of an article stating that, although the authors hated violence, it was less to be deplored when used by the Soviet Union than by capitalist countries.

When weighed against the grave harm resulting from governmental intrusion into the intellectual life of a university, such justification for compelling a witness to discuss the contents of his lecture appears grossly inadequate. Particularly is this so where the witness has sworn that neither in the lecture nor at any other time did he ever advocate overthrowing the Government by force and violence.

Progress in the natural sciences is not remotely confined to findings made in the laboratory. Insights into the mysteries of nature are born of hypothesis and speculation. The more so is this true in the pursuit of understanding in the groping endeavors of what are called the social sciences, the concern of which is man and society. The problems that are the respective preoccupations of anthropology, economics, law, psychology, sociology, and related areas of scholarship are merely departmentalized dealing, by way of manageable division of analysis, with interpenetrating aspects of holistic perplexities. For society's good—if understanding be an essential need of society—inquiries into these problems, speculations about them, stimulation in others of reflection upon them, must be left as unfettered as possible. Political power must abstain from intrusion into this activity of freedom, pursued in the interest of wise government and the people's well-being, except for reasons that are exigent and obviously compelling.

Justice Frankfurter's discussion of the Progressive Party also sets forth the precise inquiries.

Petitioner stated, in response to questions at the hearing, that he did not know of any Communist interest in, connection with, influence over, activity in, or manipulation of the Progressive Party. He refused to answer, despite court order, the following questions on the ground that, by inquiring into the activities of a political organization, they infringed upon the inviolability of the right to privacy in his political thoughts, actions and associations:

"Was she, Nancy Sweezy, your wife, active in the formation of the Progressive Citizens of America?"

"Was Nancy Sweezy then working with individuals who were then members of the Communist Party?"

"Was Charles Beebe active in forming the Progressive Citizens of America?"

"Did he work with your present wife—did Charles Beebe work with your present wife in 1947?"

"Did it [a meeting at the home of one Abraham Walenko] have anything to do with the Progressive Party?"

The Supreme Court of New Hampshire justified this intrusion upon his freedom on the same basis that it upheld questioning about the university lecture, namely, that the restriction was limited to situations where the Committee had reason to believe that violent overthrow of the Government was being advocated or planned. It ruled:

". . . That he [the attorney general] did possess information which was sufficient to reasonably warrant inquiry concerning the Progressive Party is evident from his statement made during the hearings held before him that 'considerable sworn testimony has been given in this investigation to the effect that the Progressive Party in New Hampshire has been heavily infiltrated by members of the Communist Party and that the policies and purposes of the Progressive Party have been directly

influenced by members of the Communist Party.' 100 N.H., at
111, 121 A.2d, at 790.

For a citizen to be made to forgo even a part of so basic a
liberty as his political autonomy, the subordinating interest of
the State must be compelling. . . . In the political realm, as in
the academic, thought and action are presumptively immune
from inquisition by political authority. It cannot require argument that inquiry would be barred to ascertain whether a citizen had voted for one or the other of the two major parties
either in a state or national election. Until recently, no difference would have been entertained in regard to inquiries about
a voter's affiliations with one of the various so-called third parties that have had their day, or longer, in our political history.
. . . Whatever, on the basis of massive proof and in the light of
history, of which this Court may well take judicial notice, be
the justification for not regarding the Communist Party as a
conventional political party, no such justification has been afforded in regard to the Progressive Party. A foundation in fact
and reason would have to be established far weightier than the
intimations that appear in the record to warrant such a view of
the Progressive Party. This precludes the questioning that petitioner resisted in regard to that Party.

To be sure, this is a conclusion based on a judicial judgment in balancing two contending principles—the right of a
citizen to political privacy, as protected by the Fourteenth
Amendment, and the right of the State to self-protection. And
striking the balance implies the exercise of judgment. This is
the inescapable judicial task in giving substantive content,
legally enforced, to the Due Process Cause, and it is a task ultimately committed to this Court. It must not be an exercise of
whim or will. It must be an overriding judgment founded on
something much deeper and more justifiable than personal
preference. As far as it lies within human limitations, it must
be an impersonal judgment. It must rest on fundamental presuppositions rooted in history to which widespread acceptance may
fairly be attributed. Such a judgment must be arrived at in a
spirit of humility when it counters the judgment of the State's
highest court. But, in the end, judgment cannot be escaped—
the judgment of this Court. . . . And so I am compelled to con-

clude that the judgment of the New Hampshire court must be reversed.[50]

Two years later, without any separate explanation of his reasons, Mr. Justice Frankfurter joined the majority of five in the Uphaus and Barenblatt cases, upholding convictions of contempt for refusal to answer questions put by the attorney general of New Hampshire and by a subcommittee of the House Committee on Un-American Activities. The New Hampshire case[51] concerned solely the refusal of Mr. Uphaus, who conducted a "World Fellowship's Camp" in New Hampshire, to produce a record of the guests at that camp, which was a resort or inn, furnishing board and lodgings to persons applying, and required by statute to maintain a register like a hotel register. The majority of the Supreme Court, in an opinion by Mr. Justice Clark, stated: ". . . the academic and political freedom discussed in Sweezy v. New Hampshire, *supra*, are not present here in the same degree since World Fellowship is neither a university nor a political party."

The Uphaus case aroused much sympathy; the defendant thus imprisoned for a considerable period was an elderly man, identified with liberal causes for a long time, considered by many observers to be a harmless left-winger. Nevertheless, the distinctions between the Uphaus and Sweezy cases, as the majority pointed out, were substantial; the values were not quite the same; the relative weighting of the interests of the state and of the respondent could be considered determinatively different, by a fair-minded man.

In Barenblatt, where Justice Frankfurter again joined a five-man majority without separate expression, the distinction from Watkins two years earlier is more difficult. Barenblatt had been a teacher at the University of Michigan. He was indicted under Title 2 United States Code, Section 192; the Supreme Court decided only the propriety of the following questions: "Are you now a member of the Communist Party? Have you ever been a member of the Communist Party? Were you ever a member of the Haldane Club of the Communist Party while at the University of Michigan?" The majority distinguished Watkins. Mr. Justice Harlan wrote:

> Undeniably a conviction for contempt under 2 U.S.C. sec. 192 cannot stand unless the questions asked are pertinent to the subject matter of the investigation. Watkins v. United States, *supra* (354 U.S. at 214, 215). But the factors which led us to rest decision on this ground in Watkins were very different from those involved here.
>
> In Watkins the petitioner had made specific objection to the Subcommittee's questions on the ground of pertinency; the question under inquiry had not been disclosed in any illuminating manner; and the questions asked the petitioner were not only amorphous on their face, but in some instances clearly foreign to the alleged subject matter of the investigation— "Communism in labor." *Id.* 354 U.S. at 185, 209–215.
>
> In contrast, the petitioner in the case before us raised no objections on the ground of pertinency at the time any of the questions were put to him. It is true that the memorandum which petitioner brought with him to the Subcommittee hearing contained the statement, "To ask me whether I am or have been a member of the Communist Party may have dire consequences. I might wish to . . . challenge the pertinency of the question to the investigation," and at another point quoted from this Court's opinion in Jones v. Securities & Exch. Com., 298 U.S. 1, language relating to a witness' right to be informed of the pertinency of questions asked him by an administrative agency. These statements cannot, however, be accepted as the equivalent of a pertinency objection. At best they constituted but a contemplated objection to questions still unasked, and buried as they were in the context of petitioner's general challenge to the power of the Subcommittee they can hardly be considered adequate, within the meaning of what was said in

Watkins, supra (354 U.S. at 214, 215), to trigger what would have been the Subcommittee's reciprocal obligation had it been faced with a pertinency objection.

We need not, however, rest decision on petitioner's failure to object on this score, for here "pertinency" was made to appear "with undisputable clarity."

Justice Harlan pointed out that before the questions were put to him Barenblatt had prepared a memorandum of constitutional objections which he filed with the subcommittee to justify his refusal to respond. This memorandum, Justice Harlan indicated, showed that Barenblatt understood the pertinency of the inquiries put to him. Futhermore, as the Court's opinion indicated, Barenblatt refused to answer questions concerning his own Communist Party affiliation while Watkins had freely answered the same inquiry.

Competing interests in questions of constitutionality can become so evenly balanced that they turn on a knife edge. What may appear petty differences may be sufficient to tilt the balance one way or the other. Reasonable men can differ about the weight to give factors of differentiation; but I find it hard to say that there is no substantial difference between Sweezy and Watkins of 1947 and Uphaus and Barenblatt of 1959.

## III.

The constitutional status of the American Negro has been one of the urgent questions before the Supreme Court throughout the period of Mr. Justice Frankfurter's active work. In a number of his opinions treating various aspects of this question, the Justice has demonstrated the qualities which this paper particularly examines—awareness of the multiple relevances which should bear on decision of an important public question, and scrupulous attention to the precise question presented by the complex of fact and law. An example is the Jaybird Party case[52] of 1953. Ever since Reconstruction times, one of the conspicuous policies of former Confederate states has been the attempt to bar the Negro from effective political participation. Where this exclusion does not concern any federal office, and where it is effectuated by purely private means, the ability of the United States to intervene becomes doubtful, because there may be a federal ground neither in Article I of the Constitution nor in the Fourteenth or Fifteenth Amendments with their state-action requirements. The Jaybird Party case presented such an attempt to control local politics by whites only. Since 1889, in one of the Texas counties, a group calling itself the Jaybird Democratic Association or Jaybird Party had excluded Negroes from its ranks. The Jaybirds annually conducted a pre-primary election in which they determined whom they would support for purely local offices in the Democratic primary. Selection in the primary was tantamount to final election. And, with few exceptions, between 1889 and 1953, endorsement by Jaybirds meant victory in the primary. If the Jaybirds were entirely non-governmental, having no statutory sanction as the primaries themselves have, having no other public quality, exclusion of Negroes from Jaybird ranks becomes difficult to distinguish from exclusion of Negroes from membership in, say, a golf club or a businessmen's luncheon club; conceivably in some communities endorsement by such a group might have a determinative influence in a local election. Terry and some other Negro voters of the county in question brought an action in the United States District Court against Adams and other officers of the Jaybird Association, seeking a decree declaring that the plaintiffs and others similarly situated were entitled to vote in the Jaybird pre-primary. The District Court concluded that the plaintiffs had such a right.[53] The Court of Appeals reversed.[54] On certiorari the Supreme Court of the United States reversed the Court of Appeals and reinstated the holding of the District Court that the combined Jaybird-Democratic-general election machinery had on account of race and color unconstitutionally deprived Terry and the other Negroes of their right to vote.

In this case, as in a number of other difficult constitutional controversies of the present time, the judgment of the Court did not muster in one opinion a majority of five Justices. Mr. Justice Black announced the Court's judgment and wrote an opinion in which Justices Douglas and Burton joined. Mr. Justice Clark wrote another opinion concurring in the Court's judgment and Chief Justice Vinson and Justices Reed and Jackson joined with him. Mr. Justice Frankfurter wrote a separate opinion in which he spoke for himself alone. Only Mr. Justice Minton dissented. The ground of Justice Minton's dissent points up the reasoning of Justice Frankfurter's opinion in favor of the Negroes' rights. Minton ends his dissent with these pointed words:

> In this case the majority have found that this pressure group's work does constitute state action. The basis of this conclusion is rather difficult to ascertain. Apparently it derives mainly from a dislike of the goals of the Jaybird Association. I share that dislike. I fail to see how it makes state action.

Justice Frankfurter's opinion clearly shows his mode of reasoning to reach a result contrary to Minton's, his consciousness of the inevitability of individual choice, his perception of the impossibility in such a case of finding some extraneous standard which will lift from the judge the burden of individual judgment. He wrote:

> This case is for me by no means free of difficulty. Whenever the law draws a line between permissive and forbidden

conduct cases are bound to arise which are not obviously on one side or the other. These dubious situations disclose the limited utility of the figure of speech, a "line," in the law. Drawing a "line" is necessarily exercising a judgment, however confined the conscientious judgment may be within the bounds of constitutional and statutory provisions, the course of decisions, and the presuppositions of the judicial process. If "line" is in the main a fruitful tool for dividing the sheep from the goats, it must not be forgotten that since the "line" is figurative the place of this or that case in relation to it cannot be ascertained externally but is a matter of the mind. . . . "The right of citizens of the United States to vote shall not be denied or abridged by the United States or by any State on account of race, color, or previous condition of servitude." U.S. Constitution, Fifteenth Amendment, Section 1. The command against such denial or abridgment is directed to the United States and to the individual States. Therefore, violation of this Amendment and the enactments passed in enforcement of it must involve the United States or a State. In this case the conduct that is assailed pertains to the election of local Texas officials. To find a denial or abridgment of the guaranteed voting right to colored citizens of Texas solely because they are colored, one must find that the State has had a hand in it. . . . As the action of the entire white voting community, the Jaybird primary is as a practical matter the instrument of those few in this small county who are politically active—the officials of the local Democratic party and, we may assume, the elected officials of the county. As a matter of practical politics, those charged by State law with the duty of assuring all eligible voters an opportunity to participate in the selection of candidates at the primary—the county election officials who are normally leaders in their communities—participate by voting in the Jaybird primary. They join the white voting community in proceeding with elaborate formality, in almost all respects parallel to the procedures dictated by Texas law for the primary itself, to express their preferences in a wholly successful effort to withdraw significance from the State-prescribed primary, to subvert the operation of what is formally the law of the State for primaries in this county.

Justice Frankfurter, by upholding the right of the Negro to political participation on the basis of the practical control of the Jaybird election by public officials which therefore made the pre-primary "State action," avoids the difficulty involved in saying that whenever a group becomes numerous enough it becomes "the State." His vigilance for the Negro's right to participate in the political process is part and parcel of his respect for that process, which emerges in much of his judicial self-restraint. If majoritarian control of government is to be majoritarian it must not exclude a large part of the majority by a policy of racial exclusiveness.

In 1960 many of the same values which Justice Frankfurter had considered in the Jaybird case appeared again when the Supreme Court had before it a question of the validity of a statute of Alabama which redefined the boundaries of the city of Tuskegee. Tuskegee had been a square; the statute changed the square to "an uncouth twenty-eight-sided figure" which excluded from the city all save four or five of its late four hundred Negro voters while it did not remove a single white voter or resident from the municipal boundaries. A United States District Court and, on appeal from it, the Court of Appeals for the Fifth Circuit both held that the federal judiciary had no power to supervise or change any boundaries of municipal corporations made by an Alabama legislature. A principal obstacle to granting the relief lay in a 1946 case, Colegrove v. Green, concerning congressional redistricting which had arisen in Illinois, in which the Supreme Court of the United States had refused to intervene on the ground that a "political question" was involved.[55] In Colegrove, Justice Frankfurter announced the Court's judgment and wrote an opinion for himself and Justices Reed and Burton. No one opinion gained the adherence of a majority of the Justices. The case involved a complaint that the congressional districting in Illinois grossly discriminated against the plaintiffs who, living in a city, had only a small fraction of the influence in the choice of a congressman enjoyed by dwellers in a sparsely populated rural area. Frankfurter wrote:

> The one stark fact that emerges from a study of the history of Congressional apportionment is its embroilment in politics, in the sense of party contests and party interests. . . . To sustain this action would cut very deep into the very being of Congress. Courts ought not to enter this political thicket.

In the Tuskegee case[56] Justice Frankfurter wrote the opinion of the Court, which, reversing the District Court and the Court of Appeals, upheld the rights of the plaintiff Negroes to have a declaration that the legislation was invalid.

He wrote:

> The respondents find [a] barrier to the trial of this case in Colegrove v. Green, 328 U.S. 549. In that case the Court passed on an Illinois law governing the arrangement of congressional districts within that State. The complaint rested upon the disparity of population between the different districts which rendered the effectiveness of each individual's vote in some districts far less than in others. This disparity came to pass solely through shifts in population between 1901, when Illinois organized its congressional districts, and 1946, when the complaint was lodged. During this entire period elections were held under the districting scheme devised in 1901. The Court affirmed the dismissal of the complaint on the ground that it presented a subject not meet for adjudication. The decisive facts in this case, which at this stage must be taken as proved, are wholly different from the considerations found controlling in Colegrove.
>
> That case involved a complaint of discriminatory apportionment of congressional districts. The appellants in Colegrove complained only of a dilution of the strength of their votes as a result of legislative inaction over a course of many years. The petitioners here complain that affirmative legislative action de-

prives them of their votes and the consequent advantages that the ballot affords. When a legislature thus singles out a readily isolated segment of a racial minority for special discriminatory treatment, it violates the Fifteenth Amendment. In no case involving unequal weight in voting distribution that has come before the Court did the decision sanction a differentiation on racial lines whereby approval was given to unequivocal withdrawal of the vote solely from colored citizens. Apart from all else, these considerations lift this controversy out of the so-called "political" arena and into the conventional sphere of constitutional litigation.

In sum, as Mr. Justice Holmes remarked, when dealing with a related situation, in Nixon v. Herndon, 273 U.S. 536, 540, "Of course the petition concerns political action," but "The objection that the subject matter of the suit is political is little more than a play upon words." A statute which is alleged to have worked unconstitutional deprivations of petitioners' rights is not immune to attack simply because the mechanism employed by the legislature is a redefinition of municipal boundaries. According to the allegations here made, the Alabama Legislature has not merely redrawn the Tuskegee city limits with incidental inconvenience to the petitioners; it is more accurate to say that it has deprived the petitioners of the municipal franchise and consequent rights and to that end it has incidentally changed the city's boundaries. While in form this is merely an act redefining metes and bounds, if the allegations are established, the inescapable human effect of this essay in geometry and geography is to despoil colored citizens, and only colored citizens, of their theretofore enjoyed voting rights. That was not Colegrove v. Green.

Thus to a certain extent Justice Frankfurter, by reprieving Colegrove v. Green, demonstrated again a thread of political philosophy that runs through a great many of his opinions. Despite the disillusionment that has beset many liberals since the close of the Second World War he retains a deep respect for the legislative process, for the traditional expression of the general will by elected legislators even when their elections are subject to some of the flaws which continually beset the democratic process. So radical a wrong as the disfranchisement of a race conflicts with this philosophy. But in 1962 when Baker v. Carr[57] held that the federal courts could properly entertain an action to enjoin state officials from conducting elections for the state legislature under a drastically unequal apportionment, Justice Frankfurter wrote a dissenting opinion in which Justice Harlan joined. The Supreme Court, Frankfurter said, was reversing in Baker v. Carr a uniform course of decision established by a dozen cases. He pointed out that the matter at bar was the latest in a series in which the due process and equal protection clauses of the Fourteenth Amendment were "invoked in federal courts as restrictions upon the power of the States to allocate electoral weight among the voting populations of their various geographical subdivisions." He cited a series of cases including Colegrove v. Green. He found clearly distinguishable the cases involving Negro voting because of the explicit mandate of the Fifteenth Amendment, but of the general question of reallocation of voting power with no racial connotations, the situation in Baker v. Carr, he wrote:

> A controlling factor in such cases is that, decision respecting these kinds of complex matters of policy being traditionally committed not to courts but to the political agencies of government for determination by criteria of expediency, there exists no standard ascertainable by settled judicial experience or process by reference to which a political decision affecting the question at issue between the parties can be judged.

It is quite possibly no mere coincidence that Mr. Justice Harlan and Mr. Justice Frankfurter were here associated in their opinions and that they have seen eye to eye in other somewhat comparable issues. Mr. Justice Harlan, a Rhodes scholar, is an honorary Fellow of Balliol. Mr. Justice Frankfurter, onetime Eastman professor at Oxford, has in many ways and on many occasions shown his deep respect for English constitutional ideas.[58] The Briton looks for protection of his constitutional rights to the deep-rooted traditions of the House of Commons much as Americans look to what they hope are the deep-rooted traditions of the Supreme Court of the United States. American liberals who were active in controversies concerning the role of the federal courts a generation ago had something of the same attitude toward the Congress. A somewhat similar line of thought emerges from Judge Learned Hand's 1958 Holmes lectures published in that year under the title *The Bill of Rights*. This is a trend which leads to less judicial activism than is desired by many liberals of the present day. It is perhaps out of harmony with some realities of our time. But to say this is far from suggesting that a reasonable man, deeply dedicated to the democratic theory of government, could not hold as Mr. Justice Frankfurter did.

## IV.

Quantitative analysis of constitutional litigation is difficult, and perhaps futile, but a glance at the Federal Supplement reports or the reports of the Supreme Court of the United States for any year will suggest that a very large part of the litigation concerning constitutional law now going on in the courts concerns criminal process. Many of these cases challenge the constitutional propriety of convictions in state courts, sometimes made by review in the Supreme Court of the United States and sometimes made by habeas corpus in the lower federal courts. Inevitably thus arise questions of the sort which gravely troubled Justice Frankfurter throughout his career on the bench.

Respect for the states as constitutional institutions was a strong element in his judicial logic. To make the Supreme Court a general tribunal of review of the reasonableness of state adjudications troubled him deeply, particularly where this involved a redetermination of state court findings of fact. But when review of a state criminal conviction in the Supreme Court did become necessary, Justice Frankfurter desired to retain his full power, to assume his full responsibility for determining the constitutionality of the decision below. He distrusted, as Holmes had before him, any idea that a verbal formula could make decisions for him and eliminate the hard necessity of self-reliance in judicial choice. This attitude led to his rejection of the idea that the Fourteenth Amendment "incorporated," *literatim et verbatim,* the provisions of the first eight Amendments of the federal Constitution. It gave rise to one of the most noteworthy exchanges of judicial views in the recent history of the Court.

In 1947 the Supreme Court held that California had not denied to a man named Adamson the due process of law guaranteed by the Fourteenth Amendment when permitting comment by the prosecutor on Adamson's failure to take the stand in his trial for murder. In a federal court, this comment would probably have been barred by the Fifth Amendment. Mr. Justice Black dissented in the Adamson case.[59] He stated that the Court's opinion, written by Mr. Justice Reed, assumed that the Fifth Amendment of its own force barred comment on failure to testify in federal courts. Mr. Justice Black felt that he must consider the case on that same assumption and went on to test the theory, as he wrote,

> that this Court is endowed by the Constitution with boundless power under "natural law" periodically to expand and contract constitutional standards to conform to the Court's conception of what at a particular time constitutes "civilized decency" and "fundamental liberty and justice."

Mr. Justice Black, who had been in the United States Senate during the height of the controversy between the New Deal and the Supreme Court, saw a danger of a revival of "economic due process" under the Fourteenth Amendment. He traced the history of that doctrine beginning with the Minnesota Rate case of 1890 when a railroad rate regulation was stricken down, and followed it down through Lochner v. New York of 1905,[60] in which Holmes had protested that the Fourteenth Amendment did not enact Mr. Herbert Spencer's Social Statics. Justice Black, stating that it was of course not necessary to agree in all that Mr. Charles Wallace Collins wrote in his *Fourteenth Amendment and the States* in 1912, goes on nevertheless to quote Mr. Collins concerning what Justice Black describes as the disappointments caused by the Supreme Court's interpretation of that Amendment: "It was aimed at restraining and checking the powers of wealth and privilege. . . . It has become the Magna Charta of accumulated and organized capital." Mr. Justice Black argued that what he describes as "the 'natural law'" formula should be abandoned as "an incongruous excrescence" on the Constitution. He wrote, "I believe that formula to be itself a violation of our Constitution, in that it subtly conveys to courts, at the expense of legislatures, ultimate power over public policies in fields where no specific provision of the Constitution limits legislative power." Justice Black's view was that the Fourteenth Amendment had been intended to restate in a few words the detailed provisions of the first eight Amendments constituting the Bill of Rights. By this incorporation he thought to escape reversion to economic due process.

Mr. Justice Frankfurter, who concurred in the judgment of the Court, felt it necessary to reply in his concurring opinion to the argument of Mr. Justice Black concerning literal incorporation.

For historical reasons a limited immunity from the common duty to testify was written into the Federal Bill of Rights, and I am prepared to agree that, as part of that immunity, comment on the failure of an accused to take the witness stand is forbidden in federal prosecutions. It is so, of course, by explicit act of Congress (March 16, 1878), 20 Stat. 30, c 37, 28 USC §632: see Bruno v. United States, 308 U.S. 287. But to suggest that such a limitation can be drawn out of "due process" in its protection of ultimate decency in a civilized society is to suggest that the Due Process Clause fastened fetters of unreason upon the States. . . .

And so, when, as in a case like the present, a conviction in a State court is here for review under a claim that a right protected by the Due Process Clause of the Fourteenth Amendment has been denied, the issue is not whether an infraction of one of the specific provisions of the first eight Amendments is disclosed by the record. The relevant question is whether the criminal proceedings which resulted in conviction deprived the accused of the due process of law to which the United States Constitution entitled him. Judicial review of that guaranty of the Fourteenth Amendment inescapably imposes upon this Court an exercise of judgment upon the whole course of the proceedings in order to ascertain whether they offend those canons of decency and fairness which express the notions of justice of English-speaking peoples even toward those charged with the most heinous offenses. These standards of justice are not authoritatively formulated anywhere as though they were prescriptions in a pharmacopoeia. But neither does the application of the Due Process Clause imply that judges are wholly at large. The judicial judgment in applying the Due Process Clause must move within the limits of accepted notions of justice and is not to be based upon the idiosyncrasies of a merely personal judgment. The fact that judges among themselves may differ whether in a particular case a trial offends accepted notions of justice is not disproof that general rather than idiosyncratic standards are applied. An important safeguard against such merely individual judgment is an alert deference to the judgment of the State court under review."[61]

The controversy over "literal incorporation" has extended down to the present time. The participants renewed it in Rochin v. California, the stomach pump case, in 1952.[62] It was renewed, in questioning put to counsel from the bench, as lately as the argument of the Sunday Law cases[63] on December 7 and 8, 1960—where the questions of Justices concerned the literal incorporation *vel non* of the entire First Amendment in the Fourteenth.

In criminal law matters, the Supreme Court seems to be moving in the direction of applying to the states, under the Fourteenth Amendment, standards in many respects similar to those applied to the United States by the Bill of Rights.[64] But the change appears to be coming according to Mr. Justice Frankfurter's theory that the Fourteenth Amendment due process clause is a canon of reasoned tradition, not by the route of literal incorporation.

Mr. Justice Frankfurter's application of the Fourteenth Amendment involved no renunciation of federal review of the justice of state court criminal procedures. In 1961 in Rogers v. Richmond[65] he wrote the Court's opinion on police practices in obtaining confessions, and the standards of federal review; and he announced the judgment of the Supreme Court and wrote an opinion in another case on the same subject in which there was no majority opinion, Culombe v. Connecticut.[66] The two opinions taken together constitute a treatise on Supreme Court review of state court confession cases. His Rogers opinion rejects the subtly persuasive theory that the demonstrated truth of facts in a confession, otherwise inadmissible because wrongfully elicited, may mitigate the effect of police misconduct and render the use of the confession constitutionally permissible. He sees a perspective which includes not only punishment of criminals but a worthy conduct of government.

Essays and books on the Supreme Court sometimes become regrettably sharp-edged. In the complex balance of governmental elements that make up our constitutionalism, men will necessarily differ as to the interplay of rule and discretion in the judicial function. Lawyers will reasonably differ as to desirable readiness of judges to invalidate the results of the majoritarian process. Good and reasonable and patriotic men, on the bench and off, will weigh these competing demands differently, and acrimony is unsuitable in valuing their ideas. That we have a Supreme Court, conceived and dedicated as it is, gives reason for deep satisfaction, without fretfulness because its Justices sometimes follow different trains of thought. One can disagree with some of Felix Frankfurter's conclusions, without ceasing to realize that his thought is detached and rational, that he has the great virtue of consciousness of his own predispositions. These traits have notably led him, weighing all aspects of a matter, to include high in the balance the claims of the political process, itself one of the great freedoms in our society. The ability of a majority of men to select their own legislators and to demand the laws they want for the control of their own political, social, and economic affairs has by no means been taken for granted through all centuries of our people; in much of the world this is not a matter of course today. Only a third of a century ago, most liberal Americans were much more concerned with cutting down the Supreme Court's power than with preserving it. In his judicial career Felix Frankfurter has tried to establish a reasonable balance between these two interests, cautious at judicial intervention on constitutional grounds, but declining to limit the grounds of intervention once he has decided upon it. And who can say with confidence that in years to come his doctrine will not seem to have been a wise and good one?

# Labor and the Law

## Sanford H. Kadish, *Professor,*
## *University of Michigan Law School*

The subject of labor law has a rough, practical unity for the participants in the world of industrial relations. For the Supreme Court, however, it is a congeries of disparate issues. At its touch a labor case fragments into problems of statutory interpretation, federalism, separation of powers, jurisdiction, administrative law, free speech, or due process. The form and content of the laws governing industrial relations emerge derivatively, as by-products of decisions addressed to those problems. It is a fair question, then, why it is any more appropriate to single out labor law in a volume devoted to the work of a Justice of that Court than, say, to select his decisions in the odd-numbered volumes of the United States Reports. There are at least two reasons. The first has to do with the influence of the Supreme Court's decisions and the ways in which they are reached; the other with Justice Frankfurter himself.

Plainly, to say that the Court influences labor law only derivatively is not to say that its influence is unimportant. Indeed, in the years of Justice Frankfurter's tenure the Court's decisions had a substantial influence in determining the legal ground rules in the competition between labor and capital. This was the inevitable product of its holdings on such issues as the subjection of union activities to the anti-trust laws, the constitutionality of controls over union security arrangements and picketing, the allowable area of state regulation, as well as the meaning of pivotal federal legislation, such as the Railway Labor Act, the National Labor Relations Act, and the Norris-LaGuardia Act.

Neither does it follow from the derivative character of the Court's lawmaking that the resulting shape of the substantive law has had no effect upon the Court's decisions. So to insist is to be scarcely less dogmatic than to insist that the resulting substantive law has always been controlling and the formal components of decision only rhetoric. For surely problems formally within the Court's creative competence, whether they be those of interpretation of federal statutes, definition of constitutional restraints, or adjustment of the spheres of federal and state competence, are not without organic relation to the area of social and economic life out of which they arise for decision. Nor are the social and philosophical presuppositions of the Justice, particularly in an area as unsettled and controversial as labor, unrelated to how he decides these issues. No less an authority on the significance of spheres of competence than Justice Frankfurter observed, "Particularly when dealing with legal aspects of industrial relations is it important for courts not to isolate legal issues from their workaday context."[1]

If these considerations tend generally to legitimate a study of a Justice's work in a single substantive area, certainly the scope and depth of Justice Frankfurter's social philosophy with respect to labor legitimates an examination of his labor opinions. No Justice, with the exceptions of Brandeis before him and Goldberg much later, reached the Court after so extensive an involvement in the struggles between labor and capital. As a consequence, Justice Frankfurter brought to the Court a mature and rounded philosophy of labor relations, developed, it may be added, in the period when the national policy itself was for the first time being systematically formulated. Moreover, since the Justice in his pre-judicial days was an important participant in the formation of those national policies, his labor views and activities would be worthy subjects of inquiry even if he had never reached the Supreme Court to face those issues again in the fettering robes of a Justice.

Accordingly, the following pages will deal first with the Justice's thought and action in the days before his appointment, both as prelude and for their own sake, and subsequently with his judicial opinions.

## I.

Though the term "labor lawyer" is a product of recent time, in a rudimentary sense Frankfurter practiced as one on an intermittent basis from the time of his appointment to the Harvard Law School in 1914 at least until the early 1920s. His experience as a labor lawyer stemmed from his association with Brandeis—he became Brandeis' heir apparent in the representation of labor's interests before the Supreme Court in the constitutional litigation engineered by the National Consumers' League.[2] This had prophetic significance, since the work, thought, and values of Brandeis imprinted their vital pattern upon his entire professional career.

Frankfurter's first case was Bunting v. Oregon,[3] the maximum hours for men case, in which he succeeded Brandeis as counsel for the state of Oregon upon the latter's appointment to the Supreme Court in June 1916. The transition from scholar to advocate, roles which for Frankfurter were never quite separate anyway, was accomplished without a break in stride. He had just published a law review article on the subject, "Hours of Labor and Realism in Constitutional Law."[4] Tactically, he won his case, since the Court sustained the law as a valid health measure. But it did so without so much as mentioning the apparently inconsistent holding in Lochner v. New York,[5] which Frankfurter had urged the Court to reconsider. A year later, in Stettler v. O'Hara,[6] he again appeared before the Court as Brandeis' successor, this time to sustain an Oregon minimum wage law for women. And again he won the battle but not the cause. The Court divided evenly, thereby affirming the state court's judgment upholding the law[7] without discrediting Lochner's identification of laissez-faire economics with due process of law.

The climactic effort to sustain the constitutionality of wage laws took place in 1922 when Adkins v. The Children's Hospital[8] was brought to the Supreme Court. Frankfurter participated as "of counsel" to the District of Columbia Minimum Wage Board, in defense of the validity of a minimum wage order for women. His part was the preparation of a "Brandeis" brief, the well-known innovation in advocacy originated by Brandeis which Frankfurter had occasion to develop into a high art in the Bunting and Stettler cases. Its tack was to reduce the due process challenge to a question of the reasonableness of the legislative judgment and to support that judgment, or, more properly, its reasonableness, by an overwhelming compendium of social and economic data. The utter mass of the document (more than a thousand pages in the Adkins case) and its engulfing persuasiveness suggest to a contemporary reader the image of the mountain and the molehill. But it apparently seemed otherwise to the Court—"liberty of contract" led ineluctably to the law's invalidation.[9]

For Frankfurter, participation in these cases was not merely a challenging task of professional advocacy. It was far more an act of social reform to which, as a Progressive of long standing, he was profoundly committed. While the source of his views may have been a "temperament that believed in elementary decencies," as he observed decades later,[10] it was characteristic of Frankfurter to adduce a principled justification for his position grounded on a Brandeis-ian faith in the ideals of American democracy and individuality. As he put it in 1916 in a letter to the Boston *Herald* supporting the eight-hour day for railroad workers:

> The crucial fact of modern industry is its failure to use the creative qualities of men, its deadening monotony and its excessive fatigue. . . . The result is to ensure a stunted citizenship, since only in a really adequate leisure and a training in the facility of its use can the qualities of democratic life be made manifest. For it is very certain that without facilities for the cultivation of the amenities of civilized life the mass of the people will remain incapable of disciplined democracy.[11]

Frankfurter's work as a labor lawyer went beyond the defense of social welfare legislation before the Supreme Court. In 1920 he represented the Amalgamated Clothing Workers in injunction proceedings growing out of a strike to unionize the one clothing manufacturer in Rochester, New York, who refused to sign with the union. Apparently Frankfurter was called in after a temporary injunction against picketing and boycotting had been granted and a motion to modify it had failed.[12] He entered battle with a team of lawyers and an economist in an effort to avoid a permanent injunction.[13] The trial lasted several weeks but ended in defeat.[14] For the trial court the inherent coercive effect of picketing and boycotting justified the injunction.[15] In a *tour de force* of other-worldliness the Court observed:

[T]he Amalgamated Clothing Workers, instead of endeavoring to secure recognition by an example of an enlightened and reasonable administration in other factories, chose to force their way into plaintiffs' factories by secrecy, and by a strike backed by its powerful influence and supported by acts that the law condemns. Ultimate success in the labor movement does not lie along this line, but in the direction of a peaceful exemplification of a just and reasonable administration of the affairs of the union. . . .[16]

No doubt this experience taught Frankfurter nothing new about the problems of the labor injunction; but it may have helped quicken the pulse for the later author of *The Labor Injunction*.

The First World War provided Frankfurter with another important non-academic exposure to the realities of industrial relations, this time as governmental representative. The principal problems of labor in war industries were work stoppages in the form of strikes and lockouts, and labor shortages produced by the draft and heightened industrial activity. Frankfurter played an important role in the government's response to both problems, a response founded on the policy, as he later authoritatively formulated it, of achieving "the fullest and most fruitful use of the man power of the Nation consistent with the maintenance of those standards of decent industrial life which we must preserve if we are to be honest in our professions of democracy."[17]

His participation began with the United States' entry into the war in April 1917 when Secretary of War Newton D. Baker brought Frankfurter to Washington as his assistant to handle "problems of minority groups, conscientious objectors, and industrial relations."[18] In September of that year the President established a President's Mediation Commission to settle key disputes and to "learn the real causes" of violence and industrial stoppages which had reached alarming proportions on the Pacific coast and in the Rocky Mountain mining areas.[19] This extraordinary body was created after the established mechanisms of conciliation had failed, in the hope of avoiding more drastic measures of compulsory arbitration or conscription.[20] Secretary of Labor Wilson was named chairman of the five-man Commission, and Frankfurter was transferred from the War Department to serve as its secretary and counsel. Its investigations and reports in the Mooney case and the Bisbee deportations were the most dramatic and hence best known of the Commission's activities. Among historians of the era, however, the Commission's total work is regarded, with rare unanimity, as "an important landmark in the history of American industrial relations," having "brought peace to large segments of American industries at a critical time" and having "introduced the principle of collective bargaining with its concomitant administrative machinery to make it effective in many industries which had known it only in theory."[21] Since the Commission consisted of two labor and two industry representatives, in addition to the Secretary of Labor, it requires no speculative leap to surmise that Frankfurter, as the working neutral, had much to do with the Commission's achievements. Visiting the scenes of conflict and undertaking direct negotiations with labor and management spokesmen, Frankfurter actively participated in the mediation of a number of explosive disputes—in the Arizona copper districts, the California oil fields, the telephone industry on the Pacific coast, the lumber industry in the Pacific Northwest, and the packing industry in Chicago.[22] With the exception of the lumber disputes, the efforts of the Commission were successful in each case.[23] For the later Justice this work proved to be an important source of practical experience with labor struggles at the firing line.

Of equal significance to its mediation work, the Commission produced a report on January 9, 1918,[24] analyzing the sources of industrial unrest as it had ascertained them and recommending remedial measures. On its face the report is a joint project, but its tone and Frankfurter's role in the work of the Commission stamp it as a Frankfurtian product. Whether or not it "is one of the most important documents bearing upon the problem of labor that this country has produced," as one historian believed,[25] it certainly belongs with the series of reports of governmental boards and commissions which contributed to the ultimate shape of federal labor legislation.[26] The essential insights and recommendations of the report are now accepted starting points: Since individual dealings between employers and employees are no longer possible, recognition of the principle of "collective relationship" as an accepted part of national labor policy is indispensable. Such recognition is needed to remedy "the central cause of our difficulties," the "failure to equalize the parties in adjustments of inevitable industrial contests." Moreover, "too many labor disturbances are due to the absence of disinterested processes to which resort may be had for peaceful settlement. Force becomes too ready an outlet. We need continuous administrative machinery by which grievances inevitable in industry may be easily and quickly disposed of and not allowed to reach the pressure of explosion." Beyond the correction of specific evils, the central challenge is psychological: to provide "for the release of normal feelings by enabling labor to take its place as a cooperator in the industrial enterprise."

The final recommendation of the President's Mediation Commission for a "single-headed administration" to give "unified direction of the labor administration of the United States"[27] was acted upon in January 1918 when the President designated the Secretary of Labor as War Labor Administrator to develop and administer all governmental war labor policies.[28] Two important agencies were subsequently created as part of the same program. One was the National War Labor Board, established in April 1918 to settle disputes in war industries on the basis of a code of principles previously formulated by a predecessor body, the War Labor Conference Board.[29] That code[30] extended to all in-

SANFORD H. KADISH

dustries the principles which the President's Mediation Commission had formulated to guide its resolution of particular controversies:[31] wartime strikes and lockouts were outlawed, labor's right to organize was assured,[32] discharge for union membership was prohibited, existing union shops were stabilized, and there was established a basic eight-hour day, a living wage to provide subsistence "in reasonable comfort," and equal pay for women.

The other major agency, the War Labor Policies Board, was established a month later. Composed principally of representatives of governmental production departments, it was designed as a legislative-administrative counterpart to the quasi-judicial War Labor Board[33] and was empowered to standardize wages, overtime, and methods for dealing with strikes; to regulate and rationalize the mobilization, distribution, and employment of labor; and to adopt and enforce uniform labor policies under all government war contracts.[34] For a time President Wilson gave serious thought to moving Justice Brandeis from the bench to direct this program.[35] In the end, however, he named Frankfurter chairman of the Board and assistant to the Secretary of Labor in the latter's capacity as Labor Administrator.[36]

The Board adopted as its basic policies those of the War Labor Board, which, as was said, were derived in large measure from the work of the President's Mediation Commission.[37] It implemented these policies by inserting into government contracts clauses imposing the eight-hour day, assuring the right to organize, providing for submission of disputes to arbitration[38] and, ironically, embodying the policies of the recently invalidated Child Labor Act.[39] Another accomplishment of the Board was the development of a plan to centralize the recruiting of unskilled labor in one national agency, the United States Employment Service.[40] While results were often successful, the Board proved unable to cope with skilled labor recruitment where a furious contest in competitive wage rates prevailed.[41]

The acute problems of wage disparity, labor competition, and

161

turnover[42] were to be dealt with, according to the original plan for a war labor administration, by a comprehensive wage standardization program. Chairman Frankfurter projected such a plan and took preliminary steps to carry it out.[43] However, both employer and employee groups showed distaste for the program and the Armistice in October 1918 terminated the attempt. The difficulties in making any substantial progress toward this crucial objective of the overall program, the sibling rivalries with the War Labor Board, and the resentments engendered in both labor and management corners as a result of its unpopular tasks suggest that the Board was far from the unmitigated success the President's Mediation Commission was.[44]

In February 1919, one month before the Secretary of Labor terminated the War Labor Policies Board,[45] Frankfurter resigned. Soon after, he wrote an article for the *Yale Review* in which he formulated the views on industrial unrest which he had developed from his wartime experiences and which were destined to play a governing role in many of his labor decisions as a Justice.[46] Those views had their source neither in a "throbbing sympathy for the misfortunes and struggles of his fellow men,"[47] nor in the Marxian account of the class struggle, but in a perception of the sociological and political implications of a functioning democratic system. A dominant source of difficulty, he believed, was the reaction of the workingman to the contrast between political democracy and economic autocracy. "Modern industry more and more stifles the deep creative impulses of the workers at the same time that it emphasizes how illusory is their political power and how unrelated to economic control. . . . [A]s to the essential circumstances of their lives they are but the instruments of needlessly blind chance under the direction of the heads of industry." The remedies were long familiar, though not to be forthcoming for years to come:

[W]e must carry over into the field of industry the problems of politics. Government in industry, like unto political government, must be worked out where power and responsibility are shared by all those who are participants in industry as well as the dependent "public." The task is nothing less than devising constant processes by which to achieve an orderly and fruitful way of life.

"Collective bargaining" is the starting point of the solution and not the solution itself. This principle must, of course, receive ungrudging acceptance. . . . We are confronted with mass production and mass producers; the individual, in his industrial relations, but a cog in the great collectivity. The collectivity must be represented and must be allowed to choose its representatives.

The direction of effort should be "invention and intelligence" in order to resolve the hard problem of making collective bargaining work.

The spirit and the inventive ferment of the scientist must be brought to bear in industry. We need the authoritative ascertainment of facts both by the government and by industry itself. Light must be shed on all phases of industry, business must be translated into terms of life and judged by the quality of civilization it fosters or frustrates.

These ideas were not, as Frankfurter himself observed, original contributions.[48] They were probably no more original in Justice Brandeis, who had formulated the same ideas before him in terms so parallel as to leave no doubt of their line of descent.[49] They were nonetheless essential underpinnings of Frankfurter's responses to the problems of labor and capital.

What proved to be a major obstacle to implementing these ideas in the resolution of industrial controversy was the use of the labor injunction. Frankfurter was not the first to recognize the peril of the injunction for unionization and collective bargaining and the need for remedial legislation. The labor injunction had been a fighting issue for organized labor since its inception in the latter part of the nineteenth century, and after *In re Debs*[50] was decided in 1895 it came to be labor's principal *bête noire*.[51] Proposals for legislative remedies began almost as early.[52] Indeed, in 1914 it was widely believed that with the enactment of Section 20 of the Clayton Act the cause had been won, although later interpretive decisions of the Court proved the optimism unwarranted.[53] It was Frankfurter, however, who made the most formidable intellectual contribution to the eventual demise of the labor injunction in the federal courts, both by participating in the drafting of the Norris-LaGuardia Act, which accomplished that demise, and by publishing comprehensively and definitively in favor of the proposed law.

The Norris-LaGuardia Act originated in a very different bill introduced by Senator Shipstead in the 70th Congress. This was the bill, long advocated by Andrew Furuseth and the A.F.L., which would have prevented federal courts of equity from treating as "property" any interest not "tangible and transferable." The subcommittee of the Senate Judiciary Committee, chaired by Senator Norris, to which this bill was referred, doubted the constitutionality and suitability of a bill which cut so broad a swath, and after holding hearings in March 1928 decided to report out a substitute bill.[54] Norris arranged for a group of noted attorneys and labor specialists—Frankfurter, Donald Richberg, Herman Oliphant, Edwin E. Witte, and Francis B. Sayre—to come to Washington to prepare the substitute bill.[55] Their work began in an intensive forty-eight-hour session "locked" in the Judiciary Committee's rooms, and resulted in the first form of the Norris-LaGuardia Act, reported as Senate Bill 1482 in May 1928.[56] Though it failed of passage in the 70th and 71st Congresses, the bill finally prevailed

in the 72nd by an overwhelmingly favorable vote in both houses
and was signed by President Hoover in March 1932.[57]

While Frankfurter's contribution to the bill's drafting appears
on the record to have been part of a group effort,[58] it is widely
believed that his part was substantial, if not dominating.[59] In any
event it was he, with Nathan Greene, who prepared the definitive case in support of the bill in *The Labor Injunction,* a book
whose masterful blending of scholarship and advocacy entitles
it to a place among the few classics of American legal literature.[60]
The romantic comments of a federal judge in 1937 capture
something of the influence the book and its senior author were
thought to have had:

> But there is more in the background of the Norris-LaGuardia
> Act than the Clayton Act and the conflicting interpretations
> of that act. There is more in the background than the reports of
> committees submitting the measure to the two houses. In that
> background also is the figure, sinister or saintly (the reader
> may take his choice), the figure of Professor Frankfurter of the
> Harvard Law School. From High Olympus, more than once, he
> has moved the pawns upon the nation's chess board, and it is
> whispered, on occasion has even sought to check the King. In
> part it was he who wrote the Law. . . . Over and over again the
> committees refer to his book, *The Labor Injunction.* Obviously
> that book was written to promote this law. Whatever else one
> may think of this Jupiter, certainly it will be believed that he
> knew what he meant in what he wrote.[61]

The book was in no sense a disinterested inquiry. Its authors'
commitment to the judgment that the labor injunction should be
neutralized as a legal weapon against unions gives the book its
energy and direction. It is, then, a brief, even a "downright
brief" as a critical reviewer would have it.[62] But as Edgar Durfee
observed, though a brief, "it is a work of the highest scholarship
towering in thoroughness and accuracy above most of the blood-

less works which achieve the dispassionate tone of scholarship."[63]

The first and fourth chapters, though examples of forensic craftsmanship at its best, are not the book's creative contributions. Chapter I is historical and doctrinal, tracing the development of the use of the injunction in labor disputes and of the restrictive substantive law which the courts derived "like nitrogen, out of the air," to use one of the Justice's favored figures. It is an effective demonstration of Justice Holmes's insights in his classic dissenting opinion in Vegelahn v. Guntner:[64] starting as an application of common law conceptions of conspiracy and restraint of trade, the governing law developed into a judicial assessment of the propriety of the ends and means of the labor activity in question. This entailed a process in which "sterility and unconscious partisanship readily assume the subtle guise of 'legal principles.' "[65] Chapter IV, a "study in irony,"[66] is a review of state and federal remedial legislation and the judicial response, interpretive and constitutional, which reduced the statutory efforts to futility. The fifth and concluding chapter summarizes the preceding material and offers a supporting analysis of the bill which eventually became the law.

It is the third and fourth chapters that are the book's most significant contributions. Their creativity lies not so much in the ideas advanced or in the manner of their demonstration as in the virtuosity with which the authors applied that maxim, *ex facto jus oritur*, which Brandeis had made a central precept of his own working philosophy.[67] The endemic abuses of the labor injunction are laid bare and their existence irrefragably demonstrated through a massive analysis of the detailed workings of the injunction in scores of actual controversies. In descending from consideration of the law governing the labor injunction as a body of principles to a study of its practical operation and consequences through an exhaustive examination of pleadings, proofs, and decrees, the study earns the tribute paid it at the time by Newton D. Baker: a "model for what is just on the eve of becoming a new technic in the study of law from the social point of view."[68]

The procedural abuses so overwhelmingly demonstrated have by now become common knowledge: "temporary" restraining orders, usually permanent in their impact on the strike, were granted *ex parte* on the basis of irresponsible assertions, or, where notice was granted, solely on the basis of exchanges of affidavits without resort to the traditional scrutinizing processes of fact finding. Orders were sweepingly drawn to proscribe far more than the tortious, or ambiguously drawn to terrorize innocent conduct. Commonly addressed to the public at large like criminal statutes, they were enforced through summary contempt proceedings which imposed criminal sanctions without the safeguards of a criminal trial. Naturally, it mattered much to Frankfurter that the effect of these abuses was to thwart unionism and collective bargaining. But it mattered even more that the federal judiciary had come to be viewed as a committed partisan of the ruling classes, bereft of popular respect as the disinterested administrator of the reign of law.[69]

Yet it was not solely procedural abuses which Frankfurter regarded as requiring remedy by the Norris bill. "After all," he observed, "procedural safeguards are not enough."[70] If they were, Sections 7 and 8 of the bill[71] would have sufficed, for they imposed limitations upon equity procedure in labor disputes carefully drafted to preclude all the documented procedural abuses in the limited instances in which labor injunctions were permitted by the bill. In fact the bill went beyond procedure in Section 4, which prohibited all restraint of strikes, picketing, and boycotts as such regardless of the procedure employed, with the consequence that courts were wholly precluded from passing judgment upon the lawfulness of labor's use of its economic weapons.

167

Certainly one of Frankfurter's objectives here also was to preserve judicial prestige by removing courts from a bitter social struggle. But he advanced a further argument to support the laissez-faire policy of Section 4. It was similar to that earlier articulated by Holmes[72] and Brandeis[73]: "that our economic system is founded upon the doctrine of free competition, accepting for its gains the cost of its ravages; that large aggregations of capital are not inconsistent with the doctrine of free competition, but are, indeed, inevitable and socially desirable; that the individual workers must combine in order thereby to achieve the possibility of free competition with concentrated capital." Moreover, "recognition of the social utility and, indeed, of the necessity of trade unions implies acceptance of the economic and social pressure that can come from united action." This "leaves open the most troublesome of questions—the questions of how far and when," which "raise bristling issues of policy, and, therefore, of law." But the determination "at precisely what points the cost of competition is too great . . . is the task of legislatures. Only within very narrow limits is it the functions of courts to apply their own notions of policy."[74]

The Norris bill's provision, then, that no federal court might enjoin the use of labor's traditional economic weapons, Frankfurter regarded not as the final solution, but as a tentative response pending legislative definition of what constitute excessive costs in particular circumstances. In fact, however, the Norris-LaGuardia Act provided the guiding philosophy for federal legislation in the decade and a half which followed, proving itself "one of labor's greatest and most enduring legislative victories."[75] The Wagner Act of 1935 extended its underlying policies by providing affirmative governmental protection against employers doing for themselves what, before Norris-LaGuardia, they enlisted the aid of federal courts to accomplish. As Justice Frankfurter observed, the Wagner Act "leaves the adjustment of industrial relations to the free play of economic forces but seeks to assure that the play of those forces be truly free."[76] Not until the Taft-Hartley Act of 1947 was the legislative cost-accounting made and a new direction taken.

## II.

For two years after taking his seat on the bench on January 30, 1939, Justice Frankfurter voted in mute acquiescence with the majority in a number of important labor opinions.[77] But this was the quiet before the storm. On February 3, 1941, he spoke for the Court in United States v. Hutcheson[78] in an opinion which stirred up more critical reaction than any labor decision he wrote, and probably had as much practical importance as any for the subsequent governance of labor relations. This, plus the fact that it raised issues which intimately touched his labor experience before his appointment, make it a likely starting point for a review of his judicial work.[79]

### A.

At issue in Hutcheson was the criminality under the Sherman Act of picketing and a nationwide consumer boycott directed by the Carpenters against a beer company as part of a jurisdictional dispute with the Machinists. At stake was the labor pincer of Assistant Attorney General Arnold's anti-trust blitzkrieg, which the year before had been checked by a restriction of the Act to restraints on competition in business and commercial transactions.[80] A similar disposition would have served as well in Hutcheson,[81] but Justice Frankfurter, for the Court, elected an encircling maneuver, through Section 20 of the Clayton Act and the Norris-LaGuardia Act, which effectively and finally cut off Mr. Arnold's lines of support.

The conduct in question, according to Justice Frankfurter, fell within the categories of acts defined in the second paragraph of Section 20 as non-enjoinable; and under the concluding "catch-all" clause of that paragraph, no such acts could be held violations of federal law. But the first paragraph limited the scope of the second to cases between employers and employees growing out of a dispute concerning conditions of employment, and the Supreme Court in its 1921 decision in Duplex Printing Co. v. Deering[82] had construed this to exclude disputes involving those not standing in the proximate employment relation, precisely the situation in Hutcheson. Justice Frankfurter, however, found in the considered and explicit rejection of the Duplex construction in the Norris-LaGuardia Act's own grant of injunctive immunity a basis for rejecting the Duplex construction for purposes of all of Section 20 of the Clayton Act, including its legalizing "catch-all" clause, "for Congress now placed its own meaning upon that section." To be sure, Norris-LaGuardia was explicitly directed at injunctions in labor disputes, but to argue that Duplex still governed for purposes of a criminal prosecution would be a narrow distortion of Norris-LaGuardia simply because "meticulous words are lacking." For it would be strange indeed that, although these acts could not be enjoined, "the elaborate efforts to permit such conduct failed to prevent criminal liability punishable with imprisonment and heavy fines."[83]

So it was that the Sherman Act, after a tortuous history, ceased any longer to threaten the conventional activities of labor, at least so long as labor acted alone.[84] This revolutionary consequence would have been enough to raise eyebrows; that it was accomplished through Norris-LaGuardia raised temperatures as well. After all, that Act was structured as a substitute for, rather than as an amendment of, the Clayton Act. Moreover, it dealt exclusively with the jurisdiction of federal courts to issue injunctions and, unlike Section 20 of the Clayton Act, contained no general legalizing language. Furthermore the Norris bill had been explicitly held out by Professor Frankfurter himself as withdrawing only the remedy of injunction, leaving "civil action for damages and criminal prosecution [as] available instruments."[85] As a result there was an expectable outcry of professional criticism, led by Justice Roberts' dissenting castigation of the opinion as a "usurpation by the courts of the function of the Congress not only novel but fraught, as well, with the most serious dangers to our constitutional system of division of powers."[86]

Yet some of the criticism was off target. The assertion, for example, that the statute was concerned solely with the abusiveness of the injunctive remedy[87] disregards Section 4 and Frankfurter's rationale of it in *The Labor Injunction.* We have seen that the total immunity granted by Section 4 rested on the substantive premise that labor's conventional activities should be free from legal prohibitions pending legislative rather than judicial determination of the need for restraints. The Sherman Act could hardly be viewed as such a determination, since its notorious generality gave to the courts a freedom to pursue their economic and social preferences which was scarcely less limited than the freedom derived from the powers of equity.[88] The real trouble was not that Justice Frankfurter improvised a policy foreign to the congressional will or inharmonious with the enacted law, but that he carried it to an extreme which Congress had deliberately chosen not to hazard.

Why Congress, or more accurately the guiding spirits behind the Norris bill, made this choice appears dramatically in an unpublished contemporary memorandum prepared by Professor Frankfurter, along with Oliphant and Witte.[89] This memorandum, written at Senator Norris' request, recommended against an amendment to the Norris bill proposed by the A.F.L., which would have added to Section 4 a paraphrase of Clayton Section 20: "(j) Nor shall any of the acts described in this section be considered or held to be unlawful acts."[90] The memorandum's recommendation (adopted by Senator Norris, who twice declined to accept the A.F.L. amendment)[91] was expressly put upon the ground that with that provision the bill would be harder to pilot through Congress and might be held unconstitutional.[92] The source of the constitutional concern was Truax v. Corrigan, in which Chief Justice Taft held an Arizona statute to deprive employers of the property of their business without due process, insofar as it protected active picketing and concomitant activities against all legal redress.[93] The only reason Clayton Section 20 would pass muster was, as the Chief Justice said,[94] that the Court had already construed its catalogue of non-enjoinable and legally immunized acts to embrace union "missionary" work, but not "the inevitable intimidation of the presence of groups of pickets."[95] But the Norris bill had been meticulously drafted to thwart a like emasculation,[96] so that the only defense against Truax was to argue, as Professor Frankfurter did, that the bill did not shelter conduct destructive of property from all legal redress, but merely withdrew the particular remedy of the injunction.[97]

In the light of this legislative concern, so dramatically manifested in the memorandum of Professor Frankfurter, it becomes difficult to accept Justice Frankfurter's conclusion that "the Norris-LaGuardia Act reasserted the original purpose of the Clayton Act by infusing into it the immunized trade union activities as redefined by the later Act."[98] To be sure, the Justice did not reason that this result flowed from any implied legalizing provision in Norris-LaGuardia. It was, after all, partly on his recommendation that none was enacted. He rested rather on a rejuvenated Clayton Section 20. But since Congress rejected such a clause in Norris-LaGuardia out of fear of its unconstitutionality, that body can hardly have contemplated a "rejuvenation" of the earlier Section 20 which would have opened it to the identical constitutional challenge.[99]

Admittedly, it would have been hard for Justice Frankfurter to resist the temptation of interpreting Norris-LaGuardia as it might have been written had Truax imposed no constitutional limitations, for that precedent had since been devitalized by Justice Brandeis' 1937 decision in Senn v. Tile Layers Protective Union.[100] But it is still a fair question whether Frankfurter in this opinion did not embrace that very "statesmanship" in statutory interpretation he has consistently deplored.[101] Walton Hamilton on the eve of the Justice's appointment observed: "As an interest within the commonwealth their status [i.e., that of the workers] is of conscious public concern. Here a host of problems break in a tangle of legal issues, whose formal concern is cause of action, jurisdiction, procedure, statutory interpretation, the law of the constitution. Frankfurter will consider such issues within their judicial setting, he will accord full due to all the proprieties of legal usage. But his values—set in an intellectual system that brooks no divisions between the social and the legal—will shape his judgments."[102] Though the subsequent pattern of the Justice's judicial career makes this prognostication dubious at best,[103] Mr. Hamilton may have felt his prophecy fulfilled in the Hutcheson opinion. Maintaining the equipoise between adjudication and legislation, difficult as it is, proved impossible here, where the judge had also, in effect, been the legislator.[104]

## B.

Contrary to the expectation raised by the Justice's Hutcheson opinion, he did not thereafter exercise a leadership on the bench in interpreting Norris-LaGuardia to match his great contribution to its original enactment. He wrote only three later opinions dealing directly with that Act. One was written for the Court to sustain the enjoinability of a boycott aimed at the collection of a private debt.[105] This was a business, not a labor controversy, and even for the draftsman of Norris-LaGuardia the need for confining judicial judgment could not mean obliterating it.[106] Another was his partial dissent in the United Mine Workers contempt case, in which he protested against strong-arming an exception for the United States government *qua* employer (indeed, *qua pro forma* employer under a seizure) from the limitations of the Act.[107] That the continued production of coal was important in 1946 was no warrant for mauling the "text, context, content and historical setting" of the Act.[108] This was doubly true since, as the Justice believed, the contempt conviction could be sustained despite the invalidity of the order, on the ground that the trial court had jurisdiction to determine its jurisdiction.

The third opinion was his dissent in United Brotherhood of Carpenters v. United States,[109] which involved the meaning of Section 6, precluding union responsibility for unlawful acts of "officers, members, or agents" without proof that those acts were actually authorized or ratified. The language on its face clearly applied to acts of responsible upper-echelon union officials which violated the Sherman Act. But for Justice Frankfurter the literal language was a false guide. "By talking about 'actual authorization,' Congress merely meant to emphasize that persons for whose acts a corporation or a union is to be responsible should really be wielding authority for such corporation or union." It was not designed to change the whole basis of collective responsibility, with the result that the union could not be held for the unlawful acts of responsible union officers in their official capacity unless their acts were, in effect, authorized or ratified in convention duly assembled. Of major significance to the Justice was the view that such a reading would, by virtue of the "anatomy and physiology of trade union life," sterilize the Sherman law where it still applied to labor, so far as the powerful international unions are concerned. Indeed, that unions, as legally recognized and protected centers of private power within the larger community, must be held accountable for the irresponsible exercise of their power was a recurrent first principle of his social philosophy, manifested as early as 1922 when he defended the ruling in United Mine Workers v. Coronado Coal Co.[110] that unions were suable as such. Trade unions, he wrote, as "unincorporated associations of men united for common action and acting as a unit" enjoy no "special immunity before the law, as compared with other associations, because of [their] humanitarian aims."[111]

In a number of important cases the issue turned on whether the restrictive provisions of Norris-LaGuardia should be held inapplicable ("accommodated," in the judicial euphemism) to the later provisions of the Railway Labor Act. While the Justice was silent, at least outside the conference room, he voted in each instance to subordinate the anti-injunction provisions to the later Act. In one group of cases, he apparently deemed overriding the Railway Labor Act's implied command that unions afford employees non-discriminatory representation.[112] In another group, he deemed overriding the Act's substitution of an institutionalized process of grievance adjustment for the use of economic force, even though this meant enjoining a threatened strike.[113]

Because of the unfortunate illness which led ultimately to his retirement the Justice did not participate in perhaps the most prickly of the problems of reconciling Norris-LaGuardia with later statutes. This was whether that Act could be "accommodated" to allow federal injunction of a strike in breach of an arbitration and no strike clause, in the light of Section 301 of Taft-Hartley which, as interpreted, authorized federal courts to grant specific performance of agreements to arbitrate. Would the author of Hutcheson have found, with the minority, that the literal language of the anti-injunction statute and the presumption against repeal by implication should give way to the mood, sense, and purpose of the later and differently premised legislation?[114] The answer is not really a mystery since the Justice's exchange with counsel during argument made it clear that he would stand, contrary to his position in the Railway Labor Act cases, on the text of the earlier Act and on the absence of a repealing provision in the later Act.[115] Nor is this surprising, in view of the similarity between the equity discretion of the federal courts, which Norris-LaGuardia had abolished at Professor Frankfurter's instigation, and the discretion of the federal courts under Section 301 to fashion a law of collective bargaining agreements, which Justice Frankfurter likewise deplored.[116]

## C.

Another war horse of the Justice's pre-judicial days was the constitutional power of the state to legislate in response to the problems of labor in an industrialized society. By the time he reached the bench the battle to sustain the constitutionality of protective labor legislation, which he had lost as advocate in the minimum wage cases, had been won so sweepingly that substantive due process was well on its way to complete impotency as a constitutional restraint upon economic and social legislation. When legislative patterns changed to produce the irony of labor invoking due process and liberty of contract to protect itself against state prohibitions of union security agreements, the result was foreordained, and Justice Black's opinion made short shrift of the union's arguments.[117] But for Justice Frankfurter this was not a horse soon curried. He chose to concur at length in an eloquent summing up of the philosophy of deference to the legislative judgment in the process of judicial review. The old constitutional doctrine was a laid ghost which would arise no longer even to a union's calling, for "when the tide turned, it was not merely because circumstances had changed and there had arisen a new order with new claims to divine origin. . . . Unions are powers within the State. . . . If concern for the individual justifies incorporating in the Constitution itself devices to curb public authority, a legislative judgment that his protection requires the regulation of the private power of unions cannot be dismissed as insupportable."[118] This opinion's passionate plea for ultimate self-restraint and intellectual humility in the process of judical review[119] may have seemed to some an old campaigner's reliving of battles past. But the lesson it taught had a direct though unmentioned relevance to an ongoing constitutional controversy which had arisen only after Frankfurter's accession—the constitutionality of restraints upon picketing.

In his classic statement on the rigorous confines of judicial review, the Justice himself announced an exception for matters "like censorship of the press or separation of Church and State, on which history, through the Constitution, speaks so decisively as to forbid legislative experimentation."[120] By identifying labor picketing with the speech whose freedom is implicitly protected by the due process clause of the Fourteenth Amendment, the Court in its 1940 opinions in Thornhill v. Alabama and Carlson v. California had apparently placed restraints on picketing in that exceptional category.[121] The upshot was that at least so far as picketing was concerned labor was ensconced in the bastion of its displaced antagonists. It had the best of two worlds —judicial review under substantive due process was no longer a threat to legislation which favored its cause, but it could be used as a shield against state action which restrained the use of one of its major economic weapons.

Justice Frankfurter joined Thornhill and Carlson without comment. Indeed, a year later he served as the Court's spokesman to reaffirm that restraints on picketing constitute a "ban of free communication . . . inconsistent with the guarantee of freedom of speech," thereby requiring that picketing "be guarded with a jealous eye" by the Court.[122] But there were signs of disaffection too, even at the beginning, and in the ensuing years he led the Court (the word is warranted since he wrote the bulk of the picketing decisions and he never was in the minority) on a tour which, by 1957, brought it "full circle"[123] back to where Brandeis had left it in 1937,[124] when he freed the states from the constitutional restrictions imposed by Truax v. Corrigan[125] upon their power to legislate with regard to picketing.

The lines of movement followed two ultimately converging paths. The first appeared in the Meadowmoor Dairies case[126] the year after Thornhill. Even though "peaceful picketing is the workingman's means of communication," Frankfurter observed, it is not immune from the permissible restraints on other forms of communication. Where it is sufficiently "enmeshed with contemporaneously violent conduct" to warrant a factual finding by the state court "that the momentum of fear generated by past violence would survive even though future picketing might be wholly peaceful," it loses "its significance as an appeal to reason . . . sheltered by the Constitution." Moreover, a year later in the Ritter's Café case[127] he wrote for the Court upholding state power to enjoin even wholly peaceful picketing of a restaurant whose owner hired a non-union contractor to construct a build-ing elsewhere in town. "[R]ecognition of peaceful picketing as an exercise of free speech," he stated, "does not imply that the states must be without power to confine the sphere of communication to that directly related to the dispute," excluding businesses "wholly outside the economic context of the real dispute" in order to prevent the conscription of neutrals.[128] Further, "Restriction of picketing to the area of the industry within which a labor dispute arises leaves open to the disputants other traditional modes of communication."[129]

In 1950 after a prolonged fallow period Frankfurter wrote two opinions revealing the second path of retreat. Picketing in labor disputes, he observed, even publicity picketing which is not directed to conveying threats of union discipline,[130] is a "hybrid"[131] possessing compulsive features which distinguish it from communication as an appeal to reason. A newspaper publication may convey the same information as a picket's placard, but "the very purpose of a picket line is to exert influences, and it produces consequences, different from other modes of communication. The loyalties and responses evoked and exacted by picket lines are unlike those flowing from appeals by printed word."[132] This plain fact had been recognized earlier even by the stalwart defenders of Thornhill,[133] but for Frankfurter it was the final warrant for bringing review of state picketing restraints into harmony with the review of other accommodations of competing social and economic interests. The wedge opened in Thornhill by the Giboney case[134] the year before, sustaining picketing directed to coercing an employer to commit an unlawful act, Justice Frankfurter drove all the way through. A state must be free, he held, to restrict picketing for any purpose hostile to its considered policy, whether it be racial discrimination in employment,[135] or protection of self-employers against unionization,[136] or protection of employee freedom not to join a union.[137] Speaking for the Court in 1957 in an opinion which reordered all that went before in the picketing cases, he announced that in the end the whole range of picketing cases "involved not so much questions of free speech as review of the balance struck by a State between picketing that involved more than 'publicity' and competing interests of state policy."[138] Therefore, "the clash of fact and opinion should be resolved by the democratic process and not by the judicial sword."[139]

## D.

The remaining constitutional issue of import to labor law which arose during Frankfurter's tenure was whether specific state laws were pre-empted by, or could peacefully coexist with, the comprehensive regulatory schemes of the original and amended National Labor Relations Act. For labor the stakes were high, since, now that the picketing-free speech doctrine was moribund, the pre-emption doctrine was labor's last constitutional defense against inimical state law. For the Court the question was complex. Justice Frankfurter early assayed the favored Frankfurtian doctrine of judicial humility in the face of the state legislative judgment.[140] But it would hardly do. After all, why on this ground defer to the state's judgment, rather than to that of Congress? Surely the demand that the Court umpire the federal system compelled active choice, since the question was not whether, but which. Passivity was theoretically possible in another way, for the final question was the congressional intent either to pre-empt or to coexist. But for the most part there was no such intent to be found. In effect, one had to be created from hints, moods, guesses, and perhaps even preferences.[141] For the Court, therefore, as Frankfurter recognized, the task demanded making the hard choice in each instance which Congress declined to face. Which should prevail: the nationalist interest of faithfulness and uniformity in the enforcement of the regulatory scheme, or the competing federalist interest of diversity and autonomy?[142]

The Justice wrote frequently in this area, and what he recently observed in San Diego Building Trades Council v. Garmon of the inevitable disharmonies in language and implication of the Court's opinions, which extended over more than a decade,[143] is equally true of his own. One observes toward the end some dimming of the strong federalist rhetoric to be found in the four opinions he wrote before 1955, all in defense of state coexistence.[144] Indeed toward the end, in Garmon, he became the spokesman for a five-justice majority in articulating a rationale which made significant inroads into local autonomy. Nonetheless, there is more constancy than change in the Justice's position,[145] which over the years became almost, if not quite, the median position of the Court.

One view which the Justice held at first and last was this: where the state-regulated conduct was wholly untouched by the federal law, or was only peripherally touched by it, and the state interest was rooted in solid local concerns, the absence of an explicit rejection of state authority in the federal law required that state power be sustained. Internal union affairs Justice Frankfurter consistently regarded as conduct of this character. Thus in his initial pre-emption opinion in 1945, Hill v. Florida,[146] he dissented from the Court's invalidation of a Florida licensing system for union officials. Since the Wagner Act was directed solely at protecting freedom of employee choice of bargaining representative against *employer* interference, and since Congress "with eyes wide open" refused to deal with the conduct of employees and their unions, there was no warrant for "wiping out the right of states under the police power to require qualifications appropriate for union officials having fiduciary duties" The Justice must have appreciated, as well as the majority, the unique potential for thwarting unionization in a discretionary licensing system for union representatives, but it would only be consistent with his federalist commitments not to hold an otherwise valid state law preempted in anticipation of its abuse. In 1960 in his final pre-emption case when the validity of a similar New York licensing provision was argued before the Court, the Justice was able to command a majority for its support.[147] While there were factors which distinguished the majority decision in Hill v. Florida, it is doubtful that they were substantial enough to justify a different conclusion for Justice Frankfurter unless he was still committed to the core of the reasoning in his dissent in that case.[148]

Another case falling under the same rubric was International Association of Machinists v. Gonzales[149] decided in 1958. Writing for the majority, Justice Frankfurter upheld a state award of damages and an injunction in behalf of an employee wrongfully ousted from his union, on the ground that the state's concern was with rights of union membership, a matter which the federal law explicitly left unregulated. In some circumstances where denial of employment resulted, such expulsion might constitute a federal unfair labor practice remediable by an N.L.R.B. back pay and job restoration award (though not restoration to union membership). But this could not mutilate the state power to afford a complete remedy since the federal concern with the gist of the state-regulated conduct was only "peripheral."

Even where the activity regulated fell squarely within the center of federal concern, there was a class of situations in which the congressional intent to displace state law would likewise have to be explicitly and unmistakably indicated. This was where the conduct challenged traditional local authority to maintain conditions of order within the community. Violence and other breaches of the peace belonged in this category. Hence he believed that such conduct could be dealt with by any appropriate state remedy regardless of its impact upon the federal scheme,[150] although a more consistently nationalist-minded minority would confine the state in such cases to remedies not available under federal law.[151] Labor stoppages which create emergencies within the state, such as public utility strikes, were, for Justice Frankfurter, though not for the Court, another instance of this kind, even though state regulation meant interference with the federally protected right to strike.[152] This followed because "[d]ue regard for basic elements in our federal system makes it appropriate that Congress be explicit if it desires to remove from the orbit of State regulation matters of such intimate concern to a locality as the continued maintenance of services on which the decent life of a modern community rests."

So much, then, Frankfurter conceded to state autonomy. But the competing interests of the federal scheme set outer limits. Therefore, in all other cases where the conduct regulated fell within the central concern of the National Labor Relations Act, either because it was protected by Section 7 or prohibited by Section 8, the imperative of explicit state displacement was unnecessary since to leave the states free in such cases "involves the greater danger of conflict between power asserted by Congress and requirements imposed by state law."[153] And, contrary to the more stalwart federalist minority,[154] his final position, after some wavering, was that pre-emption operated even where the state law granted a remedy unavailable under federal law for conduct prohibited by both. This followed from the premise that potential for conflict inheres not only in different rules of law but in differing procedures and remedies as well.[155] The Court's concern must be "with conflict in its broadest sense; conflict with a complex and interrelated federal scheme of law, remedy and administration."[156] Where it is not clear whether the conduct is federally protected or prohibited, the state must yield so long as the point is arguable. In such cases the principle of primary jurisdiction intersects, for it is beyond the competence of the federal courts, including the Supreme Court, as well as of the states, to make determinations within the exclusive primary competence of the National Labor Relations Board.[157] And should the Board hold, or its precedents make compellingly clear, that the conduct is neither protected nor prohibited, Justice Frankfurter, again in contrast to the more consistently federalist minority,[158] declined to say that the states could act even then, although the Frankfurter of the 1940s would probably not have hesitated to say that they could.[159]

As in the picketing-free speech course of litigation, it fell to Justice Frankfurter to write the landmark opinion, at the end of a chapter if not the volume, discarding the false leads and articulating an ordering rationale. And again, as in the picketing cases (though not to the same degree), it was the Frankfurtian direction the Court eventually took. That direction, as the Justice himself would probably have viewed it, was strongly but not dogmatically federalist, requiring a pragmatic search in each case for the alternative which would preserve for the states the maximum regulatory power consistent with the minimum demands of the federal legislative scheme.

## E.

A large number of Justice Frankfurter's opinions were addressed to the task of giving meaning to the comprehensive regulatory schemes of the National Labor Relations Act and the Railway Labor Act, as well as other legislation. It was in these cases that the Justice's social philosophy bore most directly upon the discharge of his judicial function. The statutes, it will be recalled, were the culminations of a search for policy in which Justice Frankfurter had a shaping influence. Moreover, their interpretation involved in many instances recourse to the interpreters' governing conceptions of policy, for, as the Justice early observed, "much of the life of a statute dealing with contentious social issues is determined by the general outlook with which judges view such legislation. . . . Statutory construction in doubtful cases, in the last analysis, is a choice among competing policies as starting places for reasoning."[160] Justice Frankfurter's judicial work in advancing two root policy commitments of this important labor legislation, collective bargaining and unionization, will be the primary focus of the remaining pages of this essay.

(1)

A central policy of these statutes was to encourage collective bargaining between group representative and employer as the means of achieving a realistic participation by the individual worker in his industrial life and a "collaborative self-government"[161] which would "substitute processes of justice for the more primitive method of trial by combat."[162] But this created a formidable train of problems barely dealt with by the statutes. Those problems fall into three principal categories: first, the relationship between the individual worker and the group representative; second, oversight of the processes of bargaining between union and employer; third, remedies for enforcing the bargain. Justice Frankfurter had much to say about these problems, although his words here, in contrast to the picketing and pre-emption areas, were more often heard than heeded.

a) In defining the legal relationship between workers and union out of the implications of the new statutory schemes, the Justice manifested a consistent sensitivity to the needs of the group. This did not mean that he regarded unions as entitled to a favored position under the law. Indeed, a recurrent theme in his opinions was, as suggested earlier, that unions are "powers within the State" and accountable for the exercise of their power "like the power of industrial and financial aggregations."[163] Nor did it mean that he was wholly oblivious to the interests of the individual. He concurred in affording legal protection to the individual against distortion of the representative function, as in the racial discrimination cases.[164] And in sustaining state anti-closed-shop laws he observed that union power "can come into being only when, and continue to exist only so long as, individual aims are seen to be shared in common with the other members of the group. There is a natural emphasis, however, on what is shared and a resulting tendency to subordinate the inconsistent interests and impulses of individuals. . . . At the point where the mutual advantage of association demands too much individual disadvantage, a compromise must be struck."[165] The fact remains, however, that in every statutory case in which he spoke it was to sustain the collective interest represented by the union, even where this required subordinating the claims of the individual.

The "starting places for reasoning" which led him to these conclusions the Justice set out explicitly on each occasion. In 1945 the majority decided in Elgin, Joliet & Eastern Ry. v. Burly[166] that employees could sue in the courts to enforce rights arising under the collective agreement; and could upset a prior adverse award by the Railroad Adjustment Board (partly founded on a union settlement) by showing that the recognized union representative which presented the grievance was not specifically authorized by them to do so. Since the Railway Labor Act left the authority of the bargaining representative over grievances substantially undefined, judgment rested ultimately upon assessment of the considerations of policy implicit in the Act. For Justice Frankfurter, who dissented, the dominant policy was solidification of the authority of the union both as spokesman for the group interest and as one of the principal organs of industrial government. The majority's holding would destroy the carriers' confidence in the unions' capacity to adjust grievances and thereby vitiate that "maximum pressure toward amicable settlement" between carrier and union which was a vital object of the Act. Moreover:

Not to allow the duly elected officers of an accredited union to speak for its membership in accordance with the terms of the internal government of the union and to permit any member of the union to pursue his own interest under a collective agreement undermines the very conception of a collective agreement. It reintroduces the destructive individualism in the relations between the railroads and their workers which it was the very purpose of the Railway Labor Act to eliminate.[167]

The Justice's forebodings were well grounded. On reargument the crippling impact of the decision on railroad grievance adjustment was so compellingly represented to the Court that the majority, while adhering to its original decision, apparently felt obliged to narrow the triable issue of agency to make it virtually impossible for the individual to prove the union's lack of authority.[168]

In his dissenting opinion in Bay Ridge Operating Co. v. Aaron,[169] the Justice resorted to similar considerations of policy in interpreting the less pliant language of the Fair Labor Standards Act. In order to discourage "casualization" of longshoreman employment a collective bargaining pattern had emerged over the years under which time and one half was payable for work outside weekday daytime hours. Upon the passage of the Fair Labor Standards Act in 1938, this premium rate was designated "overtime" in order to avoid inflating the employee's statutory "regular rate." The Court rejected the contract designation and determined "regular rate" by dividing the weekly compensation, including the contract "overtime" premium, by the hours worked. Since the contract "overtime" was actually a shift differential and not compensation for excessive work, the majority was on plausible ground, in terms of the statutory language and its prior interpretation.[170] Moreover, the Fair Labor Standards Act was designed to protect the individual's working conditions rather than union representation. Nevertheless, Justice Frankfurter regarded the Court's interpretation as intolerably literal, and unmindful of the values implicit in the national policy of collective bargaining as a form of industrial government and of the collective agreement "as an instrument of industrial democracy." He would have elevated these values to primacy by allowing the "regular rate" to be established by bargaining between the union and the employer, at least so long as the agreement "was an honest reflection of the distinctive conditions" of the industry. Unless the contract can be shown not to express the true interests of the union as an entity, he concluded,

> this court had better let the union speak for its members and represent their welfare, instead of reconstructing, and thereby jeopardizing, arrangements under which the union has lived and thrived and by which it wishes to abide. Collective agreements play too valuable a part in the government of industrial relationships to be cast aside at the whim of a few union members who seek to retain their benefits, but wish to disavow what they regard as their burdens.[171]

Again the Justice received a kind of vindication, this time from Congress, which amended the law in 1949 to reject the Court's ruling.[172]

The commitments revealed in these two notable dissents were long-standing ones, reaching back to the Justice's war labor experiences. Their judgmental influence manifested itself in a wide variety of contexts in his subsequent opinions. Under the Selective Service Act a veteran had a right to be restored "without loss of seniority" to the position he held before he entered the military service. Did this entitle him to exemption from a super-seniority clause for shop stewards and union chairmen negotiated during his absence? Justice Frankfurter, for the Court, predictably responded in the negative, declining to read the Act as elevating the veteran's individual interest over the collective interest in continuity of office for union representatives with important functions in the administration of the contract. "Because they are union chairmen they are not regarded as merely individual members of the union; they are in a special position in relation to collective bargaining for the benefit of the whole union. To retain them as such is not an encroachment on the seniority system but a due regard of union interests which embrace the system of seniority rights."[173]

In Brooks v. N.L.R.B.[174] the Justice held for the Court that a union's loss of support soon after its election and certification did not justify an employer in refusing to deal with the union. "In placing a non-consenting minority under the bargaining responsibility of an agency selected by a majority of the workers, Congress has discarded common law doctrines of agency." The principle of freedom of choice of representative must be accommodated, in industrial as well as in political democracy, to the interest of stability and responsible government.

In his opinion in Association of Westinghouse Salaried Employees v. Westinghouse Electric Corp.,[175] Justice Frankfurter was concerned with the scope of Section 301 of the Taft-Hartley Act, which authorized suits for breach of collective agreements in the federal courts. While deciding the case on other grounds, he paused long enough to reject the theory of labor contracts advanced in the Court of Appeals, which regarded claims of individual employees based on terms of the collective agreement as arising out of their individual contracts of hire and not out of the collective agreement itself. Since the consequence of this theory was to deny the union authority to press grievances to suit, it only served to limit the governmental contribution of the union as an instrumentality through which grievances are adjusted without resort to force. "If the union can secure only the promise and it is impotent to procure for the individual employees the promised benefits, then it is bound to lose their support. And if the union cannot ultimately resort to suit, it is encouraged to resort to strike action."[176]

The last case in which Justice Frankfurter addressed himself to this issue of the one and the many in labor context was International Association of Machinists v. Street.[177] The Supreme Court had already sustained laws authorizing closed-shop agreements where the dues and assessments were used to support negotiating and administering collective agreements.[178] But did the authorization in the Railway Labor Act entitle the union to use the obligatory payments for advancing favored causes, influencing the legislature, and supporting political candidates? And if so, was such a law an infringement of the First Amendment's guarantee of freedom of speech and assembly? Despite the fact that it meant confronting a constitutional issue, Justice Frankfurter disagreed with the Court that the permissive closed-shop provision of the Act should be read to exclude the expenditures complained of by the dissident employees. His reasoning was unassailable. The legislative history revealed Congress' concern for requiring that the beneficiaries of "union activity" share its cost. But "[t]o suggest that this language covertly meant to encompass any less than the maintenance of those activities normally engaged in by unions is to withdraw life from law and to say that Congress dealt with artificialities and not with railway unions as they were and as they functioned."[179]

On the constitutional level, the Justice could find no infirmity. The union's use of a portion of the dissident employees' dues for causes they disagreed with did not restrict their freedom to speak and act in opposition, both within the union structure and outside it. "It is a commonplace of all organizations that a minority of a legally recognized group may at times see an organization's funds used for promotion of ideas opposed by the minority," even where, as in the cases of taxes and dues in an integrated bar, payment is compulsory. And such a "miniscule" constitutional claim as could be derived from the indirect obligation to support antipathetic causes was overwhelmed by the historic relation between the advancement of the group interest through collective bargaining and through legislative and political activity. "It is not true in life that political protection is irrelevant to, and insulated from economic interests. It is not true for industry or finance. Neither is it true for labor."

In Justice Frankfurter's assessment of the interplay between private group and individual in labor matters there is an echo of his dedicated commitment to a parsimonious judicial review of legislative action under the Constitution. In both cases his judgments are bottomed on a strong majoritarianism, epitomized in the observation of a state justice in a union-employee context: "In a government based on democratic principles, the benefit as perceived by the majority prevails."[180] And there is an echo as well of his federalist preferences in the pre-emption cases, for in dealing with union as well as with state power the Justice manifests a commitment to diversified and localized group units as the proper locus of governmental power, whether private or public.

b) The issue of legal supervision of the process of collective bargaining reached the Court as a problem of interpreting the cryptic commands of the Wagner Act that the employer "bargain collectively" with the union, and of the later Taft-Hartley Act addition that both parties bargain in "good faith." As Justice Frankfurter observed, the language was "not a specific direction, but an expression of a governing viewpoint or policy."[181] The divisive issue generally was the propriety of intervention by the N.L.R.B. in the bargaining process. More particularly it was whether the statutory language authorized the Board to develop rules for a desired model of bargaining, or rather confined it to assessing in each case simply whether the parties subjectively were prepared to enter into an agreement.[182]

In two minority opinions, one involving an employer and the other a union refusal to bargain, Justice Frankfurter addressed himself to these issues. In the first, N.L.R.B. v. Truitt,[183] he dissented from a judgment upholding a finding against an employer based on the latter's rejection of the union's request to produce financial data to support the employer's claimed inability to pay higher wages. In his view the Board erred in making its finding turn automatically upon the refusal to produce the data. The Board's duty, he stated, was not to fashion a rule of law "out of one thread drawn from the whole fabric of the evidence in the case," but rather to draw an inference, from the refusal to produce the data, as well as from all the other evidence, as to whether the employer sincerely desired to compose differences and reach an agreement with the union. He apparently rejected a role for the Board as a molder of bargaining practices, even where the model pursued might be justified as a means of advancing reasoned exchange of fact and opinion.

The Justice spoke to this issue again in his separate opinion in the union refusal to bargain case, N.L.R.B. v. Insurance Agents.[184] Consistent with his views in Truitt, he agreed with the Court that the union's harassing and "unprotected" economic pressure during bargaining negotiation was not by itself sufficient to sustain the Board's finding of refusal to bargain in good faith—a union may nonetheless be desirous of reaching an agreement. But the majority suggested at one point that because resort to economic force was not inconsistent with good-faith bargaining it followed that it could not even be evidence of failure to bargain in good faith. To this Justice Frankfurter took exception, even though in several passages the majority appeared to deny that it meant so to confine the evidentiary judgment of the Board.[185] The bigger game the Justice was pursuing was what he took to be the majority's reading of the Act as idealizing the use of force in the bargaining process. The majority observed that "the use of economic pressure by the parties to a labor dispute is not a grudging exception to some policy of completely academic discussion, enjoined by the act; it is part and parcel of the process of collective bargaining." Justice Frankfurter's reply was eloquent:

The presupposition of collective bargaining was the progressive enlargement of the area of reason in the process of bargaining through the give-and-take of discussion and enforcing machinery within industry, in order to substitute, in the language of Mr. Justice Brandeis, "processes of justice for the more primitive method of trial by combat." . . . [I]t should not be the inexorable premise that the process of collective bargaining is by its nature a bellicose process. . . . The statute lays its emphasis upon reason and a willingness to employ it as the dominant force in bargaining. That emphasis is respected by declining to take as a postulate of the duty to bargain that the legally impermissible exertions of so-called economic pressure must be restricted to the crudities of brute force.[186]

To the Board, which had been attempting to formulate rules of bargaining on precisely this rationale, this must have seemed a strange way to support a conclusion that its role was confined to judging from all the evidence solely whether the union meant to frustrate chances of agreement. One is tempted to regard the statement as a *cri de coeur* from a Justice who valued the rational process too deeply to allow an apology for the bellicose process to pass without protest. For while Justice Frankfurter plainly viewed the path of progress as leading away from trial by economic combat (which at an earlier stage of labor relations he himself defended) to the use of reason and intelligence, he placed a higher value on bargaining autonomy free of undirected administrative and judicial intervention.[187]

c) Justice Frankfurter's view of the problems of judicial enforcement of the collective agreement was, in two words, negative and dissident. The issue presented itself as one of interpreting Section 301 of Taft-Hartley, which authorized federal suits for breach of collective agreements. Invariably his response was to confine the scope of the section, motivated partly by constitutional concerns, but also by two other predominant convictions. The first had its source in the Norris-LaGuardia battles and, as we have seen, continued to feed his viewpoints in a variety of contexts; namely, that the federal courts are not suitable forums for creating labor law in the vacuum or semi-vacuum produced by the absence of legislative direction. The second was his previously mentioned preference for legal abstention in all phases of the bargaining process.

In Association of Westinghouse Salaried Employees v. Westinghouse Electric Corp.,[188] which first posed the Section 301 issue for the Court, he rejected an interpretation which would have vested the federal courts with authority to develop a substantive law of the collective agreement. "To turn Section 301 into an agency for working out a viable theory of the nature of a collective bargaining agreement smacks of unreality. Nor does it seem reasonable to view that section as a delivery into the discretionary hands of the federal judiciary, finally of this Court, of such an important, complicated and subtle field." Further, as he put it in the second Section 301 case, Textile Workers v. Lincoln Mills,[189] problems of judicial power would be created "in casting upon the federal courts, with no guides except 'judicial inventiveness,' the task of applying a whole industrial code that is as yet in the bosom of the judiciary." The same considerations led him in his Westinghouse opinion to exclude from Section 301 suits by unions to enforce individual claims under the agreement despite his explicit recognition that unions must have power to sue if they are effectively to perform their role.[190] What was primary was that his awkward interpretation of Section 301 served to cut off a substantial segment of the kind of litigation the Justice regarded as inappropriate for the federal courts.

In Textile Workers v. Lincoln Mills, Justice Frankfurter dissented from the holding that agreements to arbitrate were specifically enforceable as a matter of federal substantive law judicially created under Section 301. The central ground was that since Section 301 was, as he insisted, a grant of jurisdiction to the federal courts over contracts governed by state law, it was an unconstitutional grant of jurisdiction under Article III. And his already mentioned distaste for federal courts making labor law served as an additional ground. But he rested as well on the premise that salutary neglect of the process of collective bargaining was desirable from the standpoint of the process itself. "[T]he meaning of collective bargaining for labor does not remotely derive from reliance on the sanction of litigation in the courts. . . . [J]udicial intervention is ill-suited to the special characteristics of the arbitration process in labor disputes. . . ." And he invoked the words of Dean Shulman, that the courts cannot, "by occasional sporadic decision, restore the parties' continuing relationship" but may through their intervention "seriously affect the going systems of self-government."[191]

By the time Lewis v. Benedict Coal Corp.[192] arose the commitment to developing a federal substantive law of the collective agreement under Section 301 was too firmly made for Justice Frankfurter to continue his protest.[193] But he found in the established doctrines of the law of contracts a second line of defense against that judicial "inventiveness" he distrusted. In a lone dissent he protested against the Court's rejection of the traditional third-party beneficiary doctrine which, if applied, would have allowed the employer to set off against his welfare fund contributions to the beneficiary employees the damages caused by the union promisee's breach of its no-strike commitment. The experience of judges, he concluded, "makes them much more sure-footed in applying principles pertinent to the enforcement of contracts than they are likely to be in discerning the needs of wise industrial relations."

## (2)

As a means of creating the conditions for effective collective bargaining the Wagner Act attempted to shield unionization and union activities from employer interference through a code of employer unfair labor practices administered by the National Labor Relations Board. Perhaps out of deference to the Board, which he viewed as the primary instrument for reading meaning into the Act's loose-jointed language defining employer unfair labor practices, the Justice's opinions contributed only in a minor way to the law's substantive development in this area. Because "words acquire scope and function from the history of events they summarize," in his early opinion in Phelps Dodge Corp. v. N.L.R.B.,[194] he invoked "the long history of industrial conflicts, the diagnosis of their causes by official investigations, the conviction of public men, industrialists and scholars"[195] to support the judgment that the national interest in industrial peace is no less affected by discriminatory refusals to hire than by discriminatory discharges. The Act's prohibition of anti-union discrimination, therefore, must embrace both, as the Board had held. Twelve years later a case arose involving the discharge of broadcasting company employees for publicly disparaging their employer's services in the course of a labor dispute. In a dissenting opinion he chided the majority for reading the authorization to discharge "for cause" to include acts of so-called employee "disloyalty," a ground the Board itself had not invoked to justify its order. The guaranteed right to engage in concerted activity would, he realized, stand for little if "disloyalty" to one's employer were enough for discharge.[196] Finally, in 1958, speaking for the majority, he resisted a Board rule automatically converting an otherwise valid employer no-solicitation rule into an unfair labor practice where the employer violated his own rule by engaging in prohibited anti-union solicitation.[197] The Board's primary responsibility to apply the Act "in the light of [its] special understanding of these industrial situations" is not discharged by its use of "mechanical answers . . . for this non-mechanical complex problem."[198] The final decision was for the Board to make, but only after facing deliberatively the crucial issue, which was "whether the employer's conduct to any considerable degree created an imbalance in the opportunities for organizational communication."[199]

Complementing his deference to Board expertise and experience in giving meaning and application to the substantive standards of employer misconduct, at least where its judgment was a conscientious assessment of the range of relevant considerations, Justice Frankfurter favored a loose judicial rein on the Board's statutory power to devise remedies to "effectuate the policies" of the Act. His Phelps Dodge opinion was the pace-setting decision and easily the most spacious in its definition of Board remedial power.[200] It was written at the same term as Hutcheson, when judicial caution was apparently a less compelling consideration for the Justice than expanding to their logical limits the underlying policies of the new protective labor laws. Holding refusal to hire, as well as discharge, on grounds of union activity to constitute prohibited discrimination was easy work. But there were steep hills to traverse to reach the conclusion that the Board could remedy the wrong, not simply by a cease and desist order, but also by ordering the employer to hire men, with back pay, who had never been employees. As Justice Stone stated in dissent, there was no hint in the legislative history that "Congress or any member of it thought it was giving the Board a remedial power [akin to compelling performance of personal service contracts] which few courts had ever assumed to exercise or had been thought to possess."[201] It was therefore a bold step to find such unprecedented power in the generally phrased authority "to take such affirmative action . . . as will effectuate the policies" of the Act; and the more so in view of the phrase Congress had inserted after its authorization of affirmative action; i.e., "including *re*instatement of *employees* with or without back pay." Considering the novelty of the authority being granted, the phrase had more of the earmarks of an extension beyond power already granted than of an illustrative example. Moreover, Justice Frankfurter held the power to compel hiring to extend as well to those who had obtained other equivalent employment, even though another section of the Act expressly excluded such persons from the definition of employees. For the Justice, two considerations overbore these formidable difficulties. The first was that search for meaning should proceed "by pursuing the central clue to the Board's powers—effectuation of the policies of the Act." And certainly in practical terms it was beyond doubt that compulsory hiring was the only realistic remedy against discrimination in hiring, just as compulsory reinstatement was the only realistic remedy against its "twin," discrimination in firing. The second consideration was that the task of relating remedy to policy fell peculiarly within the administrative competence of the Board. "[I]n the nature of things Congress could not catalogue all the devices and stratagems for circumventing the policies of the Act. Nor could it define the whole gamut of remedies to effectuate these policies in an infinite variety of specific situations. Congress met these difficulties by leaving the adaptation of means to end to the empiric process of administration." In subsequent opinions dealing with the authority of the Board to reach localized unfair labor practices[202] and with its computation and enforcement of back pay obligations, Justice Frankfurter adhered to the primacy of these same considerations.[203]

One is led quite naturally at this point to turn to the Justice's four opinions construing several of the union unfair labor practices added in 1947 by the Taft-Hartley Act. Unlike the provisions of the Wagner Act, however, these did not grow out of a search for policy in which the Justice participated, and they were not framed in that loose, admonitory language which invites recourse to first principles on the part of the interpreter.

Therefore, beyond exhibiting the Justice in the travail of statutory interpretation, they strike no major themes relevant to our purposes. In three he pursued meaning well beyond the surface of the language. In one of them he wrote a separate opinion justifying a strike after the time for reopening provided by the contract but prior to the contract's expiration, despite the terms of Section 8(d) which, read literally, would have precluded such a strike.[204] In two, dealing respectively with the legality of reserved-gate picketing[205] and refusals to work under a "hot cargo" clause,[206] he wrote imaginatively for the majority to construct something of an equilibrium between the often opposing policies of protecting neutrals against conscription and permitting primary pressure, both of which underlay the unartfully phrased secondary boycott provisions of Section 8(b)(4)(A). In the fourth, the Justice's oft-expressed apprehension over assuming the legislative pose gained the ascendancy. Sticking "close in the bark" of the Act's language,[207] his dissent in Mastro Plastics Corp. v. N.L.R.B.[208] invoked Bacon's Abridgment to support a reading of Section 8(d) to forbid a conventional self-help strike against an employer's unfair labor practice, although the provision was plainly addressed to the very different matter of insuring a cooling-off period during bargaining renegotiations. The tug-of-war within the Justice reflected in these cases between judicial creativity and fidelity to words is representative of a basic conflict in the Justice's approach to statutory interpretation; the factors which determined that one pull or the other would prevail in any case are properly analyzable only as part of a study of his interpretation of statutes which transcends any particular substantive area. Yet the labor cases at least suggest that his occasional choice of the method of literality is not explicable in terms of his personal preference for the result it yields.

Before leaving this survey of Justice Frankfurter's labor

opinions it must be said that there is more of relevance, much more, in the sixty-four volumes of the United States Reports which span Justice Frankfurter's tenure than has been touched on here. This review has leveled chiefly on those of the Justice's one hundred-odd labor opinions which concerned the legal rules and boundaries of competition between labor and capital.[209] Yet he participated notably as well in interpreting the reach and meaning of federal standard-setting legislation. There are his Federal Employers' Liability Act opinions, in which the Justice repeatedly deplored as anachronistic the fault principle on which the Act rested, while simultaneously opposing judicial erosion of that principle through the device of reviewing issues of fact.[210] There are his Fair Labor Standards Act opinions, in which the Justice undertook the futile, though heroic, effort of interpreting on principled and ordered grounds the fundamentally unprincipled and orderless provisions of that Act defining its scope of coverage.[211] There are still other decisions of varying degrees of relevance whose inclusion would have led into byways too ramified for unified treatment.[212] And there are, finally, the decisions already reviewed, which, rearranged and viewed from different perspectives than those here assayed, would have yielded further and different light on the subject. Yet a commentator on a Justice does not enjoy a publisher half so permissive as that of his subject,[213] and there must be a stopping point.

## III.

In his days as a scholar off the bench Justice Frankfurter was a vigorous activist in the affairs of his times. Between legal scholarship and the controversial issues of the day there could hardly be a great divide for one who viewed law not as "a system of artificial reason, but the application of ethical ideals, with freedom at the core."[214] Indeed, while others before him, such as Louis D. Brandeis and Henry L. Stimson, had developed the career pattern of the practicing lawyer as engaged citizen and public servant, it was Professor Frankfurter's example which did much to credit a similar combination of roles for the legal scholar. Since the problems of labor and capital were among the more urgent and controversial of those pressing for solution in his pre-judicial years, it was inevitable that some of his vast energies should have been directed to them. As a consequence, Professor Frankfurter figures prominently among the major influences shaping executive and legislative labor policy in its formative years. The form of his influence was that of government mediator and administrator during the First World War, counsel before the United States Supreme Court, editorial commentator in the lay journals, adviser and consultant to executive and legislative policy makers, and draftsman and intellectual champion of one of the key expressions of legislative policy, the Norris-LaGuardia Act. The direction of his influence was not an innovation. It was that of the progressive groups of his time: recognition of the imperative of unionization to redress the imbalance of power between worker and employer; promotion of the process of collective bargaining; development of orderly processes of grievance adjustment; freedom for concerted activities of labor from legal restraint, especially judicial, as well as from employer interference. And these were the ideas which finally emerged as the basic assumptions of national labor policy by the time Justice Frankfurter was appointed to the Supreme Court.

On the bench the roles of scholar and statesman combine less readily, and the Justice's search for a disciplined judicial creativity which skirts the willful as well as the wooden[215] was a central obsession of his judicial career. How near he came to achieving his goal, the impact upon his judging and opinion writing of his relentless and openly avowed quest, indeed, whether the object of the search was real or a mirage—these are the large questions only a little illumined by the fragment of his work represented by his labor opinions.[216] What does appear is that his major early labor opinions seem less tormented by the specter of willfulness than his later ones. The Hutcheson and Phelps Dodge opinions are the major examples. They suggest rather an *enfant terrible* than a "Hamlet on the bench"[217] in the grip of the contradictions in his office. Indeed, it is the dissents in those cases which more nearly approach the mood of the later Justice.

This is not to say that his later ventures in statutory interpretation were predominantly wooden and literal, though such opinions on occasion inexplicably appear, as in the Mastro Plastics case. It is rather to say that none of his later opinions approached those two early cases in boldness and unabashed judicial creativity. Certainly the Justice did not later reject the insight of his days as observer and critic, that the general outlook with which judges view statutes dealing with contentious social issues determines much of the life of those statutes, or that in the last analysis interpretation of doubtful statutes "is a choice among competing policies as starting places for reasoning."[218]

The collective bargaining cases are the clearest evidence of these propositions. How the individual would relate to the union in its representational role was left fairly at large by the governing statutes. Justice Frankfurter approached the varied specific problems which posed the general issue on the basis of a judgment that the needs of the group, as represented by the union, with only rare exceptions are entitled to prevail. In part this rested on a majoritarianism which recurs with protean diversity in his judicial work; in part on a judgment that only in this way could orderly processes of self-government in industry be assured; in part out of concern to avoid the "destructive individualism" in employment relations which the labor acts were designed to remedy. Pro-unionism, in the sense of support for the institution of unionism and the elements necessary for the exercise of what the Justice regarded as its quasi-governmental function, as distinguished from its partisan meaning of supporting the labor cause in all controversies with management, was a consistent feature of his decisions. Another major interstice in the statutory law of collective bargaining, only marginally filled by the Taft-Hartley amendments, was how far the agencies of government, the Board and the courts, could or should intervene in supervising the process of bargaining. Here also Justice Frankfurter filled the void with substance derived from the implications of a social judgment, in this case that autonomy of the collective bargaining process is a major value. This judgment, in turn, was rooted in a still more fundamental commitment to the virtues of a pluralistic order, a commitment which influenced his judgments on other issues as well, notably pre-emption and individual-union relationships in the bargaining process.

Another energy source of his judging in these cases derived from a range of commitments transcending the problems of labor and capital. The Justice's concern for preserving the prestige of the federal judiciary, fed by his intimate knowledge of the damage done when courts assumed leadership in labor law during the injunction era, led him in the Section 301 cases to oppose positions which would result in vesting federal courts with authority to create a common law to govern issues of labor relations unguided by legislative direction. His hospitality to the administrative process led him to sustain a broad remedial discretion in the National Labor Relations Board and to confine judicial oversight of its application of the statute mainly to insuring that the Board deliberatively considered all the elements appropriate for judgment. His commitment to the values of federalism led him to resist findings of federal pre-emption until interference with the federal scheme was irresistibly demonstrated. And certainly in those cases which raised the constitutional issues of due process and free speech, such as the union security and picketing cases, the controlling influence was his conception of the role and method of judicial review.

To assess his influence on the Court calls for speculation since it entails a judgment of what the Court would have done (or not done) if he had not been there. Still it is hard to imagine that any group of sentient persons could remain impervious to the force of Justice Frankfurter's presence, especially in an area which engaged his attention as fully as that of labor relations. Moreover, the record offers clues of substance. He emerges as the leader of the Court's retreat from the Thornhill picketing doctrine to a position which placed picketing under the far looser restraints of economic due process. In the pre-emption cases he changed roles from dissenter in the cause of state power to spokesman for the majority and pivotal justice in a closely divided Court. In both instances the course of the Court's decisions was wandering and uncertain, and it fell to him to write the climactic opinion ordering the import of what went before and formulating common ground for the future.

How far he influenced the interpretation of important legislation is less clear. It is a fair guess, but no more, that the use of Norris-LaGuardia in Hutcheson to effect the *coup de grâce* to Sherman Act prosecutions against labor was the Justice's work. Absent his persuasive influence, perhaps the Court would have accompanied Chief Justice Stone in his gradual erosion of the Act's application to labor. In any event, apart from Hutcheson his role in Norris-LaGuardia cases was minor. As for other legislation, the Phelps Dodge opinion was his major contribution. While there is less ground here for believing his was the crucial influence in shaping the judgment of the Court, the force and authority of the opinion were no doubt partly responsible for the Court's later adherence to a wide freedom of remedial authority for the Board. In giving concreteness to the substantive restraints of the Wagner and Taft-Hartley Acts the lead was apparently elsewhere, although he contributed imaginatively by infusing a degree of coherence into the orderless secondary boycott provisions of the latter Act. On the issue of integrity of the union as a representational medium, one which arose in a variety of statutory settings, the Justice espoused a point of view with consistency and eloquence, but on the whole it was a minority view. The same may be said of his participation in the collective bargaining cases, where his separate and dissenting opinions performed their classic function of disinterring from the soothing verbiage of majority opinions the real issues on which choice must turn.

A summary, such as this, of an account of the Justice's career, even though of one aspect of it, is a perilous venture. Justice Frankfurter's work is symphonic in its variety and contrariety and richness. An account of it can scarcely be more than an unorchestrated statement of the major themes. A summary of an account of it can offer little enlightenment and, what is more to be feared, can distort and trivialize by implying that the spirit has been speared with a word, the essence netted in a phrase. Let it then be said that, if there are such words or phrases to which the rich complexity and subtlety of Mr. Justice Frankfurter can be reduced, I canfess I do not know them.

# Adventures in
# Administrative Law

## Louis L. Jaffe,
### *Byrne Professor of Administrative Law,*
### *Harvard Law School*

Felix Frankfurter when he came to the bench brought with him, if not a system of administrative law, a generally felt philosophy or, if you will, a point of view. This fact adds a certain fillip to a study of his opinions and his votes. Did he hold, we wonder, to these views? Or did the fret and friction of time bring new instruction, cast new light? I think that we can conclude that time did not alter the landscape broadly viewed (here as elsewhere, in his judicial philosophy the similes of fields and spaces is appropriate). But the doctrinal patterns become less pronounced, their application more flexible. We can measure the difference when we set the fulsomely definitive formulations of the early Pottsville against the *dubitante* (the very label is significant) of the color television case.

The political allegiances of his youth shaped the large, organic premises of Frankfurter's public law. He was one of that brilliant group of young publicists—Walter Lippmann, Herbert Croly, Joseph Eastman come to mind—who wrote in the *Nation* and the *New Republic* and whose most immediate teacher and guide was Brandeis. Their mission was to restrain, to tame, to enlighten the capitalist system. The movement, of course, had already been under way since the seventies. The prime medium of reform was regulatory legislation, some of it (the Sherman Act, for example) directly enforced by the courts, but much more of it by administration. To the extent that the opponents of the movement failed to halt it in the political arena, they carried the attack to the courts. The courts were asked to hold legislation unconstitutional, to apply crippling constitutional limitations to its administration, to read the granted powers in a begrudging, miserly fashion. The battle in the courts was raging throughout the period of Frankfurter's public service and teaching. The courts were not as uniformly hostile as the legend would make out—their attitude varied in time and place—but there was more than enough obstruction to arouse the reformers to righteous indignation.

In this battle the business community stood on traditional notions of vested interests. They appealed to constitutional limitation. They urged narrow readings of the statutes, and when they failed, they insisted that every proposed action clear the highest hurdles of traditional procedural safeguards. The reformers countered by an insistence on the limited role of the judiciary. It was their argument that the courts could veto only where the clearest constitutional or statutory limits were violated. Administrative action, they would concede, must be fair, but traditional methods of trial were not *ipso facto* the measure of fairness. Procedure was to be shaped in terms of the overarching objective of administration action. The end in view was not the vindication of private rights but the public interest.

No one case (both the decision and the opinion) better illustrates this whole order of ideas than F.C.C. v. Pottsville Broadcasting[1] in which in his first year on the bench Justice Frankfurter spoke for a unanimous Court (McReynolds J. concurred in the result.) In this case Pottsville had applied for a broadcasting license. The application was denied on the ground of lack of financial qualification. The Court of Appeals reversed because the finding rested on a mistake of law (both the applicant and the Commission shared the mistake). On remand the F.C.C. set Pottsville's application for argument along with two rival applications filed subsequently. The Court of Appeals commanded the F.C.C. to decide Pottsville's application on the original record. Reversing, Mr. Justice Frankfurter said:

> This was not a mandate from court to court but from a court to an administrative agency. What is in issue is not the relationship of federal courts *inter se*—a relationship defined largely by the courts themselves—but the due observance by courts of the distribution of authority made by Congress as between its power to regulate commerce and the reviewing power which it has conferred upon the courts under Article III of the Constitution. . . . The technical rules derived from the interrelationship of judicial tribunals forming a hierarchical system are taken out of their environment when mechanically applied to determine the extent to which Congressional power, exercised through a delegated agency, can be controlled within the limited scope of "judicial power" conferred by Congress under the Constitution. Courts, like other organisms, represent an interplay of form and function. The history of Anglo-American courts and the more or less narrowly defined range of their staple business have determined the basic characteristics of trial procedure, the rules of evidence, and the general principles of appellate review. Modern administrative tribunals are the outgrowth of conditions far different from those. . . . Perhaps the most striking characteristic of this movement has been the investiture of administrative agencies with power far exceeding and different from the conventional judicial modes for adjusting

conflicting claims—modes whereby interested litigants define the scope of the inquiry and determine the data on which the judicial judgment is ultimately based. Administrative agencies have power themselves to initiate inquiry, or, when their authority is invoked, to control the range of investigation in ascertaining what is to satisfy the requirements of the public interest in relation to the needs of vast regions and sometimes the whole nation in the enjoyment of facilities for transportation, communication and other essential public services. These differences in origin and function preclude wholesale transplantation of the rules of procedure, trial, and review which have evolved from the history and experience of courts. . . .

It is, however, urged upon us that if all matters of administrative discretion remain open for determination on remand after reversal, a succession of single determinations upon single legal issues is possible with resulting delay and hardship to the applicant. It is always easy to conjure up extreme and even oppressive possibilities in the exertion of authority. But courts are not charged with general guardianship against all potential mischief in the complicated tasks of government. The present case makes timely the reminder that "legislatures are ultimate guardians of the liberties and welfare of the people in quite as great a degree as the courts." Missouri, K. & T. Ry. Co. v. May, 194 U.S. 267, 270. . . .[2]

Thus all the big doctrinal guns are marshaled against the petitioner and fired with a raking generality which leaves no avenue of escape. "The Court of Appeals laid bare [the] error, and in compelling obedience to its correction exhausted *the only power* which Congress gave it." So there we have it: judicial review is a very scrawny power, a power simply to lay bare error. It derives whatever scope it may have from specific congressional grant. The Court of Appeals in construing its mandate had drawn upon the analogy of upper to lower court. But reliance on the alien analogies will cause courts "to stray outside their province." These grand propositions were small comfort to the angry plaintiff, who had at considerable expense gone to court and won out only to find himself presented with two Johnny-come-lately rivals and a costly comparative hearing. In answer to his bitter complaint he was admonished with a "timely reminder."

In this matter the legislature did, indeed, respond (though too late, of course, to help Pottsville) by providing that on remand "unless otherwise ordered by the Court" the Commission shall give effect to the judgment "upon the basis of the proceedings already had." It is fair, I think, to say that the predicament of a Pottsville would appeal more to the average man on the street and the average lawyer (to whom the congressmen are akin) than to Frankfurter. He had lived most of his young and later adult life in government and university, always among a group that took its task in a heady, rather lofty spirit. The winning and losing of money was not in the forefront of his intensities; at best Pottsville's interest rated only as a factor in a public problem. Nor should the Justice's "timely reminder" be taken as simply a rhetorical flourish. It reflects his basic concept of the role of judicial review to which I shall return later.

But first let us look at one other of the significant themes stated in Pottsville:

> Administrative agencies have power themselves to initiate inquiry, or, when their authority is invoked, to control the range of investigation in ascertaining what is to satisfy the requirements of the public interest in relation to the needs of vast regions. . . . These differences in origin and function preclude wholesale transplantation of the rules of procedure . . . which have evolved from the history and experience of courts. . . . To be sure, the laws under which these agencies operate prescribe the fundamentals of fair play.

Here the Justice asserts that the rules evolved for fair judicial trials should not be transplanted to a proceeding to determine the application for a broadcast license. Why not? Because the principal objective of the proceeding is the public interest in providing an effective broadcasting system; and so rules devised to try issues for the vindication of private rights may not be appropriate. The upshot? The Commission, some years after the trial of plaintiff's application and a judicial determination that the denial of the application was not well founded, is permitted to reopen the proceeding to admit two new applicants. The Court does not totally deny that the private interest is relevant (after all, *some* private person must under the scheme do the broadcasting): it admits, for example, that there must be "fair play" but not, it would seem, fair play by the standards of the common man.

The boldest of Frankfurter's expressions of this point of view is his dissent in the well-known Ashbacker case.[3] The Communications Act provides that the Commission may *grant* a license without hearing but before *denying* a license must accord a hearing. In Ashbacker there were two applicants for a single available license. The Commission granted the application of Fetzer and set down the application of Ashbacker for hearing. Ashbacker succeeded in convincing five of the seven sitting judges of the Court that the grant to Fetzer was equivalent in its practical consequence to a denial of its application without hearing. Frankfurter, dissenting for himself and Rutledge, does not deny that this is the likely consequence. He says only that the grant to Fetzer is conditional and may be either "adjusted" (I do not understand what that means) or revoked "if the hearing should develop considerations not disclosed by the prior scrutiny of the Commission." He does, however, note that "presumably" the Commission before granting an application prior to setting another for hearing has carefully scrutinized the competing applications. When it then grants the one application without hearing, it has decided that the public interest will be best served by an immediate grant, as it similarly does in other cases when it decides that none of the applications should be granted without hearing. This solution, he argues, is "within the explicit provisions" and "wholly consonant with the scheme of the legislation." It is reinforced by the notion that the objective of the legislation is "the public interest": the primary purpose of the hearing in short is not to protect the applicant but to implement the Commission's responsibility for the public interest. The weakness (not necessarily fatal) of the argument is that under the statute the Commission is not free to dispense with a hearing where it proposes to deny an application, even though it is of the opinion that the hearing is not necessary in the public interest. This is, perhaps, another way of saying that the congressional scheme *does* manifest a regard for the private interest which Frankfurter is prepared rather summarily to discount. But anyone who has followed the vast, wasteful, and inconclusive consequences of that behemoth, the comparative hearing, is inclined to credit the Justice with prophetic insight.[4] The flexible scheme devised by the Commission is to my mind superior to that forced upon it by the Court's majority, and if it be conceded that the Court's interpretation is more sensitive to the specific "intent" of the legislation, Frankfurter's is at least within the tolerance open to a judge choosing to decide on the basis of a more general "principle" derived from the overall meaning of the statute.

In immigration cases where the personal concern of the resident alien is acutely involved, Frankfurter has been less inclined to sanction the ways and devices of administrative convenience or so broadly to equate administrative objectives with the public interest. In Colyer v. Skeffington,[5] a case arising out of the "Deportations Delirium" of 1919, Professors Frankfurter and Chafee had acted as *amici curiae* and had seen the reckless brutality with which the resident alien could be victimized. The Justice has *not* felt himself as free as some other judges to impugn the constitutionality of legislation directed against the alien,[6] but where a procedure of doubtful fairness was being questioned, he has been prepared, as he was not in Ashbacker, to find it lacking in statutory warrant, though, again as in Ashbacker, his reading may be thought to have strained the probable statutory "intent."[7] My assertion suggests, incidentally, that something more than a "neutral" search for the statutory intent would seem at times to have motivated Frankfurter. And that is in fact my opinion. Frankfurter, to be sure, is in the forefront of those whose legal philosophy sets a high value on the statute as a source of law and as presumptively the ultimate source of law, a presumption only to be overcome by a convincing and circumstantial demonstration of unconstitutionality or *ultra vires*. His is not a mere profession of allegiance to statutory intention lightly to be disregarded because he prefers a different purpose than the legislature had in view. But this principle of choice, as is true of almost any principle of choice, is relative. He is among those judges who holds most firmly to an objective standard of statutory interpretation, but he shares with all judges the disposition occasionally to find in a statute or outside of it general purposes and principles sufficient to overcome apparently authoritative specifics. So much for procedure.

The chief question of administrative law, at least for the judge, is the role of judicial review. The Justice, as we have already noted, was at the time of his accession to the bench among those who would give this role the most limited function and the narrowest legal definition. This was manifested in his early votes and opinions on standing, ripeness, and scope of review. The two most developed expressions of his general position are in Stark v. Wickard and Pottsville. In Stark v. Wickard[8] a milk producer attacked the legality of a pricing order, an order allegedly reducing his returns from a fund into which the purchasers (handlers) of the milk paid the cost of the milk. The order operated "against" the purchasers in the sense that it was they who must pay the price set by the order. The statute granted to "any handler subject to the order" a right of judicial review. In the opinion of the majority of the Court this did not by implication exclude the producer's right to judicial review. The statute meant to create on behalf of the producer a "personal right" and the protection of personal rights from *ultra vires* action is a judicial function, at least in the absence of its express statutory exclusion. To this Mr. Justice Frankfurter, dissenting, attacks the majority with the very general proposition that "judicial review" (the quotes are the Justice's) apart from "the text and texture of a particular law in relation to which judicial review is sought" is a "mischievous abstraction." There is no such thing as "a natural law" (again his quotes) or "a common law" of judicial review in the federal courts: ". . . whether judicial review is available at all, and if so, who may invoke it, under what circumstances, in what manner, and to what end, are questions that depend for their answer up the particular enactment under which judicial review is claimed."[9]

These surprising statements are the consequence in part of a certain characteristic argumentative exuberance with which the Justice was wont to make his point, but their tenor reveals the intensity with which he was still fighting the battle against what he and many others regarded as the undue, ill-advised intrusion of the judiciary into the area of administration. I characterize the statements as "surprising" for two reasons. First, because they ignore an enormous corpus of decisions which can only be explained on the ground of "a common law" of "judicial review." The federal courts quite without any specific statutory warrant had often reviewed certain alleged administrative "mistakes of law." Were it otherwise, said Peckham J. in American School of Magnetic Healing v. McAnnulty,[10] the individual would be "left to the absolutely uncontrolled and arbitrary action of a public and administrative officer." And in Gegiow v. Uhl,[11] though the statute declared that the decision of the immigration officer to exclude an alien was "final," the Court by Mr. Justice Holmes was unwilling to read this as denying the right to a review of legality. It would make the case for Frankfurter's position no better to argue that particularly in Gegiow v. Uhl an important personal interest was involved. The very meaning and operation of "common law" is to decide when a large principle does and does not apply. The provision for review of "orders" of the Commerce Commission did not define the nature of an order or who had standing to seek review. To give body to this general statute Mr. Justice Brandeis in a series of decisions developed a cluster of ideas more or less derived from the common law; and these decisions have governed review not only of Commerce Commission orders but of other administrative actions.[12]

The second reason for surprise is that characteristically Frankfurter is deeply aware that no important institution or area of the law can be coherently administered without a pre-existing and prevailing order of general ideas. You may, if you wish, argue that Congress itself (whatever it says or leaves unsaid in a specific statute) impliedly adopts this order of ideas; that, however, is but another way of saying that there is a common law of judicial review. Indeed, the Justice had already had occasion in this way to find in a judicial review statute what Congress had either neglected or chosen not to include. In Scripps-Howard Radio v. F.C.C.,[13] speaking for a majority, he had held that a reviewing court had by implication the power to stay the administrative decision pending review. However, unwilling as he usually was to concede that anything but the public interest could be involved in an administrative proceeding ("the rights to be vindicated are those of the public and not of the private litigants"), he argues that to deny the power to grant a stay where necessary "would stultify the purpose of Congress to utilize the courts as a means for vindicating the public interest." As warrant for reading in the power, he referred to "the historic procedure for preserving rights" of a "court of equity."[14] By 1951 he was prepared in his concurrence in Joint Anti-Fascists Refugee Committee v. McGrath[15] to write—drawing on the entire field of administrative law—a treatise-in-little on "standing" and "finality," and it fell out that the great clue to the whole was not the federal statutes but the concept of "justiciability" as it derived "from the business of the Colonial courts and the courts of Westminster when the Constitution was framed."[16] You could say, perhaps, that the subject of his essay was perforce extra-statutory since the question was justiciability under the Constitution. But that only goes to prove the point that the statutes do not operate *in vacuo*. Furthermore, his conclusion was that, despite the absence of a judicial review statute, the plaintiff *did* on the basis of the general common law have standing.[17]

Frankfurter, indeed, could be approvingly aware of the creative, systematizing role of the judiciary when as in the famous Abilene[18] case its effect was to *limit* the courts' jurisdiction. Here in the face of statutory language preserving a common law jurisdiction Justice White had sharply qualified it by devising the doctrine of primary jurisdiction. In Far East Conference[19] Frankfurter warmly espoused, even perhaps extended, the doctrine. White's decision was, he said, "one of those creative judicial labors whereby modern administrative law is being developed as part of our traditional system of law."[20]

Far East Conference emphasizes again one of the principal aspects of the Justice's approach to judicial review, particularly in his first few years on the Court, namely, the limited function which he assigns to it. He is not ordinarily prepared to see its function as the protection of "private" rights. Even where as in Scripps-Howard he finds that there is an implied power of stay pending appeal, the rights "to be vindicated are those of the public and not of the private litigants." In a number of other cases, without denying that there are private rights entitled to protection, he rejects the notion that the courts are particularly to be looked to for that protection. Hardship "there may well come through action of an administrative agency," he says, dissenting, in Columbia Broadcasting, "[b]ut to slide from recognition of hardship to assertion of jurisdiction is once more to assume that only the courts are the guardians of the rights and liberties of the people."[21]

And again to quote his words in Pottsville:

> It is always easy to conjure up extreme and even oppressive possibilities in the exertion of authority. But courts are not charged with the general guardianship against all potential mischief in the applicated tasks of government. The present case makes timely the reminder that "legislatures are ultimate guardians of the liberties and welfare of the people in quite as great a degree as the courts." [Citing Holmes J. in Missouri, K. & T. Ry. Co. v. May, 194 U.S. 267, 270 (1904).] Congress which creates and sustains these agencies must be trusted to correct whatever defects experience may reveal. Interference by the courts is not conducive to the development of habits of responsibility in administrative agencies. Anglo-American courts as we now know them are themselves in no small measure the product of a historic process.[22]

The point which Frankfurter was making here is important and it is well to make it. If fair treatment is to be available on a day-to-day basis our legislatures and our administrations must *believe* in fair treatment. In the absence of a political system based on this conviction the occasional judicial intervention cannot do much more than defeat an occasional inequity and keep alive hope for a better day. Frankfurter in these statements is pointing out to us where we can most effectively direct our energies. But there are overtones here which belie our traditional wisdom, which ignore the expectations of *the very people itself* (those whom legislatures represent). His appeal to the "historic process" which has formed our courts cannot fail to remind us that the courts in the minds of the people do have a special role, a role certified by an almost flamboyant historical warrant, in protecting the rights of the *individual*. Power, it is said, corrupts, and one form of corruption is to sacrifice the individual in the name of "the public interest." A strong legislature and a strong administration are not inconsistent with a strong judiciary. If a major and desirable strength of administration is zealotry, a judiciary alert to protect the individual from excess is a most appropriate complement. The argument of the Court in Pottsville was that if the result were harsh the legislature could remedy the injustice. But that will not help the individual whose ox has been gored. The question in such a case is not simply whether the legislature should remedy the general situation (whatever the Court does, the legislature can remedy the general situation) but whether an individual who is presently the suffering object of an excess of zeal should and can be relieved.

Of course, the plaintiff will be told that, however great the outrage, the Court is limited by a statutory strait jacket. We have noted Frankfurter's statement in Pottsville that the Court of Appeals "laid bare [the] error, and in compelling obedience to its correction exhausted *the only power* which Congress gave it." There have been times, too, where his insistence on agency expertise would exclude the courts even from adjudicating an alleged "error of law." In the tax field at least (relying on the Jackson decision in the famous Dobson case)[23] he would have had the courts eschew "sterile attempts at differentiation between 'fact' and 'law in the abstract.' "[24] But unless the courts are to revise all administrative judgments whether of fact or law or to revise none—these discriminations, however difficult, must be made. Statements of this sort do no more, perhaps, than indicate a mood—and a mood which for the most part works in what I would regard as the right direction, the maximizing of administrative discretion. The Justice can, of course, differentiate "law" from "fact" when he thinks he should,[25] and his record in that respect is admirable. His actual rulings on the substantive issues involved in administrative rulings on balance show, first, a sensitive respect for statutory intention both in affirming[26] and overruling agency decisions[27] and, second, a broad deference to the exercise of administrative discretion where the statute leaves open a choice.[28]

It would not do to say that in his first decade on the bench Frankfurter uniformly indulged the agencies either by always espousing general principles increasing their power or by approving their specific conclusions. A famous example to the contrary on both scores is the Chenery litigation. In the first Chenery[29] case he reformulated with considerable force the requirement that "the orderly functioning of the process of review requires that the grounds upon which the administrative agency acted be clearly disclosed and adequately sustained." "The Commission's action cannot be upheld merely because findings might have been made and considerations disclosed which would justify its order. . . ."[30] This surely was not surprising, and it is a thoroughly correct position for a judge who is prepared to give wide tolerance to administrative discretion. It is a characteristic of many administrative situations that they can be resolved consistently with the statute in a great variety of ways. But it must appear that the decision was not based on considerations which the statute means to exclude or make irrelevant. This is not merely a matter of couching the results in the correct words. It is assumed that public servants wish to be guided by the law, and even a formulation which is not sincerely felt today is likely to become a guiding principle for the future.

The sequel to the first Chenery case *was*, however, rather surprising. On remand the Securities Commission *did* formulate an elaborate rationalization. No doubt one could disagree with it, but when the case came once more to the Court,[31] a majority of which upheld the Commission, Mr. Justice Jackson in a dissent for himself and Frankfurter went so far as to say that the Court "approves the Commission's assertion of power to govern . . . *without* law." (Italics in original.) The decision is "ominous" to one who believes "that men should be governed by law."[32] Jackson's anathema was directed to the application of a rule first explicitly formulated in the decision itself; but perhaps this rule was sufficiently grounded in emerging principles so that its *ex post facto* application was within the accepted common law power to innovate. The whole opinion, indeed, is hyperbolic, and perhaps Frankfurter went along because he was unable to find a tactful way to temper his partner's excess. Ordinarily where he has been unwilling to support an administrative claim to power his tone is measured.[33]

It was in RCA v. United States,[34] that Mr. Justice Frankfurter in a *dubitante* made, for the moment at least, one brilliant, flashing break for freedom from the imprisoning categories of judicial abstention. He saw the case as exceptional. "I am no friend of judicial intrusion into the administrative process," he began (at 427). "I have no doubt that if Congress chose to withdraw all court review from the Commission's orders it would be constitutionally free to do so." But if the factual situation was exceptional, the doctrinal terms in which it must be presented to the Court (and in which it was decided) made intervention nearly impossible. The *dubitante* was the maximum that Frankfurter could muster and—ah, Scylla, ah, Charybdis!—a *dubitante* might be thought to be perilously close to the advisory opinion which Frankfurter so deprecates.

RCA and CBS had both been hard at work to develop and perfect color television. CBS's system was more nearly ready for use but was "non-compatible"; i.e., it required a change in existing equipment to be received. The F.C.C. promulgated a rule prescribing standards for transmission of color television which accepted CBS's system. It was argued that this would seriously set back RCA's development of a compatible system. The F.C.C. decided that the public's interest in the immediate if limited gain overcame its interest in a "rosier but indeterminate future" even with the possible setback which the choice would entail. Here is par excellence a reasoned "exercise of discretion" by an "expert" body. "[C]ourts should not overrule an administrative decision merely because they disagree with its wisdom,"[35] said Mr. Justice Black, citing Frankfurter's statements to that effect in NBC v. United States.[36] And yet in some sense, in a very substantial sense, this is just what Frankfurter finds himself tempted to do. He strains valiantly to elude the standard categories. It is not "a *mere* exercise of *conventional* discretion." Why? Because it "may so profoundly affect the public interest." The question is not "one of those expert matters as to which courts should properly bow to the Commission's expertness." Why not? Because the public's interest in the speedy development of color television is a great social question involving the philosophy of progress. Even the Commission's prediction as to the likely prospect of the early attainment of compatibility is "hardly in the domain of expertness so long as scientific and technological barriers do not make the prospect fanciful." And then the final volte-face. "In any event, this Court is not without experience in understanding the nature of such complicated issues. We have had occasion before to consider complex scientific matters" (citing the Court's decisions in patent matters).

It was precisely an acute feeling of the profound *unwisdom* of the Commission's determination (as contrasted with "legal error") which moved Frankfurter to redefine and to reverse so drastically his usual premises.

"One of the more important sources of the retardation or regression of civilization is man's tendency to use new inventions indiscriminately or too hurriedly without adequate reflection of long-range consequences. No doubt the radio enlarges man's horizon. But by making him a captive listener it may make for spiritual impoverishment." The whole passage is eloquent and worth reading.

It cannot be said that the Justice thus meant to abandon or did abandon his general premises as to the role of judicial review. The Court continues to be a limited partner in formulating policy, and occasionally, as in Color Television, were the *dubitante* to prevail it would be a partner with a sense of its positive potentialities. It can do more (on occasion) than "lay bare [an] error." Administrative expertise must no longer be "puffed up," and the judges themselves are wise old bodies ever and anon worth heeding. Thus the stark, strict outlines of a philosophy formed in a time of battle, in a period when he was himself a protagonist, have softened. The war is over (for the time being at least) and he has become a judge.[37] As the grist of the administrative mill comes to the courts over the years to be assayed, the weaknesses of expertise appear—not just the "wrong" decisions but the endemic, the characteristic faults and distortions which it is the judges' role to ameliorate. The judges can justly believe that they are not barely licensed intruders but a useful, integral part of the system. This, it seems to me, is what Frankfurter saw and said in RCA v. United States. It is inspiring to observe a man of Frankfurter's degree of maturity and sophistication continuing to learn and to respond, and to summon the courage to confront unsettling insights.

# The Justice
# and His Law Clerks

Andrew L. Kaufman,
*Former Law Clerk to Justice Frankfurter*

My pleasant assignment for this book is an essay from the law
clerk's point of view. Others are writing of Justice Frankfurter
as a person, as a lawyer and professor, and as a judge. This essay
deals with a relationship—the relationship established each year
between Justice Frankfurter and first one and then two recent
law school graduates.

The Justice loves his law clerks. His friendship with some of
them goes back over a quarter of a century; with each it is
close and lasting, varying only in degree from warm to intimate.
Yet, with a few exceptions, the law clerks knew the Justice only
after he came on the bench. His prior career as student, lawyer,
teacher, defender of Sacco and Vanzetti, and adviser to Presi-
dents was historical knowledge only. However, selection by
Professor Henry Hart and later by Professor Albert Sacks, both
of the Harvard Law School, virtually assured for each law clerk
not only love but also immediate acceptance as a colleague in

what might be, but never was, called the search and pursuit of the ends of the law. This recognition was naturally highly flattering to novice lawyers and, though it entailed obligations, they were probably not regarded as such by anyone.

Perhaps the only personal qualification for a law clerk was fondness for discussion and a willingness to express his own opinions. Any viewpoint expressed by the Justice, even the most cherished, was an open subject for debate, and the more exuberant the better. The shouts of the Justice and his law clerks could often be heard through closed doors in the hallways of the Supreme Court. Discussions with the Justice and providing intellectual companionship were the most important parts of the law clerks' function. From the Justice's point of view, talks with his clerks may have helped him arrange his own thoughts on particular cases, especially if a clerk happened to emphasize considerations that the parties had not stressed. But perhaps even more importantly, each discussion, whether legal or not, constituted a mental exercise for the Justice which was as much a part of his life as reading newspapers, English and American, keeping abreast of current non-fiction literature, and engaging in a vast correspondence. These endeavors were essential to his job as judge; they were part of the background, the intellectual atmosphere that he brought to bear upon each case.

The law clerk's feeling that he was the Justice's junior partner, an associate Associate Justice, was enhanced by the work the Justice wanted him to do. The law clerk rarely read a petition for certiorari and he worked on only a relatively few cases. These were the cases that intrigued the Justice and were generally the most interesting and challenging. And if a law clerk at some time during his tenure spent long hours working on a lengthy appendix, it was good for him to be aware that law, even in the Supreme Court, often involves the tedious process of collecting facts. The law clerk, however, was not restricted to cases in which the Justice had expressed interest. Often the most thought-provoking discussions might arise out of a law clerk's chance remarks concerning a particular case.

In all of this I have been dealing only in generalities. The confidential nature of the law clerk's job of course forbids any "inside story" about the details of the Court and its work. But the formal work performed by Justice Frankfurter's law clerks was merely a part of the experience. The real flavor can be conveyed only by a sample of other events in the law clerk's life. The day started with coffee at the Justice's house on Dumbarton Avenue in Georgetown before driving with him to the Court or meeting him at the corner of Fifteenth and H after his morning walk with Mr. Acheson. The New York *Times* was early on the daily schedule; familiarity with current events was necessary for conversation with the Justice. There were also random conversations and a stream of questions at any time of day, and sometimes of night, about history, the law, philosophy, politics, personalities, the Harvard Law School, music—in short, any subject whatever. These were followed by numerous reading suggestions and, often, the books themselves from the library. The day ended with the evening drive back to Georgetown. Despite extreme dawdling by the law clerks, the time was always too short for the subjects of conversation which would then be concluded in the driveway or in the library. An occasional Sunday would also be spent in Georgetown when work was pressing. The work would be done, but with dinner and wine and perhaps a stroll through Georgetown and Dumbarton Oaks as well.

What law clerk will forget listening to the sextet from *Lucia* being whistled somewhat off key in the corridor of the Court, followed by the Justice bursting in the door of the law clerks' room fresh from conference or a court session with the news of the day. What Supreme Court page will forget the constant procession to the Frankfurter law clerks whenever the Court was in session with notes requesting information or merely informing the clerk of some interesting repartee in the courtroom or telling him to come in and listen to a good argument. There also comes to mind an occasional whole day spent on some such topic as selecting the ten or fifteen milestones in the history of private law and defending and discussing the choices. One can imagine the debate that would ensue were a selection to include the Coke-Ellesmere dispute in preference to the publication by Holmes of *The Common Law*. Finally the annual dinners of the law clerks should be mentioned. They are wonderful evenings, cherished both by the Justice and by the clerks. As Commissioner Philip Elman of the F.T.C., a former clerk, writes: "The Justice does not regard the dinners as gatherings of former apprentices to salute their old master. We are his children and heirs to whom he feels an obligation to render periodic accountings of his judicial stewardship. And so, as cigars and brandy come around, the Justice rises. But what begins as a message on the state of the Court finishes as a joyously uninhibited free-for-all in which it is utterly futile to try to enforce any rule of germaneness or uninterrupted discourse. Only at 3:00 or 4:00 A.M., after one of the older clerks seizes him *vi et armis* to take him home—the Justice protesting all the while that the evening is still young—does the party end."

A brief incident that comes to mind may provide further illustration. A particularly heated discussion between a law clerk and the Justice ended early one evening with the Justice charging the law clerk with intellectual arrogance for use of a particular line of argument. The law clerk departed for home and the Justice telephoned the law clerk's wife immediately to tell her that he had been hard on her husband in the heat of discussion and hoped that he had not given unintended offense. His advice: "Meet your husband at the door with martini in hand."

The only thing missing was the recipe for the drink. We can supply it—heated discussion mixed with concern, humor, and confidence in the wife's ability to put everything right. That is a recipe for the Felix Frankfurter cocktail, and there are many others.

This compact catalogue of events indicates that being a law clerk involved not only a professional but an intensely personal relation—one in which the law clerk's wife was not only included but even made to feel that she was superior to her husband in the affections of the Justice. After a law clerk had finished his term at the Court, a stream of letters, notes, and memoranda with comments, questions, and reading suggestions would follow him wherever he went. Once a law clerk, forever a colleague and friend.

One cannot write as a law clerk about the Justice without also mentioning some other people close to the Justice and to the law clerks. Most special and in a class by herself is of course Mrs. Frankfurter, the only person whose wit and charm are sufficient to take the center of attraction away from the Justice at the law clerks' dinners. (And no one is prouder of that occurrence than the Justice himself.) Then there is the Justice's secretary, Elsie Douglas, who has been so invaluable to him. She and her predecessors, the Watters sisters, ran the office with quiet smoothness and were the law clerks' friends. There were also various court personnel with whom the law clerks were thrown into close contact because the Justice believed that his law clerks should get to know the librarians, the printers, the clerk's office, the marshal's office, and the reporter's office. It would not be amiss to name the two persons among these with whom the clerks, through the Justice, had the closest contact at the Court: Helen Lally, librarian-lawyer-researcher for the Justice, and Buck Row, head of the Government Printing Office unit in charge of the countless drafts, memoranda, opinions, and appendices that flowed from the Frankfurter office. Also at the Court was Tom Beasley, the Justice's jack-of-all-trades and the law clerks' friend. Finally, but not least, at Dumbarton Avenue one could always enjoy the pleasant companionship and wisdom of Matilda Williams and Ellen Smith, who looked after the law clerks as well as the Frankfurters.

Henry Hart and Herbert Wechsler have dedicated their monumental work on *The Federal Courts and the Federal System* "To Felix Frankfurter who first opened our minds to these problems." Mark Howe has written in his Foreword to Volume I of his Holmes biography, "So many authors have expressed their gratitude to Mr. Justice Frankfurter that it is becoming almost a ritual of scholarship to acknowledge the indebtedness." This is the man to whom we, his law clerks, were exposed each day. If we have not profited, the fault is our own. But even a sloth would be moved by Justice Frankfurter. His brain is constantly and restlessly inquiring, learning, and communicating, and it forces those around him to bestir their own brains to do the same. No one can be smug or complacent in his presence. He is one of those rare individuals who inspires minds, who invests people with a savage desire to develop their latent abilities. The dedication to the present volume could well be, "No one who knows Felix Frankfurter is the same thereafter."

# Notes

## Separation of Powers: The Justice Revisits His Own Casebook, *Nathaniel L. Nathanson*

1. 3 Dall. 386.
2. 3 Dall. at 394.
3. 3 Dall. at 388–389.
4. 4 Dall. 14 (1800).
5. 4 Dall. at 18.
6. 4 Dall. at 19.
7. 4 Wall. 333 (1867).
8. 4 Wall. 277 (1867).
9. 328 U.S. 303 (1946).
10. 328 U.S. at 315–316.
11. 328 U.S. at 319.
12. 328 U.S. at 321–322.
13. 328 U.S. at 312–313.
14. 328 U.S. at 313.
15. 328 U.S. at 314.
16. 328 U.S. at 325.
17. 328 U.S. at 318.
18. 328 U.S. at 330.
19. See Nathanson, *The Supreme Court as a Unit of the National Government: Herein of Separation of Powers and Political Questions,* 6 JOUR. OF PUBLIC LAW 331, 336 (1958).

20. 103 U.S. 168 (1880).
21. 273 U.S. 135 (1926).
22. 269 Mass. 23, 171 N.E. 82 (1930).
23. 354 U.S. 234 (1957).
24. 354 U.S. 178, 225 (1957).
25. 65 Cong. Rec. 9082.
26. 65 Cong. Rec. 9081.
27. 345 U.S. 41 (1953).
28. 345 U.S. at 43–44.
29. 345 U.S. at 46.
30. 345 U.S. at 47.
31. *Id.*
32. 354 U.S. at 217.
33. 354 U.S. at 208.
34. 360 U.S. 109 (1959).
35. 360 U.S. at 124.
36. Nathanson, *supra* note 19, at 348 *et seq.*
37. 321 U.S. 414 (1943).
38. United States v. National Dairy Products Corp., 372 U.S. 29 (1963). Compare United States v. Cohen Grocery Co., 255 U.S. 81 (1921).
39. Bickel, The Least Dangerous Branch 158 (1962).
40. People v. Tremaine, 252 N.Y. 27, 168 N.E. 817 (1929).
41. Frankfurter and Davison, Cases and Other Materials on Administrative Law 113 (1932).
42. 272 U.S. 52 (1926).
43. Humphrey's Executor v. United States, 295 U.S. 602 (1936).
44. 357 U.S. 349 (1958).
45. 357 U.S. at 352.
46. 357 U.S. at 355.
47. 357 U.S. at 356.
48. 343 U.S. 579 (1952).
49. 343 U.S. at 593.
50. 343 U.S. at 589.
51. 343 U.S. at 593.
52. 343 U.S. at 595.
53. See Freund, *The Supreme Court, 1951 Term-Foreword: The Year of the Steel Case*, 66 HARV. L. REV. 89 (1952).
54. 343 U.S. at 595.

55. 343 U.S. at 596.
56. 277 U.S. 189, 209.
57. 343 U.S. at 597.
58. 343 U.S. at 597.
59. 343 U.S. at 610.
60. 343 U.S. at 613.
61. 272 U.S. 52, 240, 293.
62. 343 U.S. at 702.
63. 267 U.S. 87 (1925).
64. 253 U.S. 245 (1920).
65. 2 Dall. 409 (1792).
66. 13 How. 40 (1851).
67. 117 U.S. 697 (1864).
68. 219 U.S. 346 (1911).
69. 273 U.S. 70 (1927).
70. 367 U.S. 497 (1961).
71. 277 U.S. 274 (1928).
72. 277 U.S. at 289. Other sentences in the opinion make it clear that Mr. Justice Brandeis meant this in a constitutional, as well as a statutory, sense.
73. 328 U.S. 549, 552 (1946).
74. 288 U.S. 249, 262 (1933).
75. 319 U.S. 293, 300 (1943).
76. 330 U.S. 75 (1946).
77. 367 U.S. 497 (1961).
78. 367 U.S. at 501.
79. 367 U.S. at 502.
80. State v. Nelson, 126 Conn. 412, 11A. 2d 856.
81. 367 U.S. at 505.
82. Professor Bickel does draw the contrary conclusion: "The consequence of the opinion nevertheless, must be that a prosecution of persons situated as are Dr. Buxton and his patients would fail on the ground of desuetude." (Bickel, *supra* note 39, at 154.) He suggests, however, that the issue is clouded by the fact that Mr. Justice Frankfurter did not speak for a majority, and that Mr. Justice Brennan's concurrence "gives reasons that are none too scrutable." (*Id.*) Leaving Mr. Justice Brennan's opinion out of account, I find it difficult to believe that this is the implication of Mr. Justice Frankfurter's opinion. If it is to be enforced by the Supreme

Court it would require constitutional rationalization, presumably on the basis of denial of equal protection. This itself would be no mean addition to constitutional law doctrine.

83. 248 U.S. 215 (1918).
84. 262 U.S. 553 (1923).
85. Publications of Permanent Court of International Justice, Series A-24.
86. 7 How. 1 (1949).
87. 307 U.S. 433 (1939).
88. 328 U.S. 549 (1946).
89. 369 U.S. 186 (1962).
90. Government Under Law 19 (1956).
91. 369 U.S. at 267.
92. 369 U.S. at 282.
93. 369 U.S. at 283.
94. 369 U.S. at 289.
95. 369 U.S. at 287.
96. 369 U.S. at 300.
97. *Id.*
98. 290 U.S. 398 (1934).
99. These shoals are devastatingly described and analyzed in Neal, *Baker v. Carr: Politics in Search of Law*, SUPREME COURT REV. 252 (1962).
100. 369 U.S. at 237.
101. 369 U.S. at 265.
102. Since this passage of the text was written, the Court has already indicated, over the dissent of both Mr. Justice Stewart and Mr. Justice Harlan, that it is not likely to stop with such a compromise. Wesberry v. Sanders, decided Feb. 17, 1964.
103. Jaffe and Nathanson, Administrative Law 38 (1961).

# Mr. Justice Frankfurter and the Reading of Statutes, *Henry J. Friendly*

1. Frankfurter, *Mr. Justice Brandeis and the Constitution*, 45 HARV. L. REV. 33, 104 (1931).
2. The lecture has been printed in 2 Record Assn. of the Bar of the

City of New York 213 (1947), as a separate volume published by the Association, in 47 COLUM. L. REV. 527 (1947), and in Frankfurther, Of Law and Men 44 (1956). I shall cite it simply as Reflections, and the page references will be to Of Law and Men.

3. Freund, Competing Freedoms in American Constitutional Law, U. of Chi. Conference on Freedom and the Law, 26 (1953).

4. Mendelson, *Mr. Justice Frankfurter and the Construction of Statutes,* 43 CALIF. L. REV. 652 (1955). See also Mendelson, Justices Black and Frankfurter: Conflict in the Court, 14–36 (1961).

5. See Freund, Introduction to Bickel, The Unpublished Opinions of Mr. Justice Brandeis, xvi (1957).

6. See Friendly, *The Gap in Lawmaking: Judges Who Can't and Legislators Who Won't,* 63 COLUM. L. REV. 787, 788–789 (1963).

7. 304 U.S. 64 (1938).

8. Reflections, 45. This estimate, of course, included cases involving the constitutionality of statutes, but the problems of constitutionality and of construction are not unrelated, as we shall see.

9. *Id.,* 44. Also, "My business throughout most of my professional life has been with statutes," 48.

10. One feels this intimacy, for example, in his early opinion in Rochester Tel. Corp. v. United States, 307 U.S. 125 (1939), and, a decade later, in United States v. Interstate Commerce Commission, 337 U.S. 426, 444 (1949) (dissenting).

11. 2 Holmes-Pollock Letters 13 (Howe ed. 1941); 1 Holmes-Laski Letters 204–205 (Howe ed. 1953).

12. Towne v. Eisner, 245 U.S. 418, 425 (1918).

13. Reflections, 51-52.

14. *Id.,* 51.

15. None of this is meant to minimize Mr. Justice Brandeis' contribution in developing the use of legislative materials as an aid to the ascertainment of meaning—for an outstanding example of which see his unpublished opinion in Strathearn S.S. Co. v. Dillon, 252 U.S. 348 (1920), printed in Bickel, The Unpublished Opinions of Mr. Justice Brandeis, 35, 47-50 (1957)—or his architectural skill in marshaling all possible considerations favorable to his view, for an example of which see his dissent in King Manufacturing Co. v. Augusta, 277 U.S. 100, 115 (1928). The labors incident to the preparation of this opinion are still rather vivid to the writer, his law clerk during that term. These included thumbing through each volume of the U. S.

Reports—happily then a hundred less in number—a process indicative of the Justice's demand for precision and his lack of confidence in digests and indices. Many of Mr. Justice Frankfurter's opinions show that he was bred in that same thorough school. See, e.g., the two appendices in Commissioner v. Estate of Church, 335 U.S. 632, 687, 690 (1949) (dissenting).

16. See, particularly, How Far Is a Judge Free in Rendering a Decision? in Hand, The Spirit of Liberty 103, 104-110 (1952 ed.); *Is There a Common Will?*, 28 MICH. L. REV. 46, 52 (1929); Cox, *Judge Learned Hand and the Interpretation of Statutes*, 60 HARV. L. REV. 370 (1947); and Diamond, *Learned Hand and Federal Taxation*, 3 SYRACUSE L. REV. 81 (1951).

17. Hand, Thomas Walter Swan, in The Spirit of Liberty, 209, 213.

18. Reflections, 60. See also Collected Legal Papers 207 (1920).

19. United States v. Whitridge, 197 U.S. 135, 143 (1905).

20. United States v. Johnson, 221 U.S. 488, 496 (1911).

21. Brooklyn Nat. Corp. v. Commissioner, 157 F. 2d 450, 451 (2 Cir.), cert. denied, 329 U.S. 733 (1946).

22. Reflections, 48.

23. The Spirit of Liberty, 108 (1952).

24. Reflections, 48. Compare the statement in F.H.A. v. The Darlington, 358 U.S. 84, 92 (1958) (dissenting), "The task is imaginatively to extrapolate the contemporaneous answer that the Legislature would have given to an unconsidered question. . . ."

25. This view is expressed in Reflections, 52, 53, 60, 67, and in countless opinions. Addison v. Holly Hill Fruit Products, Inc., 322 U.S. 607, 617 (1944), will suffice as an example: "To let general words draw nourishment from their purpose is one thing. To draw on some unexpressed spirit outside the bounds of the normal meaning of words is quite another."

26. Summers, *Frankfurter, Labor Law and the Judge's Function*, 67 YALE L. J. 266, 282–83 (1957).

27. See 1 Warren, The Supreme Court in United States History, 158-209 (rev. ed. 1926); Levi, *An Introduction to Legal Reasoning*, 33, 56-57 (1961 ed.).

28. Professor Summers mentions also the Justice's belief that courts "should not act as a clean-up crew for sloppy legislation but should increase the pressure on [legislators] to discharge their responsibilities," *supra* note 26, at 283. See, e.g., Commissioner v. Wodehouse,

337 U.S. 369, 409 (1948) dissenting: "Free judicial rendering of needlessly unprecise legislation is sufficiently undesirable in that it encourages Congress to be indifferent to the duty of giving laws attainable definiteness." *Sed quaere* how effective judges can thus be as schoolmasters to the legislature.

29. Reflections, 56.

30. F.T.C. v. Bunte Brothers, 312 U.S. 349, 350 (1941). See also Shapiro v. United States, 335 U.S. 1, 39 (1948) (dissenting): "To ascertain what Congress meant . . . we would do well to begin by carefully attending to what Congress said."

31. Pope v. Atlantic Coast Line R.R. Co., 345 U.S. 379, 390 (1953) (dissenting).

32. *Ex parte* Peru, 318 U.S. 578, 596 (1943) dissenting.

33. Stark v. Wickard, 321 U.S. 288, 319 (1944) (dissenting) discussed below.

34. Elgin, J. & E. R. Co. v. Burley, 325 U.S. 711, 760 (1945) (dissenting).

35. Utah Junk Co. v. Porter, 328 U.S. 39, 44 (1946).

36. Mastro Plastics Corp. v. N.L.R.B., 350 U.S. 270, 293 (1956) (dissenting). See also Commissioner v. Wodehouse, 337 U.S. 369, 410–11 (1949) (dissenting).

37. Estep v. United States, 327 U.S. 114, 136 (1946) (concurring); see also Addison v. Holly Hill Fruit Products, Inc., 322 U.S. 607, 618 (1944); Commissioner v. Culbertson, 337 U.S. 733, 754 (1949) (concurring).

38. McDonald v. Commissioner, 323 U.S. 57, 64 (1944); see also United States v. Ogilvie Hardware Co., 330 U.S. 709, 721 (1947) (dissenting).

39. United States v. Maher, 307 U.S. 148, 155 (1939). See also United States v. John J. Felin & Co., 334 U.S. 624, 626 (1948): ". . . we must translate the idiom of the industry into vernacular English."

40. N.L.R.B. v. Highland Park Mfg. Co., 341 U.S. 322, 326 (1951) (dissenting). By insisting that the question whether words have a special industry meaning must be asked, the Justice does not prejudge the answer; this may well be negative. See F.C.C. v. Columbia Broadcasting System, 311 U.S. 132, 135–36 (1940); Elgin, J. & E. R. Co. v. Burley, 325 U.S. 711, 749 (1945) (dissenting).

41. United States v. Union Pacific R. Co., 353 U.S. 112, 122 (1957) (dissenting).

42. Interstate Commerce Commission v. J-T Transport Co., 368 U.S. 81, 94, 127 (1961) (dissenting).

43. Monroe v. Pape, 365 U.S. 167, 244 (1961) (dissenting).

44. United States v. Union Pacific R. Co., *supra*, 353 U.S. at 122 (dissenting).

45. Standard Oil Co. v. United States, 337 U.S. 293, 311-313 (1949); Amalgamated Clothing Workers v. Richman Brothers, 348 U.S. 511, 515-516 (1955).

46. United States v. Monia, 317 U.S. 424, 431 (1943) (dissenting).

47. Massachusetts Bonding & Ins. Co. v. United States, 352 U.S. 128, 138 (1956) (dissenting). The "knockout" was thought to have been administered by Mr. Justice Holmes's statement in Boston Sand & Gravel Co. v. United States, 278 U.S. 41, 48 (1921), and followed by Judge Learned Hand's in Guiseppi v. Walling, 144 F. 2d 608, 624 (2 Cir. 1944) (concurring), aff'd *sub nom.* Gemsco, Inc. v. Walling, 324 U.S. 244 (1945).

48. United States v. Witkovich, 353 U.S. 194, 199 (1957). Compare the wise observation of Plowden: "sometimes the Sense is more confined and contracted than the Letter, and sometimes it is more large and extensive." Eyston v. Studd, Plowd. 459, 465 (1573).

49. Sullivan v. Behimer, 363 U.S. 335, 358 (1960) (dissenting). See also Interstate Commerce Commission v. J-T Transport Co., 368 U.S. 81, 107 (1961) (dissenting): "Words are seldom so plain that their context cannot shape them."

50. United States *ex rel.* Knauff v. Shaughnessy, 338 U.S. 537, 548-549 (1950) (dissenting).

51. Romero v. International Terminal Operating Co., 358 U.S. 354, 379 (1959). See also Pope v. Atlantic Coast Line R.R. Co., 345 U.S. 379, 392 (1953) (dissenting), and Florida Lime & Avocado Growers v. Jacobsen, 362 U.S. 73, 95 (1960) (dissenting).

52. Compare Lord Bramwell in Hill v. East and West India Dock Co., 9 A.C. 448, 464-465 (1884), and Lord Atkinson in Vacher & Sons, Ltd. v. London Society of Compositors [1913] A.C. 107, 121-122, with Holy Trinity Church v. United States, 143 U.S. 457 (1892).

53. Caminetti v. United States, 242 U.S. 470, 485 (1917).

54. United States v. Sullivan, 332 U.S. 689, 705 (1948) (dissenting).

55. Caminetti v. United States, *supra* note 53.

56. Reflections, 45.

57. The Nature of the Judicial Process, 32 (1922).

58. Reflections, 53. For an instance see J. C. Penney Co. v. Commissioner, 312 F. 2465 (2 Cir. 1962).

59. D. A. Schulte, Inc. v. Gangi, 328 U.S. 108, 121-122 (1946) (dissenting); compare Reflections, 55-56, 60, and the quotation from Addison v. Holly Hill Fruit Products, Inc., *supra* note 25.

60. See, e.g., Utah Junk Co. v. Porter, 328 U.S. 39, 44 (1946).

61. River Wear Commissioners v. Adamson, 2 A.C. 743, 746 (1877).

62. Panama Refining Co. v. Ryan, 293 U.S. 388, 439 (1935) (dissenting). See also Duparquet Co. v. Evans, 297 U.S. 216, 218 (1936).

63. N.L.R.B. v. Lion Oil Co. 352 U.S. 282, 297 (1957) (concurring and dissenting). See also United States v. Ruzicka, 329 U.S. 287, 292 (1946).

64. Achilli v. United States, 353 U.S. 373, 379 (1957). See also Federal Maritime Board v. Isbrandtsen Co., 356 U.S. 481, 513 (1958) (dissenting); Lewyt Corp. v. Commissioner, 349 U.S. 237, 249 (1955) (dissenting).

65. Palmer v. Massachusetts, 308 U.S. 79, 83 (1939). See Barr v. United States, 324 U.S. 83, 100 (1945) (dissenting).

66. Youngstown Sheet & Tube Co. v. Sawyer, 343 U.S. 579, 609 (1952) (concurring).

67. Reflections, 68-69. Holmes's observation, in Boston Sand & Gravel Co. v. United States, 278 U.S. 41, 48 (1928), that the plain meaning doctrine "is rather an axiom of experience than a rule of law, and does not preclude consideration of persuasive evidence if it exists," is the single statement most frequently quoted or cited in Frankfurter's opinions on statutory construction.

68. Phelps Dodge Corp. v. N.L.R.B., 313 U.S. 177, 189 (1941). Compare Professor Summers' interesting comment on this opinion, 67 YALE L. J. at 283-284. See also Miles v. Illinois Central R.R. Co., 315 U.S. 698, 714 (1942) (dissenting).

69. Singer v. United States, 323 U.S. 338, 346 (1945) (dissenting)

70. Hawkins, Pleas of the Crown, 192 (4th ed. 1762).

71. United States v. Dege, 364 U.S. 51, 52 (1960), quoting United States v. Union Supply Co., 215 U.S. 50, 55 (1909). See the earlier statement in United States v. Hood, 343 U.S. 148 (1952).

72. Singer v. United States, *supra*, 323 U.S. at 346.

73. Bell v. United States, 349 U.S. 81, 83 (1955).

74. United States v. Turley, 352 U.S. 407, 418 (1957) (dissenting). [Dyer Act should not be construed to include conversion and interstate transportation of automobile, possession of which had been lawfully obtained.]

75. Bell v. United States, *supra*, 349 U.S. at 83-84.

76. 364 U.S. 587 (1961).

77. *Id.*, at 596. It was a particularly unkind cut for the Justice to have applied to the dissenters' reliance on a rule whose recent Supreme Court career he had done not a little to promote, Holmes's statement, "To rest upon a formula is a slumber that, prolonged, means death." Collected Legal Papers, 306 (1920).

78. In United States v. Shirey, 359 U.S. 255 (1959), four Justices thought the rule of lenity required a construction of a criminal statute less severe than that expounded by Frankfurter for the majority.

79. See United States v. Sobell, 314 F. 2d 314, 327 (2 Cir.), cert. denied 374 U.S. 857 (1963).

80. Callanan v. United States, *supra*, 364 U.S. at 593.

81. United States v. Johnson, 323 U.S. 273, 276 (1944). [Federal Denture Act construed as requiring trial of sender in district of deposit and of importer in district of receipt rather than as allowing trial in any district through which dentures are carried, although the latter was within Congress' constitutional power.]

82. Textile Workers Union v. Lincoln Mills, 353 U.S. 448, 477 (1957) (dissenting). The Justice had previously applied the rule, in a related context, in Association of Salaried Employees v. Westinghouse Elec. Corp., 348 U.S. 437, 453 (1955). This has been criticized as "seizing upon a restrictive interpretation which he tacitly recognized had little foundation in logic, legislative history or the practicalities of collective bargaining," whereby "The day of reckoning could only be postponed, and in the meantime a disruptive dichotomy was injected into the law of collective agreements." Summers, *supra* note 26, at 272, 274. Westinghouse was overruled in Smith v. Evening News Assn., 371 U.S. 195 (1962).

83. See, in addition to the extract from the *Lincoln Mills* dissent quoted above, United States v. Lovett, 328 U.S. 303, 320 (1946) (dissenting); United States v. Rumely, 345 U.S. 41, 45 (1953).

84. Trop v. Dulles, 356 U.S. 86, 118-119 (1958) (dissenting); Inter-

national Assn. of Machinists v. Street, 367 U.S. 740, 800 (1961) (dissenting). See also United States v. U.A.W., 352 U.S. 567, 589 (1957).

85. It has the backing of Holmes, Blodgett v. Holden, 275 U.S. 142, 148 (1927) (concurring); of Taft, Richmond Screw Anchor Co. v. United States, 275 U.S. 331, 346 (1928); of Brandeis, Ashwander v. TVA, 297 U.S. 288, 341 (1936) (concurring); of Stone, Lucas v. Alexander, 279 U.S. 573, 577 (1929); of Hughes, Crowell v. Benson, 285 U.S. 22, 62 (1932); and of many others, in addition to the Justice himself.

86. United States v. Lovett, *supra*, 328 U.S. at 319.

87. See the statements in United States v. Lovett, *supra*, 328 U.S. at 319-320, 329-330, and in United States v. Rumely, *supra*, 345 U.S. at 48.

88. See Summers, *supra* note 26, at 273; and Wellington, *Machinists v. Street; Statutory Interpretation and the Avoidance of Constitutional Issues*, 1961 SUPREME COURT REV., 49. A quite different and, to my mind, utterly sound occasion for refusal to face a constitutional issue is when the question arises on a motion to dismiss an indictment, as in United States v. U.A.W., 352 U.S. 567, 590 (1957). There, indeed, wisdom dictates postponement—both because of the possibility of an acquittal, see United States v. Petrillo, 332 U.S. 1 (1947) and 75 F. Supp. 176 (N.D. Ill., 1948), and because, in the event of a conviction, the Court will have before it not merely the bare words of the statute but the facts to which it has been applied. The same principle would apply to a motion to dismiss a civil complaint.

89. Griffiths v. Commissioner, 308 U.S. 355, 358 (1939).

90. United States v. Shirey, 359 U.S. 255, 260-261 (1959).

91. See also Nardone v. United States, 308 U.S. 338, 340 (1939); United States v. Dotterweich, 320 U.S. 217, 280 (1943); Phelps Dodge Corp. v. N.L.R.B., 313 U.S. 177, 185 (1941); Reed v. Pennsylvania R.R. Co., 351 U.S. 502, 510 (1956) (dissenting); Local 1976, United Brotherhood of Carpenters and Joiners v. N.L.R.B., 357 U.S. 93, 100 (1958); Monroe v. Pape, 365 U.S. 161, 244 (1961) (dissenting); Local 671 v. N.L.R.B., 366 U.S. 667, 672 (1961); Reflections, 59-61.

92. Reflections, 55.

93. See Yntema, *The Hornbook Method and the Conflict of Laws*, 37 YALE L. J., 468–480 (1928); Hutcheson, *The Judgment Intuitive: The Function of the "Hunch" in Judicial Decisions*, 14 CORNELL L. Q. 274, 285 (1929).

94. United States v. Johnson, 221 U.S. 488, 496 (1911), quoted and relied on in United States v. Dotterweich, 320 U.S. 227, 284 (1943).

95. Van Vranken v. Helvering, 115 F. 2d 709, 711 (2 Cir. 1940), cert. denied, 313 U.S. 585 (1941).

96. Reflections, 47. "On the question you ask depends the answer you get." Bay Ridge Operating Co. v. Aaron, 334 U.S. 446, 478 (1940) (dissenting).

97. 3 Co. 7a, 76 Eng. Rep. 637 (1584).

98. Reflections, 65-66.

99. Interstate Commerce Commission v. J-T Transport Co., 368 U.S. 81, 107 (1961) (dissenting).

100. United States v. Rabinowitz, 339 U.S. 56, 70 (1950) (dissenting). The comment that "Some words are confined to their history, some are starting points for history," Reflections, 59, belongs with Maitland's famous sentences, "Time will show what these words shall mean. Some will perish in the struggle for existence; others have long and adventurous careers before them." Domesday Book and Beyond, 8 (1897).

101. Phelps Dodge Corp. v. N.L.R.B., 313 U.S. 177, 186 (1941).

102. United States v. Monia, 317 U.S. 424, 432 (1943) (dissenting).

103. See, e.g., the use of subsequent legislative materials in N.L.R.B. v. Lion Oil Co., 352 U.S. 282, 299-301 (1957) (concurring), and in United States v. United Mine Workers, 330 U.S. 258, 331-328 (1947) (concurring).

104. A good example is United States v. U.A.W., 352 U.S. 567 (1957) [political contributions by corporations and unions].

105. St. Joe Paper Co. v. Atlantic Coast Line R.R. Co., 347 U.S. 298, 306 (1954).

106. Bay Ridge Operating Co. v. Aaron, 334 U.S. 446, 478 (1948) (dissenting).

107. Local 1976, United Brotherhood of Carpenters and Joiners v. N.L.R.B., 357 U.S. 93, 100 (1958); Local No. 761 v. N.L.R.B., 366 U.S. 667, 672 (1961).

108. International Assn. of Machinists v. Street, 367 U.S. 740, 800 (1961) (dissenting).

109. Romero v. International Terminal Operating Co., 358 U.S. 354, 370-371 (1959).

110. Interstate Commerce Commission v. J-T Transport Co., 368 U.S. 81, 114-115 (1961) (dissenting).

111. See Radin, *Statutory Interpretation*, 43 HARV. L. REV. 863 (1930), and Landis, *A Note on "Statutory Interpretation,"* 43 HARV. L. REV. 886 (1930). It may not be an altogether wild speculation that Professor Landis' Note was stimulated by his senior Harvard colleague.

112. See his concurring opinions in Schwegmann Bros. v. Calvert Distillers Corp., 341 U.S. 384, 395 (1951), and United States v. Public Utilities Commission, 345 U.S. 295, 319-321 (1953), and his article, *The Meaning of Statutes: What Congress Says or What the Court Says*, 34 A.B.A.J. 535 (1948), reprinted in 8 F.R.D. 121 (1948).

113. See Landis, *supra* note 111, at 888-890; Cox, *supra* note 16, at 381.

114. There is, of course, the fear that the "intention" expressed even in committee reports and sponsors' statements may have been manufactured—perhaps, indeed, placed there for the very reason that it was known that the language could *not* be placed in the act itself. But is it not going too far to ask the courts to police such abdication of legislative responsibility?

This problem is quite different from the smuggling of "intention" into hearing materials, which the legislators cannot prevent. The Justice protested against undue reliance on such materials in United States v. Shapiro, 335 U.S. 1, 48-49 (1948) (dissenting), discussed below.

115. Utah Junk Co. v. Porter, 328 U.S. 39, 42 (1946); Schwegmann Bros. v. Calvert Distillers Corp., 341 U.S. 384, 402-411 (1951) (dissenting); United States v. Orloff, 345 U.S. 83, 98 (1953) (dissenting); Phillips Petroleum Co. v. Wisconsin, 347 U.S. 672, 686 (1954) (concurring); Palermo v. United States, 360 U.S. 343 (1959).

116. Standard Oil Co. v. United States, 337 U.S. 293, 312 (1949); Commissioner v. Acker, 361 U.S. 87, 94 (1959) (dissenting).

117. Commissioner v. Estate of Church, 335 U.S. 632, 678-679 (1949) (dissenting) [see the comprehensive Appendix, 335 U.S. at 687, "Decisions During the Past Decade in which Legislative History was Decisive of the Construction of a Particular Statutory Provision"]; United States v. Orloff, *supra* note 115; Phelps Dodge

Corp. v. N.L.R.B., 313 U.S. 177, 186 (1943); Bindczyck v. Finucane, 342 U.S. 76, 82 (1951) [overruled by Sec. 340 (j) of the Immigration and Nationality Act of 1952, 66 Stat. 163]; Galvan v. Press, 347 U.S. 522, 526 (1954); Federal Maritime Board v. Isbrandtsen Co., 356 U.S. 481, 501 (1954) (dissenting); Interstate Commerce Commission v. J-T Transport Co., 368 U.S. 81, 111 (1961) (dissenting). See also United States v. Public Utilities Commission, 345 U.S. 295, 321 (1953) (concurring)

118. Carlson v. Landon, 342 U.S. 524 (1952).

119. Universal Camera Corp. v. N.L.R.B., 340 U.S. 474, 483 (1951).

120. Bok, *The Tampa Electric Case*, 1961 SUPREME COURT REV., 267, 290.

121. Shapiro v. United States, 335 U.S. 1, 46, 48-49 (1948) (dissenting). But hearing materials are sometimes helpful—e.g., if there are no committee reports and the statute has rather clearly resulted from a felt need voiced by sponsors at a hearing or otherwise. See Greenwood v. United States, 350 U.S. 366 (1956) [report of committee of the Judicial Conference of the United States].

122. United States v. United Mine Workers, 330 U.S. 258, 319 (1947) (concurring). See also Baltimore & Ohio R.R. Co. v. Kepner, 314 U.S. 44, 60 (1941) (dissenting); Reflections, 67.

123. F.C.C. v. Columbia Broadcasting System, 311 U.S. 132, 136-137 (1940). See also Greenwood v. United States, *supra* note 121, where the Justice wrote in another connection, 350 U.S. at 374: "But this is a case for applying the canon of construction of the wag who said, when the legislative history is doubtful, go to the statute." Compare Reflections, p. 67.

124. Utah Junk Co. v. Porter, 328 U.S. 39, 42 (1946).

125. 361 U.S. 87 (1959).

126. *Id.* at 93-94, quoting United States v. Calamaro, 354 U.S. 351, 359 (1957).

127. *Id.* at 94.

128. Reflections, 67.

129. Boston Sand & Gravel Co. v. United States, 278 U.S. 41, 48 (1928).

130. The contrary would seem indicated by the contrast in the provisions of Sec. 3611(d)(1) for failure to file a return with those of Sec. 3611(d)(2) for false or fraudulent returns.

131. The *Acker* case would seem to fit the statement of Mr. Justice

Brandeis in Iselin v. United States, 270 U.S. 245, 251 (1926), of which the Justice is fond, Reflections, 54, that "What the Government asks is not a construction of a statute, but, in effect, an enlargement of it by the court, so that what was omitted, presumably by inadvertence, may be included within its scope." He would doubtless distinguish this on the ground of the absence of probative legislative history in *Iselin*. But in his dissent in Schwegmann Bros. v. Calvert Distillers Corp., 341 U.S. 384, 402 (1951), he went only so far as to say: "Where both the words of a statute and its legislative history clearly indicate the purpose of Congress, it should be respected." His *Acker* dissent also seems to run counter to the views that he expressed, dissenting in Commissioner v. Wodehouse, *supra*, 337 U.S. at 409, as to the undesirability of courts picking up the pieces left by the legislature. See note 28, *supra*.

132. Reflections, 44.

133. Pope v. Atlantic Coast Line R.R. Co., 345 U.S. 379, 390 (1953) (dissenting). He maintained in this dissent that by adopting, in 1948, the transfer provision, 28 U.S.C. Sec. 1404(a), held applicable to FELA suits in *Ex parte* Collett, 337 U.S. 55 (1949), Congress had removed the "judicial gloss" placed on Sec. 6 of the FELA by Baltimore & Ohio R.R. Co. v. Kepner, 314 U.S. 44 (1941), and Miles v. Illinois Central R.R. Co., 315 U.S. 698 (1942), forbidding state court injunctions against or dismissals of FELA suits brought in an inconvenient forum. See also Reflections, 61, and Landis, Statutes and the Sources of Law, in Harvard Legal Essays in Honor of Beale and Williston, 213, 218-222, 226-227 (1934).

134. 306 U.S. 381 (1939).

135. *Id.* at 389, 394.

136. Mr. Justice Holmes in Johnson v. United States, 163 Fed. 30, 32 (1908). "Congress had a right to assume that the characteristic energies for corporate enterprise with which a few months previously it had endowed Reconstruction would now radiate through Reconstruction to Regional." 306 U.S. at 393-394.

137. 312 U.S. 219 (1941).

138. 254 U.S. 443 (1921).

139. Mr. Justice Stone concurred in an opinion to the effect that, quite apart from any inferences from the Norris-LaGuardia Act, the indictment did not state an offense under the Sherman Act. Mr. Justice Roberts dissented for himself and Chief Justice Hughes.

140. 312 U.S. 235. This is followed by a citation of Keifer & Keifer v. R.F.C., *supra* note 134.

141. United States v. United Mine Workers, 330 U.S. 258, 309 (1947) (concurring). See also United Brotherhood of Carpenters and Joiners v. United States, 330 U.S. 395, 414 (1947) (dissenting).

142. See Frankfurter and Greene, The Labor Injunction 200 (1930).

143. 257 U.S. 312 (1921).

144. See note 139, *supra*.

145. 274 U.S. 37 (1927).

146. F.T.C. v. Bunte Bros., 312 U.S. 349, 357 (1941). The two cases were *sub judice* together.

147. Phelps Dodge Corp. v. N.L.R.B., 313 U.S. 177, 191 (1941).

148. Houston, E. & W. T. Ry. Co. v. United States, 234 U.S. 342 (1914). Indeed, the Interstate Commerce Act had explicitly denied jurisdiction over transportation "wholly within one state."

149. 41 Stat. 484 (1920).

150. E.g., Palmer v. Massachusetts, 308 U.S. 79, 83-84 (1939); Cloverleaf Co. v. Patterson, 315 U.S. 148, 172 (1942); Bethlehem Steel Co. v. New York State Board, 330 U.S. 767, 780 (1947) (concurring); Leiter Minerals, Inc. v. United States, 352 U.S. 220, 236 (1956).

151. For a case where Mr. Justice Frankfurter insisted on giving a word in one statute the same meaning it had been adjudged to have in a cognate statute, "where obvious reasons do not compel divergent treatment," see Merrill v. Fahs, 324 U.S. 308, 313 (1945). See also Communist Party v. S.A.C. Control Board, 367 U.S. 1, 39-40 (1961).

152. 312 U.S. at 351, citing National Labor Relations Act Secs. 2(7), 9(c), 10(a), 49 Stat. 450, 453; Bituminous Coal Act, Sec. 4-A, 50 Stat. 83; Federal Employers' Liability Act, Sec. 1, 35 Stat. 65, as amended, 53 Stat. 1404.

153. 321 U.S. 288 (1944).

154. 321 U.S. at 313.

155. Jaffe, *The Right to Judicial Review*, 71 HARV. L. REV. 401, 432 (1958); 3 Davis, Administrative Law Treatise, 278 (1958).

156. Board of Governors v. Agnew, 329 U.S. 441 (1947), over a dissent by Mr. Justice Rutledge joined by Mr. Justice Frankfurter; United States v. Interstate Commerce Commission, 337 U.S. 426 (1949), over a dissent by Mr. Justice Frankfurter joined by Justices Jackson and Burton; see also Leedom v. Kyne, 358 U.S. 184 (1958),

over a dissent by Mr. Justice Brennan joined by Mr. Justice Frankfurter. Frankfurter himself seems to have relied on a principle similar
to that followed by the majority in Stark v. Wickard when he gave
an affirmative answer to the question whether a court may stay an
administrative order in the absence of a specific provision in the directly relevant statute and despite the presence of such provisions in
cognate statutes. Scripps-Howard Radio v. F.C.C., 316 U.S. 4, 10-17
(1942).

157. See note 151, *supra*.

158. United States v. Johnson, 323 U.S. 273, 277 (1944); Cornell
Steamboat Co. v. United States, 321 U.S. 634, 643-649 (1944) (dissenting). Professor Summers thinks the Justice has sometimes attributed too much legal knowledge to Congress; see his criticisms of
the dissent in Mastro Plastics Corp. v. N.L.R.B., 350 U.S. 270, 293
(1956), in 67 YALE L. J. at 688.

159. Polish National Alliance v. N.L.R.B., 322 U.S. 643, 647 (1944).

160. United States v. Monia, 317 U.S. 424, 443 (1943) (dissenting).
See also Snyder v. Buck, 340 U.S. 15, 23 (1950) (dissenting).

161. *Infra*.

162. F.T.C. v. Ruberoid Co., 343 U.S. 470, 486 (1952) (dissenting).

163. See, e.g., Phelps Dodge Corp. v. N.L.R.B., 313 U.S. 177, 194
(1941).

164. Interstate Commerce Commission v. J-T Transport Co., 368
U.S. 81, 127 (1961) (dissenting).

165. Addison v. Holly Hill Fruit Products, Inc., 322 U.S. 607, 616-
617 (1944).

166. N.L.R.B. v. Coca-Cola Bottling Co., 350 U.S. 264, 269 (1956).
This decision, for a unanimous Court—with the quoted passage perhaps rather a dictum since the N.L.R.B.'s construction accorded
with "lay understanding" and with indications in the statute itself—
respected N.L.R.B. v. Highland Park Mfg. Co., 341 U.S. 322 (1951),
as to the precise point there decided. However, it seems to have
vindicated the views of the Justice's dissent in that case, there joined
only by Mr. Justice Douglas, 341 U.S. at 327, as to the weight to
be given the N.L.R.B.'s interpretation of technical terms in the National Labor Relations Act. In Social Security Bd. v. Nierotko, 327
U.S. 358, 370 (1946) (concurring), the Justice wrote a separate
opinion to make clear that he joined in reversing the Board's refusal to consider back pay as wages only because he thought the

Board had excluded "from wages what as a matter of law are wages." Compare Addison v. Holly Hill Fruit Products, Inc., 322 U.S. 607 (1944). The principle of deference to an agency's construction of statutory terms is limited to the agency's own area of expertise— ". . . the Bureau's expertness does not extend to the Copyright Law." Commissioner v. Wodehouse, 337 U.S. 369, 414 (1949) (dissenting).

167. Compare Mendelson, Justices Black and Frankfurter: Conflict in the Court, 39-40.

168. F.T.C. v. Bunte Bros., 312 U.S. 349, 352 (1941); see also Inland Waterways Corp. v. Young, 309 U.S. 517, 524 (1940).

169. Kirschbaum v. Walling, 316 U.S. 517, 523 (1942); Tennessee C. I. & R.R. Co. v. Muscoda Local, 321 U.S. 590, 604 (1944) (concurring); Mitchell v. Zachry Co., 362 U.S. 310, 314 (1960).

170. See Mr. Justice Jackson's opinion in Skidmore v. Swift & Co., 323 U.S. 134 (1944). There had been no adversary process in the non-action of the Comptroller of the Currency so heavily—and, in my view, rightly—relied on by the Justice in Inland Waterways Corp. v. Young, *supra* note 168. The F.L.S.A. does present the problem of the private suit but, if the pattern had been established in suits brought by the administrator, the former ought not occasion too much difficulty.

171. United States v. Interstate Commerce Commission, 337 U.S. 426, 446 (1949) (dissenting).

172. In other opinions, discussed below, the Justice has emphasized the lack of realism in supposing, in the absence of evidence, that Congress' failure to alter procedural or jurisdictional provisions to overcome judicial construction is significant. Toucey v. New York Life Ins. Co., 314 U.S. 118 (1941); Florida Lime & Avocado Growers v. Jacobsen, 362 U.S. 73, 97-98 (1960) (dissenting). Compare Scripps-Howard Radio v. F.C.C., 316 U.S. 4, 11 (1942) and the comment of Professor Summers, note 158 *supra*.

173. 307 U.S. 125 (1939). Mr. Justice Butler, joined by Mr. Justice McReynolds, thought the order under attack was in substance "affirmative," hence there was "no occasion to review earlier decisions dealing with affirmative and negative administrative orders and obviously none to overrule any of them or to repudiate or impair the doctrine they establish." 307 U.S. at 147-148 (concurring).

174. The jab is administered at 357 U.S. 439-440, fn. 8. Of the four precedents relied on by Frankfurter, only one, a *per curiam*, Ashland

Coal & Ice Co. v. United States, 325 U.S. 840 (1945), was subsequent to *Rochester Telephone;* see 357 U.S. 438-40. I am not suggesting that the dissent in United States v. Interstate Commerce Commission may not have been well justified for other reasons. Here, as often, the Justice did not put all his eggs in one basket! Mr. Justice Frankfurter's analysis of Congressional purpose was vindicated by §207 of the Technical Changes Act of 1953, 67 Stat. 615, overruling the *Church* decision.

175. 337 U.S. at 467.
176. Scott Paper Co. v. Marcalus Mfg. Co., 326 U.S. 249, 261 (1945) (dissenting).
177. Commissioner v. Estate of Church, 335 U.S. 632, 674 (1949) (dissenting). [See the comprehensive appendix, 335 U.S. at 690, "Opinions During the Past Decade Resting Upon the Rule That the Reenactment of a Statute Carries Gloss of Construction Placed Upon it by this Court."]
178. 281 U.S. 238 (1930).
179. 46 Stat. 1516.
180. 335 U.S. at 682.
181. Reider v. Thompson, 339 U.S. 113, 119-120 (1950) (dissenting) [application of Carmack Amendment to rail carriage of ocean shipment from non-adjacent foreign country].
182. Toolson v. New York Yankees, 346 U.S. 356 (1953). Other cases in which the Justice joined, on the basis of *stare decisis,* in refusing to overturn a settled construction which he scarcely would have approved are Girouard v. United States, 328 U.S. 61 (1946), and Cleveland v. United States, 329 U.S. 14 (1946). See also Andres v. United States, 333 U.S. 740, 757 (1948) (concurring), where he extends the principle of supposed congressional acquiescence to a Court of Appeals decision, and even uses decisions construing similar state statutes to aid in the interpretation of a federal statute, in this case dealing with jury recommendations against capital punishment, "a statute which has such wide scope throughout the country and the incidence of which is far greater in the State courts than in the federal courts."
183. United States v. International Boxing Club, 348 U.S. 236, 249 (1955) (dissenting).
184. South-Eastern Underwriters Assn. v. United States, 322 U.S. 533 (1944); see also Helvering v. Griffiths, 318 U.S. 371 (1941).
185. Helvering v. Hallock, 309 U.S. 106, 118-119, 120-121, fn. 7

(1940). See his later characterization of this decision in Commissioner v. Estate of Church, 335 U.S. 632, 683 (1949) (dissenting): ". . . Congress is not charged either with seeking out and reading decisions which reach conflicting views in the application of a sound principle or with taking steps to meet such decisions."

186. Toucey v. New York Life Ins. Co., 314 U.S. 118, 139-140 (1941); the Justice also noted that the last re-enactment antedated the decisions he deemed unsound. Three Justices dissented. The decision was in effect overruled by the 1948 revision of the Judicial Code, 28 U.S.C. Sec. 2283; see Reviser's Note.

187. Monroe v. Pape, 365 U.S. 167, 186-187, 220-221 (1961) (dissenting).

188. Kesler v. Dept. of Public Safety, 369 U.S. 153 (1962).

189. These are collected in the dissent, 369 U.S. at 176, fn. 5.

190. 369 U.S. at 157, 158. The Justice will not be surprised to learn that I regard the *Kesler* decision as regrettable. No one can quarrel with the "verbal logic" of his position that a claim that a state statute conflicts with a federal statute raises a constitutional question under the supremacy clause as much as a claim of conflict with the Constitution itself—a point that judges of the "inferior" courts, applying the distinction, had not failed to recognize. See Bell v. Waterfront Commission, 279 F. 2d 853, 858 (2 Cir. 1958). But the contrary had been the common understanding, apparently entertained by the Supreme Court in Florida Lime & Avocado Growers v. Jacobsen, 362 U.S. 73 (1960) only two years before, where the majority characterized a claim that a state statute contravened a federal statute as a "nonconstitutional ground of attack," 362 U.S. at 80, and Mr. Justice Frankfurter advocated restriction of the three-judge requirement "to those cases where state legislation is challenged *simpliciter* as directly offensive to some specific provision of the Constitution," 362 U.S. at 97-98. But see 362 U.S. at 90. The Justice does not document his assertion in *Kesler*, 369 U.S. at 156, that "the purpose which gave rise" to the three-judge requirement, namely, the abuse of a single district judge's enjoining rate statutes, ordinances, or orders (see Mr. Justice Whittaker's opinion for the majority in Florida Lime & Avocado Growers, 362 U.S. at 77-78), carried over to claims of conflict between state and federal statutes. There had been no protest over the limited application given to the three-judge requirement in this respect; and the statute had been recognized as one that was to be approached "as a procedural technicality and not as

the embodiment of a more or less broadly phrased social policy," and whose coverage was not to be expanded in view of its "dislocation of the normal structure and functioning of the lower federal courts" and its increase in the obligatory jurisdiction of the Supreme Court. See Mr. Justice Frankfurter's dissent in Florida Lime & Avocado Growers, 362 U.S. at 92-94.

If the distinction between a claim of unconstitutionality based on conflict with the Constitution and one based on conflict with a federal statute was to be abandoned, it would have been better judicial administration to do away with it altogether than to require a district judge, faced with the need of quickly deciding whether to request the convoking of a three-judge court, to make a preliminary determination whether a claim of conflict between state and federal statute will require the construction of either—a formula which the Chief Justice, dissenting in *Kesler*, characterized as "plainly unworkable." 369 U.S. at 178. Indeed, I cannot understand how Kesler's case itself can be said not to have involved "construction" of a federal statute, to wit, Sec. 17 of the Bankruptcy Act relating to the effect of a discharge. See note, *The Three-Judge District Court: Scope and Procedure under Section 2281*, 77 HARV. L. REV. 299, 313-314 (1963).

The scope of the three-judge requirement in suits to enjoin the application of state statutes, perhaps not too clear from the outset, seems to have gotten into such confusion that Congress ought to review the whole subject—a review which could well embrace other areas of mandatory Supreme Court appellate jurisdiction such as suits to enjoin orders of the Interstate Commerce Commission, the Expediting Act, and the Criminal Appeals Act. See, as to the second, Mr. Justice Harlan's comment in Brown Shoe Co. v. United States, 370 U.S. 294, 364-365 (1962) (dissenting), now adopted, over Mr. Justice White's disagreement, in United States v. Singer Mfg. Co., 374 U.S. 174, 175 fn. 1, 197, 202 (1963) and s. 1811 (88th Cong. 1st Sess.); and as to the first and third, Friendly, *supra* note 6, at 801, Kurland, *The Mersky Case and the Criminal Appeals Act: A Suggestion for Amendment of the Statute*, 28 U. CHI. L. REV. 419 (1961), and United States v. Ketchum, F. 2d 3 (2 Cir. 1963). The lack of leadership by the Court in seeking to curtail or abolish these anachronisms is surprising, especially in the light of the role it played in the last great jurisdictional reform, that of 1925; see Frankfurter and Landis, The Business of the Supreme Court (1927), Ch. VII.

Meanwhile the Court is busily making new and confusing distinctions, as in Shenandoah Valley Broadcasting Co. v. ASCAP, 371 U.S. 540, 375 U.S. 39 (1963), 375 U.S. 994 (1964), where it dismissed an appeal in a case under the Expediting Act because of an "unexpressed view" that the Act contained an unexpressed exception for orders "outside the main stream of the litigation in which the Government is directly concerned," and Bailey v. Patterson, 369 U.S. 31 (1962), creating a "converse substantiality" exception to Sec. 2281.

191. 344 U.S. 344 (1953).

192. N.L.R.B. v. Gullett Gin Co., 340 U.S. 361, 366 (1951).

193. 344 U.S. at 351-352.

194. But see Andres v. United States, *supra* note 182. Perhaps the statement in the text should be qualified to except a continued and unanimous construction by several courts of appeals.

195. See, in addition to the cases cited in notes 176 and 177, *supra*, F.T.C. v. Bunte Bros., 312 U.S. 349, 352 (1941), and DiBella v. United States, 369 U.S. 121, 130 (1962).

196. See Friendly, *supra* note 6, at 801-802.

197. Marshall, C.d., in United States v. Fisher, 2 Cranch (6 U.S.) 358, 386 (1805), quoted in Reflections, 65-66, and in many opinions, e.g., United States v. Universal C.I.T. Credit Corp., 344 U.S. 218, 221 (1952).

198. Summers, *supra* note 26, at 285.

199. The Spirit of Liberty (1952 ed.), 109.

200. Reflections, 53.

201. *Supra* note 199.

202. Mr. Justice Jackson in Brown v. Allen, 344 U.S. 443, 540 (1953) (concurring).


# Voice of a Modern Federalism,
## *Louis Henkin*

1. Among those who have said that "the epoch of federalism is over" was Justice Frankfurter's intimate friend Harold Laski, in *The Obsolescence of Federalism*, NEW REPUBLIC, 367-368, May 3, 1939.

2. Frankfurter, The Public and Its Government 76 (1930).

3. Frankfurter, *Some Reflections on the Reading of Statutes,* 47 COLUM. L. REV. 527, 535 (1947).

4. Holmes, "The Path of the Law," in Collected Legal Papers 195 (1920), quoted in Frankfurter, Law and Politics 291 (Prichard and MacLeish, eds. 1939).

5. Bartkus v. Illinois, 359 U.S. 121, 137 (1959).

6. San Diego Bldg. Trades Council v. Garmon, 359 U.S. 236, 243 (1959).

7. Tocqueville, 1 Democracy in America 40 (Bradley ed. 1945).

8. Frankfurter, "Mr. Justice Brandeis and the Constitution" in Mr. Justice Brandeis 84-85 (Frankfurter ed. 1932); also *id.* at 65. See also The Public and Its Government, *supra* note 2, at 48-49, 61-64.

9. Frankfurter, Mr. Justice Holmes and the Supreme Court 68-69 (1938); Law and Politics, *supra* note 4, at 11-15, 22-23, 52.

10. Mr. Justice Holmes and the Supreme Court, *supra* note 9, at 75-76.

11. Frankfurter and Landis, The Business of the Supreme Court 318 (1928).

12. Law and Politics, *supra* note 4, at 86.

13. Holmes, "Law and the Court," in Collected Legal Papers 295-296 (1920).

14. Compare, e.g., "Does Law Obstruct Government?" The Public and Its Government, *supra* note 2, Chap. II.

15. *In re* Groban, 352 U.S. 330, 335-337 (1957) (concurring). Compare Mr. Justice Holmes: "We fear to grant power and are unwilling to recognize it when it exists." Tyson & Bro. v. Banton, 273 U.S. 418, 445 (1927) (dissenting), quoted in Mr. Justice Holmes and the Supreme Court, *supra* note 9, at 40.

16. The Public and its Government, *supra* note 2, at 80.

17. Compare Frankfurter, Of Law and Men 34 (Elman ed. 1956); The Public and Its Government, *supra* note 2, Chap. II.

18. See, e.g., Cooper v. Aaron, 358 U.S. 1, 20 (1958).

19. United States v. Kahriger, 345 U.S. 22, 37 (1953) (dissenting). Compare Law and Politics, *supra* note 4, at 206-208.

20. National Mut. Ins. Co. v. Tidewater Transfer Co., 337 U.S. 583, 646 (1949) (dissenting); Textile Workers v. Lincoln Mills, 353 U.S. 448, 460 (1957) (dissenting).

In a different kind of conflict between state and nation, the

Justice, also, could not find that the United States had proprietary rights and could exclude California from submerged offshore lands. United States v. California, 332 U.S. 19, 43 (1947) (dissenting).

21. Of Law and Men, *supra* note 17, at 5.

22. *Id.* at 15.

23. E.g., Perez v. Brownell, 356 U.S. 44 (1958). See quotation from Justice Cardozo in Law and Politics, *supra* note 4, at 100-101.

24. Polish Nat'l Alliance v. N.L.R.B., 322 U.S. 643, 650-651 (1944).

25. See Cooper v. Aaron, 358 U.S. 1, 20 (1958).

26. See notes 56 and 86 below.

27. Graves v. New York *ex rel.* O'Keefe, 306 U.S. 466, 487, 489-490 (1939) (concurring).

28. City of Detroit v. Murray Corp., 355 U.S. 489, 495 (1958) (opinion of Frankfurter J.); but cf. Offutt Housing Co. v. Sarpy County, 351 U.S. 253 (1956).

29. Graves v. New York *ex rel.* O'Keefe, 306 U.S. 466, 487 (1939) (concurring); United States v. Allegheny County, 322 U.S. 174, 195 (1944) (dissenting); Board of County Comm'rs v. United States, 308 U.S. 343 (1939); New York v. United States, 326 U.S. 572 (1946) (opinion of Frankfurter J.).

30. Even as of thirty years ago; see The Public and Its Government, *supra* note 2, Chap. II.

31. *Ibid.* See, e.g., The Federal-aid Highway Acts (23 U.S.C. [1959]) as amended 23 U.S.C. (Supp. IV, 1963); The Federal Unemployment Tax Act (1954) (26 U.S.C. Secs. 3301-3308 [1959]) as amended 26 U.S.C. Secs. 3301-3308 (Supp. IV, 1963); also 24 Stat. 379, as amended 49 U.S.C. Sec. 13 (1959).

32. E.g., *In re* Rahrer, 140 U.S. 545 (1891); see Prudential Insurance Co. v. Benjamin, 328 U.S. 408 (1946).

33. Pacific Coast Dairy v. Department of Agriculture of California, 318 U.S. 285, 296 (1943) (dissenting). Compare the Offutt case, *supra* note 28.

34. Frankfurter, *Some Reflections on the Reading of Statutes*, 47 COLUM. L. REV. 544 (1947).

35. *Id.* at 539-540. Compare Kirschbaum Co. v. Walling, 316 U.S. 517, 521 (1942).

36. F.T.C. v. Bunte Bros., Inc., 312 U.S. 349, 351 (1941).

37. A word which the Justice uses also to describe the role of the

Supreme Court, perhaps borrowed from Marshall. See Mr. Justice Holmes and the Supreme Court, *supra* note 9, at 30.

38. F.T.C. v. Bunte Bros., Inc., 312 U.S. 349 (1941); cf. 10 East 40 St. Bldg., Inc. v. Callus, 325 U.S. 578 (1945).

39. Cornell Steamboat Co. v. United States, 321 U.S. 634, 641 (1944) (dissenting).

40. The Business of the Supreme Court, *supra* note 11, at 2.

41. Lumberman's Mut. Casualty Co. v. Elbert, 348 U.S. 48, 53, 59 (1954) (concurring); Frankfurter, *Distribution of Judicial Power Between United States and State Courts*, 13 CORNELL L. Q. 499, 515-516 (1928); The Business of the Supreme Court, *supra* note 11, at 251.

42. *Id.* at 293; 13 CORNELL L. Q. at 516-517. See also Amalgamated Clothing Workers v. Richman Bros. Co., 348 U.S. 511, 518 (1955).

43. See 13 CORNELL L. Q. at 520 *et seq.*; Lumberman's Mut. Casualty Co. v. Elbert, 348 U.S. 48, 53 (1954) (concurring); also Sutton v. Leib, 342 U.S. 402, 412 (1952) (concurring).

44. Indianapolis v. Chase National Bank, 314 U.S. 63, 76 (1941). Compare The Business of the Supreme Court, *supra* note 11, at 292.

45. Palmer v. Massachusetts, 308 U.S. 79 (1938); cf. Williams v. Austrian, 331 U.S. 642, 662 (1947) (dissenting); Romero v. International Terminal Operating Co., 358 U.S. 354 (1959); Baltimore & Ohio R.R. v. Kepner, 314 U.S. 44, 54 (1941) (dissenting); Miles v. Illinois Central R.R., 315 U.S. 698, 708 (1942) (dissenting); Brown v. Gerdes, 321 U.S. 178, 188 (1944) (concurring); Dice v. Akron, C. & Y. R.R., 342 U.S. 359, 364 (1952) (concurring). Compare Brillhart v. Excess Insurance Co. of America, 316 U.S. 491, 495 (1942) (federal courts should avoid "gratuitous interference with the orderly and comprehensive disposition of a state court litigation"); also Stefanelli v. Minard, 342 U.S. 117 (1951).

46. Phillips v. United States, 312 U.S. 246 (1941).

47. Association of Westinghouse Salaried Employees v. Westinghouse Electric Corp., 348 U.S. 437, 439 (1955) (opinion of Frankfurter J.); Textile Workers v. Lincoln Mills, *supra* note 20, where he went so far as to hold that Congress did not have the power. Cf. D'Oench, Duhme & Co. v. F.D.I.C., 315 U.S. 447, 462 (1942) (concurring); Vanston Bondholders Protective Committee v. Green, 329 U.S. 156, 167 (1946) (concurring).

48. The adjectives are Justice Frankfurter's. Frankfurter, *Some Re-*

*flections on the Reading of Statutes,* 47 COLUM. L. REV. 527, 529 (1947).

49. Screws v. United States, 325 U.S. 91, 138 (1945) (dissenting); Monroe v. Pape, 365 U.S. 167, 202 (1961) (dissenting). Compare United States v. Williams, 341 U.S. 70 (1951) (opinion of Frankfurter J.).

50. See note 83.

51. Screws v. United States, *supra* note 47, 325 U.S. at 138, 141, 142, 144, 145-146. The dissenting opinion is by Justices Roberts, Frankfurter, and Jackson, but the voice is the voice of Justice Frankfurter.

52. Monroe v. Pape, 365 U.S. 167, 222 (1961) (dissenting).

53. See, e.g., Farmers Educational & Cooperative Union v. WDAY, Inc., 360 U.S. 525, 535, 546 (1959) (dissenting). Compare text at note 52.

54. DeVeau v. Braisted, 363 U.S. 144, 152 (1960) (opinion of Frankfurter J.).

55. See text *infra* at note 73.

56. Cloverleaf Butter Co. v. Patterson, 315 U.S. 148, 177, 178 (1942) (dissenting); Rice v. Santa Fe Elevator Corp., 331 U.S. 218, 238, 246-247 (1947) (dissenting).

57. Bethlehem Steel Co. v. New York State Labor Relations Board, 330 U.S. 769, 777, 779-780 (1947) (opinion of Frankfurter J.). See also Hill v. Florida, 325 U.S. 538, 548 (1945) (dissenting); Rice v. Santa Fe Elevator Corp., 331 U.S. 218, 238 (1947) (dissenting); Farmers Educational & Cooperative Union v. WDAY, Inc., 360 U.S. 525, 535 (1959) (dissenting).

Of course, in many cases Justice Frankfurter also found congressional intent to supersede, even in this field of labor regulation. He set forth some of the cases on both sides in San Diego Bldg. Trades Council v. Garmon, 359 U.S. 236 (1959).

58. Bethlehem Steel Co. v. New York State Labor Relations Board, 330 U.S. 767, 777, 780 (1947) (opinion of Frankfurter J.).

59. See United States v. South-Eastern Underwriters Ass'n, 322 U.S. 533, 583 (1944) (dissenting) and 59 Stat. 33 (1945), as amended 15 U.S.C. Secs. 1011-1015 (1959); Bethlehem Steel Co. v. New York State Labor Relations Board, 330 U.S. 767, 777 (1947) (opinion of Frankfurter J.), and Labor-Management Relations Act, 1947, Sec. 101, 61 Stat. 136, as amended 29 U.S.C. 160(a) (1959); F.P.C. v. East Ohio Gas Co., 338 U.S. 464, 476 (1950) (Frankfur-

ter J. joins in Mr. Justice Jackson's dissenting opinion), and 68 Stat. 36 (1954), 15 U.S.C. 717(c) (1959). Compare Jewell Ridge Coal Corp. v. Local 6167, 325 U.S. 161, 170 (1945) (Frankfurter J. joins in Mr. Justice Jackson's dissenting opinion) and Portal-to-Portal Act of 1947, 61 Stat. 84, 29 U.S.C. Secs. 251-262 (1959); Schwegmann Bros. v. Calvert Distillers Corp., 341 U.S. 384, 397 (1951) (dissenting) and McGuire Act of 1952, 66 Stat. 632, 15 U.S.C. Sec. 45(a)(3) (1959); also United States v. California, 332 U.S. 19, 43 (1947) (dissenting) and Submerged Lands Act of 1953, 67 Stat. 29, and scattered sections of U.S.C.

60. Law and Politics, *supra* note 4, at 246.

61. Gibbons v. Ogden, 22 U.S. (9 Wheat.) 1, 238 (1824).

62. Toomer v. Witsell, 334 U.S. 385, 407-408 (1948) (concurring).

63. See *infra* note 134.

64. Dyer v. Sims, 341 U.S. 22 (1951). Professor Frankfurter wrote at length about compacts in Frankfurter and Landis, *The Compact Clause of the Constitution—A Study in Interstate Adjustments*, 34 YALE L. J. 685 (1925). See also The Public and Its Government, *supra* note 2, at 69-71.

65. New York v. O'Neill, 359 U.S. 1, 5-6, 9, 11-12 (1959).

66. See California v. Zook, 336 U.S. 725, 738 (1949) (dissenting).

67. McCarroll v. Dixie Greyhound Lines, Inc., 309 U.S. 176, 183, 186 (1940) (Black, Frankfurter, and Douglas JJ. dissenting).

68. Union Brokerage Co. v. Jensen, 322 U.S. 202, 212 (1944).

69. Freeman v. Hewit, 329 U.S. 249, 253-254 (1946).

70. See Mr. Justice Jackson concurring in Duckworth v. Arkansas, 314 U.S. 390, 397, 400-401 (1941).

71. LeRoy Fibre Co. v. Chicago, Mil. & St. P. Ry., 232 U.S. 340, 352, 354 (1914). Compare *In re* Groban, 352 U.S. 330, 335, 337 (1952) (concurring).

72. E.g., H. P. Hood & Sons, Inc. v. Du Mond, 336 U.S. 525, 564 (1949) (dissenting).

73. The Public and Its Government, *supra* note 2, at 74.

74. See Northwestern States Portland Cement Co. v. Minnesota, 358 U.S. 450, 470 (1959).

75. E.g., Freeman v. Hewit, 329 U.S. 249 (1946).

76. Northwestern States Portland Cement Co. v. Minnesota, 358 U.S. 450, 470, 476 (1959) (dissenting).

77. Freeman v. Hewit, 329 U.S. 249, 256, 257 (1946).

78. Braniff Airways, Inc. v. Nebraska Board of Equalization, 347 U.S. 590, 603, 605-606 (1954) (dissenting).

79. McLeod v. J. E. Dilworth Co., 322 U.S. 327, 330 (1944).

80. See Freeman v. Hewit, 329 U.S. 249, 253, 255-256 (1946).

81. Northwestern States Portland Cement Co. v. Minnesota, 358 U.S. 450, 470 (1959) (dissenting); compare 73 Stat. 555 (1959), 15 U.S.C. 381 (Supp. IV, 1963).

82. Mr. Justice Holmes in Missouri, Kansas & Texas Ry. v. May, 194 U.S. 267, 270 (1904), quoted in The Public and Its Government 76. Compare Minersville School District v. Gobitis, 310 U.S. 586, 600 (1940); cf. Milk Wagon Drivers Union v. Meadowmoor Dairies, Inc., 312 U.S. 287, 299 (1941); compare Monroe v. Pape, 365 U.S. 167, 202, 238 (1961) (dissenting).

83. Compare Jennings v. Illinois, 342 U.S. 104, 112 (1951) (dissenting); Sweeney v. Woodall, 344 U.S. 86, 90, 91 (1952) (concurring); *In re* Groban, 352 U.S. 330, 335-337 (1957) (concurring); Beilan v. Board of Public Education, 357 U.S. 399, 409, 410-411 (1958) (concurring); Shelton v. Tucker, 364 U.S. 477, 490, 496 (1960) (dissenting). See also quotations in text at notes 123, 124.

84. AFL v. American Sash & Door Co., 335 U.S. 538, 542, 553-557 (1949) (concurring).

85. Leland v. Oregon, 343 U.S. 790, 802, 807 (1952) (dissenting).

86. West Virginia Board of Education v. Barnette, 319 U.S. 624, 646, 667 (1943) (dissenting); Marsh v. Alabama, 326 U.S. 501, 510, 511 (1946) (concurring). Compare note 56, *supra*.

87. See note 128, *infra*.

88. Mr. Justice Holmes and the Supreme Court, *supra* note 9, at 88. See also "Mr. Justice Brandeis and the Constitution," *supra* note 8, at 74-75; also The Public and Its Government, *supra* note 2, at 50.

89. See text at note 94.

90. Anderson v. Dunn, 19 U.S. (6 Wheat.) 204, 226 (1821), quoted in Law and Politics, *supra* note 4, at 246.

91. The Public and Its Government, *supra* note 2, at 46-47.

92. Of Law and Men, supra note 17, at 16.

93. "Mr. Justice Brandeis and the Constitution," *supra* note 8, at 74. See also *id*. at 49.

94. Law and Politics, *supra* note 4, at 16.

95. But cf. Morey v. Doud, 354 U.S. 457 (1957); Justice Frankfurter was in dissent.

96. E.g., Cafeteria Employees Union v. Angelos, 320 U.S. 293 (1943); Marsh v. Alabama, 326 U.S. 501, 510 (1946) (concurring); Barsky v. Board of Regents 347 U.S. 442, 467 (1954) (dissenting); Schware v. Board of Bar Examiners, 353 U.S. 232, 247 (1957) (concurring); also Wolf v. Colorado, 338 U.S. 25, 27-28 (1949). See also note 102.

97. Kovacs v. Cooper, 336 U.S. 77, 89, 95 (1949) (concurring).

98. E.g., Harris v. United States, 331 U.S. 145, 155 (1947) (dissenting); Wolf v. Colorado, 338 U.S. 25, 27-28 (1949); Irvine v. California, 347 U.S. 128, 142 (1954) (dissenting); On Lee v. United States, 343 U.S. 747, 758 (1952) (dissenting). Even here his respect for the states showed in the construction of federal statutes. Compare Nardone v. United States, 308 U.S. 338 (1939), with Schwartz v. Texas, 344 U.S. 199, 204 (1952) (concurring).

Also Wieman v. Updegraff, 344 U.S. 183, 194 (1952) (concurring); Sweezy v. New Hampshire, 354 U.S. 234, 255 (1957) (concurring); cf. Martin v. Struthers, 319 U.S. 141, 152 (1943) (dissenting); Public Utilities Comm'n v. Pollak, 343 U.S. 451, 466 (1952) (statement of Frankfurter J.). But cf. Frank v. Maryland, 359 U.S. 360 (1959). And compare note 103.

99. See quotation in text at note 110.

100. Law and Politics, *supra* note 4, at 86.

101. See Maryland v. Baltimore Radio Show, Inc., 338 U.S. 912, 919-920 (1950) (opinion of Frankfurter J.); Irvin v. Dowd, 366 U.S. 717, 729 (1961) (concurring). Also Bridges v. California, 314 U.S. 252, 279 (1941) (dissenting); Craig v. Harney, 331 U.S. 367, 384 (1947) (dissenting); In re Sawyer, 360 U.S. 622, 647 (1959) (dissenting). Compare Martin v. Struthers, 319 U.S. 141, 152 (1943) (dissenting).

102. AFL v. American Sash & Door Co., 335 U.S. 538, 542, 550 (1949) (concurring). See McCollum v. Board of Education, 333 U.S. 203, 212 (1948) (concurring); Zorach v. Clauson, 343 U.S. 306, 320 (1952) (dissenting). See Law and Politics, *supra* note 4, at 129. Compare Butler v. Michigan, 352 U.S. 380 (1957).

103. West Virginia Board of Education v. Barnette, 319 U.S. 624, 646 (1943) (dissenting); compare McGowan v. Maryland, 366 U.S. 420, 459 (1961) (opinion of Frankfurter J.).

104. E.g., Adamson v. California, 332 U.S. 46, 59 (1947) (concurring).

105. Malinski v. New York, 324 U.S. 401, 412, 414 (1945) (opinion of Frankfurter J.).

106. *Id.* at 418.

107. Wolf v. Colorado, 338 U.S. 25 (1949); Mapp v. Ohio, 367 U.S. 643, 672 (1961) (Frankfurter J. joins in Mr. Justice Harlan's dissenting opinion); cf. Elkins v. United States, 364 U.S. 206, 233 (1960) (dissenting).

108. Louisiana *ex rel.* Francis v. Resweber, 329 U.S. 459, 466, 471 (1947) (concurring).

109. E.g., Watts v. Indiana, 338 U.S. 49 (1949) (opinion of Frankfurter J.); Stein v. New York, 346 U.S. 156, 199 (1953) (dissenting); Culombe v. Connecticut, 367 U.S. 568 (1961) (opinion of Frankfurter J.); Rochin v. California, 342 U.S. 165 (1952); Leland v. Oregon, 343 U.S. 790, 802 (1952) (dissenting); Smith v. Baldi, 344 U.S. 561, 570 (1953) (dissenting); cf. Fisher v. United States, 328 U.S. 463, 477 (1946) (dissenting).

110. Law and Politics, *supra* note 4, at 192-193; see also 26-27. Also Carter v. Illinois, 329 U.S. 173, 175-176 (1946); Paterno v. Lyons, 334 U.S. 314, 322 (1948) (concurring).

111. The Business of the Supreme Court, *supra* note 11, at 189.

112. See note 37.

113. Uveges v. Pennsylvania, 335 U.S. 437, 442 (1948) (dissenting).

114. Hale v. Bimco Trading, Inc., 306 U.S. 375, 380 (1939).

115. Adamson v. California, 332 U.S. 46, 59, 68 (1947) (concurring).

116. Terminiello v. Chicago, 337 U.S. 1, 8, 11 (1949).

117. Uveges v. Pennsylvania, 335 U.S. 437, 442, 447 (1948) (dissenting).

118. Compare Williams v. Georgia, 349 U.S. 375 (1955), with Staub v. City of Baxley, 355 U.S. 313, 325 (1958) (dissenting).

119. E.g., Watts v. Indiana, 338 U.S. 49 (1949) (opinion of Frankfurter J.); compare Wolf v. Colorado, 338 U.S. 25 (1949).

120. For a recent and perhaps extreme example, see Poe v. Ullman, 367 U.S. 497 (1961) (opinion of Frankfurter J.).

121. Railroad Comm'n of Texas v. Pullman Co., 312 U.S. 496 (1941); Spector Motor Service Co. v. McLaughlin, 323 U.S. 101 (1944); Propper v. Clark, 337 U.S. 472, 493 (1949) (dissenting); Louisiana Power and Light Co. v. Thibodaux, 360 U.S. 25 (1959); *In re* Oliver, 333 U.S. 257, 283 (1948) (dissenting); Konigsberg v.

State Bar, 353 U.S. 252, 274 (1957) (dissenting); Rogers v. Richmond, 365 U.S. 534 (1961). Compare Jennings v. Illinois, 342 U.S. 104, 112 (1951) (dissenting); Irvin v. Dowd, 359 U.S. 394, 407 (1959) (dissenting); Lynum v. Illinois, 368 U.S. 908, 911 (1961) (dissenting); also Terminiello v. Chicago, 337 U.S. 1, 8 (1949) (dissenting).

122. Clay v. Sun Ins. Office, 363 U.S. 207 (1960).

123. Williams v. Kaiser, 323 U.S. 471, 479, 482 (1945) (dissenting).

124. Uveges v. Pennsylvania, 335 U.S. 437, 442, 449-450 (1948) (dissenting).

125. Law and Politics, *supra* note 4, at 207.

126. Bartkus v. Illinois, 359 U.S. 121 (1959).

127. Knapp v. Schweitzer, 357 U.S. 371, 381 (1958).

128. *Id.*, at 375, 378, 380. Compare Feldman v. United States, 322 U.S. 487 (1944); Elkins v. United States, 364 U.S. 206, 233 (1960) (dissenting); also Malinski v. New York, 324 U.S. 401, 412, 413, 418 (1945) (opinion of Frankfurter J.).

129. Osborn v. Ozlin, 310 U.S. 53 (1940).

130. State Tax Comm'n v. Aldrich, 316 U.S. 174, 182, 183-184 (1942) (concurring).

131. Watson v. Employers Liability Corp., 348 U.S. 66, 74 (1954) (concurring).

132. Morris v. Jones, 329 U.S. 545, 554 (1947) (dissenting).

133. Compare Morris v. Jones, 329 U.S. 545, 554, 558 (1947) (dissenting); Hughes v. Fetter, 341 U.S. 609, 614, 620 (1951) (dissenting); see note 134. In some contexts, at least, it requires the Court to balance the interests of the competing states. Carroll v. Lanza, 349 U.S. 408, 414 (1955) (dissenting).

134. Williams v. North Carolina, 325 U.S. 226 (1945); see note 135; cf. Kovacs v. Brewer, 356 U.S. 604, 609 (1958) (dissenting). But cf. Vanderbilt v. Vanderbilt, 354 U.S. 416, 419 (1957) (dissenting).

135. Sherrer v. Sherrer, 334 U.S. 343, 356, 363, 377 (1948) (dissenting); cf. Cook v. Cook, 342 U.S. 126, 129 (1951) (dissenting).

136. E.g., Standard Oil Co. v. New Jersey, 341 U.S. 428, 443 (1951) (dissenting).

137. Colegrove v. Green, 328 U.S. 549 (1946) (opinion of Frankfurter J.); Baker v. Carr, 369 U.S. 186, 266 (1962) (dissenting).

138. Frankfurter, The Commerce Clause Under Marshall, Taney and Waite 43 (1937).

139. See Graves v. New York *ex rel.* O'Keefe, 306 U.S. 466, 487 (1939) (concurring). Compare Mr. Justice Johnson: "In questions of great importance and great delicacy, I feel my duty to the public best discharged by an effort to maintain my opinions in my own way." Gibbons v. Ogden, 22 U.S. (9 Wheat.) 1, 223 (1824).
140. Law and Politics, *supra* note 4, at 44-45.


# All Sides of the Question, Felix Frankfurter and Personal Freedom, *Archer E. Sutherland*

1. The Common Law, 35.
2. Justice Frankfurter made a scholarly survey of this difficult question in Culombe v. Connecticut, 367 U.S. 568, 603 (1961).
3. See Sullivan v. New York *Times*, 144 So. 2d 25 (1962); New York *Times* v. Sullivan, #39, October Term, 1963.
4. 285 U.S. 393, 410 (1932).
5. The phrase is Frankfurter's in Louisiana *ex rel.* Francis v. Resweber, 329 U.S. 459, 466 (1947).
6. An example is Justice Frankfurter's opinion in Wolf v. Colorado, 328 U.S. 25 (1949). Another, in an entirely different field, is Judge Stephens' opinion in Cushing v. Rodman, 82 F 2d 864 (CADC 1936).
7. The words are taken from Justice Frankfurter's skeptical comment on the law-fact distinction, in Bingham's Trust v. Com'r of Internal Revenue, 325 U.S. 365, 378. (1945).
8. Holmes in "Law and the Court" (1913) Collected Legal Papers 291 at 295 (1952 ed.).
9. He took his seat January 30, 1939.
10. 310 U.S. 586.
11. The mills of justice grind somewhat slowly. The children were five years older when their case reached the Supreme Court.
12. On which, I hope, I should also have taken a stand. To deny the children public education because they refused to engage in what seemed to them a sinful ritual seems to me a uselessly drastic measure, the sort of thing that is inconsistent with due process. But states have some autonomy. Reasonable men could and did differ.
13. 310 U.S. 586, 593, 600 (1940).

14. 194 U.S. 267, 270.
15. In United States v. Carolene Products Co., 304 U.S. 144, 152.
16. 319 U.S. 624 (1943).
17. 319 U.S. 646.
18. *Ex parte* Quirin, 317 U.S. 1 (1942).
19. 4 Wall. 2 (1866).
20. This book is now largely forgotten except by a few antiquarians who are curious about the turnings of intellectual history. It was written in 1936 by Drew Pearson and Robert S. Allen and was, in brief, a demonstration that the Supreme Court was A Bad Thing.
21. 198 U.S. 45 (1905).
22. My colleague Paul Freund has some wise reflections on the efficaciousness *vel non* of saying clear-and-present-danger with sufficient speed, in his book On Understanding the Supreme Court 27 (1949).
23. 330 U.S. 1.
24. 343 U.S. 306.
25. Saia v. New York, 334 U.S. 558.
26. Kovacs v. Cooper, 336 U.S. 77 (1949).
27. 336 U.S. 90.
28. 301 U.S. 242.
29. 323 U.S. 516.
30. 336 U.S. 96 (1949).
31. *John Marshall and the Judicial Function*, 69 HARV. L. REV. 217, 219 (1955). The Marshall quotation comes, of course, from McCulloch v. Maryland, 4 Wheaton 316, 407 (1819).
32. 57 Stat. at L. 431, 450.
33. United States v. Lovett, 328 U.S. 303 (1946).
34. For a bill of attainder by a state, see Act of 22 October 1779, Laws of N.Y. Third Session, c 25.
35. Dennis v. U.S., 341 U.S. 494; see page 517 and following for the Frankfurter opinion.
36. 341 U.S. 518.
37. 341 U.S. 520.
38. See, e.g., American Communications Association C.I.O. v. Douds, 339 U.S. 382 (1950); Osman v. Douds, 339 U.S. 846 (1950); Garner v. Board of Public Works, 341 U.S. 716 (1951); Wieman v. Updegraff, 344 U.S. 183 (1952).
39. Beside the samples discussed in this paper there were, of course,

a great number of others. To list them would be tedious for writer and reader alike. Recent instances are Wilkinson v. U.S., 365 U.S. 399 (1961) and Braden v. U.S., 365 U.S. 431 (1961).

40. Adler v. Board of Education, 342 U.S. 485 (1952).

41. T. 50 U.S. Code S786; see Communist Party of the United States v. Subversive Activities Control Board, 367 U.S. 1 (1961).

42. See Adler, 342 U.S. 485 (1952).

43. 354 U.S. 178.

44. 354 U.S. 234.

45. 360 U.S. 109 (1959).

46. 360 U.S. 72 (1959).

47. 354 U.S. 178 (1957).

48. 354 U.S. 234 (1957).

49. Sweezy v. New Hampshire, 354 U.S. 234, 255 (1957).

50. 354 U.S. 264.

51. Uphaus v. Wyman, 360 U.S. 72 (1959).

52. Terry v. Adams, 345 U.S. 461.

53. 90 F. Supp. 595 (D.C.S.D. Tex. 1950).

54. 193 F. 2d 600 (5th Cir. 1952).

55. 328 U.S. 549.

56. Gomillion v. Lightfoot, 364 U.S. 339 (1960).

57. 369 U.S. 186.

58. See, e.g., his opinion concerning contempt by newspaper in Maryland v. Baltimore Radio Show, 338 U.S. 912 (1950), an elaborate opinion respecting denial of a petition for certiorari, with an appendix setting forth the course of a number of recent English decisions, and referring to the report of a Royal Commission on the Press, and debate thereon in the House of Commons in 1949.

59. 332 U.S. 46.

60. 198 U.S. 45.

61. 332 U.S. 61, 67–68.

62. 342 U.S. 165.

63. Gallagher v. Crown Kosher Super Market of Massachusetts, 366 U.S. 617 (1961).

64. See, e.g., Wolf v. Colorado, 338 U.S. 25 (1949) (opinion by Justice Frankfurter); overruled in Mapp v. Ohio, 367 U.S. 643 (1961); the Court thus now holds that a search and seizure conducted by state officers, which would have been unconstitutional if made by federal officers, renders evidence so acquired inadmissible

under the Fourteenth Amendment. In Mapp Justices Frankfurter and Burton joined Mr. Justice Harlan in a dissent. See also Gideon v. Wainwright, 372 U.S. 335 (1963), overruling Betts v. Brady, 316 U.S. 455 (1942).
65. 365 U.S. 534.
66. 367 U.S. 568 (1961).


# Labor and the Law, *Sanford H. Kadish*

1. Bethlehem Steel Co. v. New York State Labor Relations Board, 330 U.S. 767, 779 (1947).
2. Phillips, Felix Frankfurter Reminisces 114 (1960). Hereafter cited, Reminisces.
3. 243 U.S. 426 (1916).
4. 29 HARV. L. REV. 353 (1916).
5. 198 U.S. 45 (1905).
6. 243 U.S. 629 (1917).
7. Justice Brandeis, of course, took no part.
8. 261 U.S. 525 (1923).
9. It was not until 1937 that the decision was overruled. West Coast Hotel Co. v. Parrish, 300 U.S. 379 (1937).
10. Reminisces at 94.
11. Law and Politics, Occasional Papers of Felix Frankfurter, 1913–1938, 203–204 (MacLeish and Prichard eds., 1939). Hereafter cited, Law and Politics.
12. Michaels v. Hillman, 111 Misc. 284, 181 N.Y. Supp. 165 (S. Ct. Monroe Co., 1920).
13. Reminisces at 172.
14. However, the Justice believed that the complaint's chief aim of dissolving the Amalgamated was successfully averted. *Id.* 173.
15. Michaels v. Hillman, 112 Misc. 395, 183 N.Y. Supp. 195 (S. Ct. Monroe Co. 1920). The use of the epithet "scab," for example, was thought an enjoinable excess. See Frankfurter and Greene, The Labor Injunction 114 n. 131 (1930). Justice Frankfurter comments on this case in Reminisces at 173.
16. 183 N.Y. Supp. at 198.
17. Address by Felix Frankfurter, Chairman of the War Labor

Policies Board, "The Labor Policy of the United States," in U.S. Dept. Labor, Report of Proceedings of the National War Labor Conference 7 (1918).

The story of the wartime efforts of the national government in the labor area is told in J. Lombardi, Labor's Voice in the Cabinet, A History of the Department of Labor from Its Origin to 1921 (1942); E. Berman, Labor Disputes and the President of the United States, Chap. V (1924); A. Bing, War Time Strikes and Their Adjustment (1921); W. F. Willoughby, Government Organization in Wartime and After, Chaps. IX and X (1919); G. S. Watkins, Labor Problems and Labor Administration in the United States During the World War, Part I, The Development of War Labor Administration (1919); L. C. Marshall, The War Labor Program and Its Administration, 26 J. POLI. ECON. 425 (1918).

18. Reminisces at 115.

19. The letter of President Wilson establishing the Commission is reprinted in Berman, *supra* note 17 at 126-127.

20. Lombardi, *supra* note 17, at 210.

21. *Id.* at 221. See the similarly laudatory judgments in Bing, *supra* note 17, at 57; Berman, *supra* note 17, at 127-128; Willoughby, *supra* note 17, at 213; Watkins, *supra* note 17, at 153.

22. See Report of President's Mediation Commission to the President of the United States (1918). An excellent account of the work of this Commission appears in Lombardi, *supra* note 17, at 212-227. Justice Frankfurter himself colorfully describes his experiences in Reminisces 117-129.

23. Report, *supra*, at 13.

24. See *supra* note 22.

25. Willoughby, *supra* note 17, at 213. He further concluded that nowhere else "can there be found in so brief a compass such an acute analysis of the causes of industrial discontent and the steps that should be taken to remove it. Furthermore, the principles of action here laid down constitute the ones which the National Government, acting through its other agencies, has consistently sought to put into execution." *Id.* at 217.

26. For a review of these documents see Cox and Bok, Cases on Labor Law 84-87, 118-119 (5th ed. 1962).

27. A similar recommendation for a unified war labor administration was formulated by Justice Brandeis about the same time. See

Mason, Brandeis—A Free Man's Life 523-524 (1946). The Council of National Defense had made a similar recommendation. See Marshall, *supra* note 17, at 436-437. Frankfurter later restated the compelling reasons as follows: "Since the outbreak of the war, the United States Government has come to be the greatest single employer of labor in the country. . . . But it has had no operating policy with regard to the plants as a whole. Each one has been operated individually as a separate enterprise, quite apart from others and, so far as the labor supply has been concerned, in active competition with the others." Monthly Labor Review, U.S. Bureau Labor Stat., July 18, pp. 25-26.

28. Lombardi, *supra* note 17, at 244; Willoughby, *supra* note 17, at 225.

29. Proclamation of the President Creating the National War Labor Board, in U.S. Department of Labor, Bur. Lab. Stat. Bull. No. 287 at 34 (1922).

30. Principles and Policies to Govern Relations Between Workers and Employers in War Industries for the Duration of the War. *Id.* at 32-33.

31. Lombardi, *supra* note 17, at 250; Berman, *supra* note 17, at 152.

32. The code's first principle is apparently a direct lineal antecedent of Section 7 of the National Labor Relations Act: "The right of workers to organize in trade-unions and to bargain collectively, through chosen representatives, is recognized and affirmed. This right shall not be denied, abridged, or interfered with by the employers in any manner whatsoever." *Supra* note 30, at 32.

33. See Ordway Tead, *The New Place of Labor*, 122 Atlantic Monthly 178, 182 (1918).

34. Remarks of Director General Densmore, in Report of Proceedings of the National War Labor Conference 7 (1918); Address by Felix Frankfurter, *id.* at 7-10; Lombardi, *supra* note 17, at 266-267; Willoughby, *supra* note 17, at 235-238.

35. See Mason, Brandeis—A Free Man's Life, 254-256 (1946).

36. The appointment was favorably received. See, e.g., editorial, *Our Developing Labor Policy*, 21 The Public 622 (1918).

37. See Resolution of the War Labor Policies Board, July 12, 1918, quoted in Willoughby, *supra* note 17, at 237-238.

38. Lombardi, *supra* note 17, at 276, and sources cited.

39. Hammer v. Dagenhart, 247 U.S. 251 (1918). See Lombardi, *supra* note 17, at 179.

40. William B. Wilson, *The Problem of the War Labor Policies Board*, 60 Forum 267, 268 (1918).

41. Wehle, *War Labor Policies and Their Outcome in Peace*, 33 Q. J. Eco. 321, 341 (1919).

42. See W. B. Wilson, *supra* note 40, at 268-269; G. S. Watkins, *supra* note 17, at 59-63.

43. Frankfurter, Address, *supra* note 34, at 10; Frankfurter, Official Bulletin, July 25, 1918, quoted in Willoughby, *supra* note 17, at 241-242.

44. The fullest treatment of the War Labor Policies Board, based in large part on relevant documents in the National Archives, is Lombardi, *supra* note 17, at 277-292.

45. Report of the Secretary of Labor, 1919, at 129.

46. *Law and Order*, 4 Yale Rev. 230 (1920), reprinted in Law and Politics at 211.

47. The words of Senator George W. Norris describing Andrew Furuseth. Norris, Fighting Liberal 311 (1945).

48. "This familiar analysis suggests its own familiar remedies." Law and Politics at 214.

49. Compare Lerner, "The Social Thought of Mr. Justice Brandeis," in Frankfurter (ed.), *Mr. Justice Brandeis* 7, 18 (1932); Richberg, "The Industrial Liberalism of Mr. Justice Brandeis," *id.* at 129, 131-133 (1932); Luney, Mr. Justice Brandeis and the Problems of Labor 2 (Abstract of Thesis, University of Illinois, 1932).

50. 158 U.S. 564 (1895).

51. Witte, The Government in Labor Disputes 83-84 (1932). For an example of labor's outrage over the injunction, see Report of the Executive Council, A.F.L., 42nd Annual Convention, 1922, at 23 and 32, quoted in Witte, *Social Consequences of Injunctions in Labor Disputes*, 24 Ill. L. Rev. 772, 783-784 (1929).

52. See Witte, The Government in Labor Disputes, 265-276 (1932); Frankfurter and Greene, The Labor Injunction, Chap. IV (1930) (hereafter cited Labor Injunction).

53. E.g., Duplex Printing Co. v. Deering, 254 U.S. 443 (1921); American Steel Foundries v. Tri-City Trade Council, 257 U.S. 184 (1921). Labor Injunction 145-148, 163-176, 191-194.

54. Norris, Fighting Liberal, 310-312 (1945).

55. *Id.* 312-313; Sen. Rep. No. 1060, Part 2, 71st Cong., 2d Sess. at 5.
56. The bill is reproduced in Labor Injunction, Appendix IX, 279-288.
57. The vote was 75-5 in the Senate, and 362-14 in the House. Neuberger and Kahn, Integrity—The Life of George W. Norris 256 (1947). How it was that a bill of such radical character [Gregory in Labor and the Law at 191 (rev. ed. 1949) refers to it as a "revolutionary piece of Labor legislation"], which was handily blocked in the two prior Congresses, was overwhelmingly enacted by the 72nd Congress and signed by President Hoover without overt protest is itself a revealing episode in the legislative process. The story is best told in Bernstein, The Lean Years 391-415 (1960).
58. See Labor Injunction at 226 n. 61: "Having long entertained the views expressed herein, one of the present writers, at the suggestion of the Senate Subcommittee on the Judiciary, collaborated with others like-minded in drafting the bill under discussion."
59. See, e.g., Gregory, *supra* note 57, at 185 to the effect that the Act was "reputedly drafted by Professor Frankfurter." It was perhaps not accidental that Senator Norris repeatedly listed Frankfurter's name first among the group consulted by the Judiciary Subcommittee. See *supra* note 55.
60. The preparation of the book in its early stages immediately preceded Frankfurter's work in behalf of Senator Norris' committee. The first three chapters appeared as a three-part article in the LAW QUARTERLY REVIEW in April and July 1928 and January 1929, under the title, *The Use of the Injunction in American Labor Controversies*, 44 L. Q. REV. 164, 353 (1928); 45 L. Q. REV. 19 (1929). The last two chapters bearing on legislative remedies apparently followed his legislative work; they appeared in two separate American law reviews later in 1929: *Legislation Affecting Labor Injunctions*, 38 YALE L. J. 879 (1929); *Labor Injunctions and Federal Legislation*, 42 HARV. L. REV. 766 (1929).
61. Otis J., dissenting in Donnelly Garment Co. v. I.L.G.W.U., 21 F. Supp. 807, 817 (W.D. Mo. 1937).
62. Book review, Young, 78 U. PA. L. REV. 798 (1930).
63. Book review, 29 MICH. L. REV. 1126, 1128 (1931).
64. 167 Mass. 92, 104, 44 N.E. 1077, 1079 (1896).
65. Labor Injunction at 46.
66. *Id.* at 175.

67. See Lerner, *supra* note 49, passim. The Labor Injunction is dedicated "To Mr. Justice Brandeis for whom law is not a system of artificial reason, but the application of ethical ideals, with freedom at the core."

68. 35 Am. Hist. Rev. 897 (1930). Cf. Witte, 20 Am. Econ. Rev. 522, 523 (1930): "Altogether, it is likely to prove one of the most influential studies ever made of any socio-legal question."

69. Labor Injunction at 131.

70. *Id.* at 203.

71. These formed the basis of Sections 7 through 12 of the Norris-LaGuardia Act.

72. Vegelahn v. Guntner, *supra* note 64.

73. Duplex Printing Co. v. Deering, 254 U.S. 443, 479 (1921) (dissenting).

74. Labor Injunction at 203-205.

75. Aaron, *The Labor Injunction Reappraised*, 10 U.C.L.A. L. Rev. 292, 297 (1963).

76. Phelps Dodge Corp. v. N.L.R.B., 313 U.S. 177, 183 (1941).

77. These cases raised such issues of consequence as the scope of coverage of the National Labor Relations Act [N.L.R.B. v. Fainblatt, 306 U.S. 601 (1939)]; the scope of review of Board orders by Courts of Appeal [N.L.R.B. v. Waterman S. S. Co., 309 U.S. 206 (1940); N.L.R.B. v. Link-Belt Co., 311 U.S. 584 (1941)]; the extent of the remedial powers of the Board [N.L.R.B. v. Newport News Co., 308 U.S. 241 (1930); National Licorice Co. v. N.L.R.B., 309 U.S. 350 (1940); Republic Steel Co. v. N.L.R.B., 311 U.S. 7 (1940)]; the picketing-free speech relationship [Thornhill v. Alabama, 310 U.S. 88 (1940); Carlson v. California, 310 U.S. 106 (1940)]; the applicability of the Sherman Act [Apex Hosiery Co. v. Leader, 310 U.S. 469 (1940)]; the interpretation of the Norris-LaGuardia Act [Milk Wagon Drivers' Union v. Lake Valley Farm Products, 311 U.S. 91 (1940)].

78. 312 U.S. 219 (1941).

79. In the December 1957 issue of the Yale Law Journal, Professor Summers treated Justice Frankfurter's labor opinions in an article entitled, *Frankfurter, Labor Law and the Judge's Function*, 67 Yale L. J. 266 (1957). I am pleased to observe that in several places we share comparable points of view; pleased because while this gives

to Mr. Summers the claim to priority, it gives to me the claim to his authority.

80. Apex Hosiery Co. v. Leader, 310 U.S. 469 (1940).

81. See Justice Stone's concurring opinion, 312 U.S. at 237; Cavers, *And What of the Apex Case Now?* 8 U. CHI. L. REV. 516, 518 (1941).

82. 254 U.S. 443 (1921).

83. United States v. Hutcheson, *supra* note 78, at 234-236.

84. United States v. Brims, 272 U.S. 549 (1926); Allen Bradley Co. v. Local Union No. 3, I.B.E.W., 325 U.S. 797 (1945).

85. Frankfurter and Greene, *Congressional Power Over the Labor Injunction*, 31 COLUM. L. REV. 385, 408 (1931); Labor Injunction 215, 220.

86. United States v. Hutcheson, *supra* note 78, at 246. Chief Justice Hughes joined in this dissenting opinion. See Steffen, *Labor Activities in Restraint of Trade: The Hutcheson Case*, 36 ILL. L. REV. 1 (1941); Landis, *The Apex Case, Addendum*, 26 CORN. L. Q. 212A (1941); Tunks, *A New Federal Charter for Trade Unionism*, 41 COLUM. L. REV. 969 (1941); Teller, *Federal Intervention in Labor Disputes and Collective Bargaining: The Hutcheson Case*, 40 MICH. L. REV. 24 (1941); Gregory, *The New Sherman-Clayton-Norris-LaGuardia Act*, 8 U. CHI. L. REV. 503 (1941); Cavers, *And What of the Apex Case Now?* 8 U. CHI. L. REV. 516, 517 (1941) ("Mr. Gregory has not spared the rod in castigating Mr. Justice Frankfurter's opinion in the Hutcheson case. If [it] could be made required reading for the American bar and a Gallup poll taken of their reactions, I think an overwhelming majority would register their approval of the author's strictures and, if the yardstick could measure attitudes qualitatively, I should expect a high degree of vehemence"); Newman, *Restraint of Trade: Labor Disputes and the Sherman Act*, 29 CALIF. L. REV. 399 (1941). But see Nathanson and Wirtz, *The Hutcheson Case: Another View*, 36 ILL. L. REV. 41 (1941). Even this defense regrets what it regards as the opinion's excesses. *Id.* at 51.

87. See, e.g., Gregory, Labor and the Law 187, 276 (1949 ed.); McNaughton and Lazar, Industrial Relations and the Government 72 (1954); Jaffe, *The Judicial Universe of Mr. Justice Frankfurter*, 62 HARV. L. REV. 357, 406 (1949); Newman, *supra* note 86, at 403 n. 18.

88. See Nathanson and Wirtz, *supra* note 86, at 54-56. The key questions had come to be whether the conduct was "reasonable" or "legitimate." Cf. Frankfurter J. in United States v. Hutcheson, *supra* note 78, at 236-237: "It was precisely in order to minimize the difficulties to which the general language of the Sherman Law in its application to workers had given rise, that Congress cut through all the tangled verbalisms and enumerated concretely the types of activities which had become familiar incidents of union procedure."

89. It is entitled "Observations on Amendments Proposed by the American Federation of Labor to the Injunction Bill Drafted by the Sub-Committee of the Senate Committee on the Judiciary," and is signed "Felix Frankfurter, Herman Oliphant and E. E. Witte." No date appears on the typewritten manuscript. George W. Norris Papers, Manuscript Division of the Library of Congress.

90. The proposal and the floor discussion at the convention from which it emerged appear in American Federation of Labor, Proceedings (1929) 194-198, 317-333, 340-352.

91. See Bernstein, The Lean Years 401-403, 411 and notes 7, 8 and 15 at pp. 549-550 (1960).

92. The text of the memorandum bearing upon this proposal of the American Federation of Labor reads as follows:

"I. The following proposals in the bill endorsed by the A.F. of L. seem to us to jeopardize the constitutionality of the entire measure:

"1. Sub-section (j) of Section 4 of the endorsed bill adds an entirely new provision to the bill as drafted by the Senate sub-committee. The sub-committee's bill withdraws the remedy of injunction for various acts in view of the *Hitchman* case (245 U.S. 229) and *Truax v. Corrigan* (257 U.S. 312). It will be a sufficiently heavy load to pilot any such measure through Congress and to save it from attack before the Supreme Court. It is one thing, however, merely to withdraw the remedy of injunction for a given act; it is a wholly different thing to take away all remedies, including civil action for damages which sub-section (j) does. This provision should be eliminated."

93. 257 U.S. 312 (1921). This was the alternative holding, on the assumption that the state statute fully legalized the conduct. 257 U.S. at 330. On the contrary assumption that it foreclosed only the

remedy of injunction and was aimed solely against employee conduct, it was held violative of equal protection. *Id.* at 330, 339.

94. *Id.* at 340.

95. American Steel Foundries v. Tri-City Central Trade Council, 257 U.S. 184, 207 (1921).

96. Labor Injunction at 219-220.

97. See, e.g., Frankfurter and Greene, *Congressional Power Over the Labor Injunction*, 31 COLUM. L. REV. 385, 408 (1931): "2. Is the denial of all adequate judical remedies in case of an illegal strike a denial of due process of law? The question is not pertinent, for the bill only withdraws the remedy of the injunction." Even so it was not clear sailing, since Truax also invalidated the Arizona statute on the alternative assumption that only the remedy of injunction was withdrawn. Frankfurter's response was as follows: "Certainly the Truax case did not maintain that withdrawal of injunctive relief alone denied due process of law. Insofar as it found an invasion of the guarantee by the Fourteenth Amendment of equal protection of the laws, the Court will hardly derive such an objection from the Fifth Amendment, alone applicable to federal legislation, which contains no such guarantee of equal protection of the laws." *Id.* at 408-409.

98. United States v. Hutcheson, *supra* note 78, at 236.

99. This argument would not apply if Hutcheson were read (in flat opposition to Justice Frankfurter's statements) to hold that while Norris-LaGuardia eliminated the gloss of Duplex from Section 20, it did not at the same time eliminate the restrictive interpretation of the American Steel Foundries decision concerning the type of activities protected. Whether or not such a holding would have sustained the result in Hutcheson is arguable. It would depend on whether the union's activities were "coercive" within the meaning of American Steel Foundries. But even if it would have, the effort would have been rather pointless. The activities protected by Clayton Section 20, had been so narrowed by American Steel Foundries as to make the Herculean rationale of Hutcheson scarcely worth the candle. Justice Stone's more conventional approach would have done as well to decide that case alone.

100. 301 U.S. 468 (1937).

101. E.g., Frankfurter, *Some Reflections on the Reading of Statutes*, 47 COLUM. L. REV. 527, 533-5 (1947). See *id.* at 535: "Statutes

come out of the past and aim at the future. They may carry implicit residues or mere hints of purpose. Perhaps the most delicate aspect of statutory construction is not to find more residues than are implicit nor purposes beyond the bound of hints."

102. Hamilton, *Preview of a Justice*, 48 Yale L. J. 819, 828 (1939).

103. Mr. Hamilton certainly would agree. Compare Mr. Hamilton less than a decade later, Book Review, 56 Yale L. J. 1458, 1460 (1947): "Mr. Justice Frankfurter has no feel for the dominant issues; he operates best when weaving crochet patches of legalism on the fingers of the case."

104. Mason reports the following exchange between Justices Stone and Frankfurter in the deliberations preceding the issuance of the opinions in the Hutcheson case [Mason, Harlan Fiske Stone—Pillar of the law 501–502 (1956)]. Stone wrote: "But apart from my desire to pursue the peaceful rather than the warpath, I have the uncomfortable feeling that the quotation [from Stone's 1936 Harvard Tercentenary address] does not fit the situation created by the passage of the Norris-LaGuardia Act. I suspect that Roberts could make a more powerful showing than he has that the Norris-LaGuardia Act was a compromise by which the proponents of the bill gained much and the opponents yielded something but not all." Mason summarizes Frankfurter's reply as follows: "At this latter observation Frankfurter lashed out fiercely, claiming personal knowledge as to the drafting and the passage of the Act. He refused to regard this legislation as a compromise of conflicting viewpoints and maintained that correction of the Duplex and Bedford constructions was its chief objective. As any further argument must seem to question Frankfurter's knowledge or his candor, direct debate came to a halt."

105. Bakery Sales Drivers Union v. Wagshal, 333 U.S. 437 (1948).

106. See also the dissenting opinions in Hunt v. Crumboch, 325 U.S. 821 (1945), in which Frankfurter joined, finding a revenge boycott unsheltered from the Sherman Act by the immunities of Norris-LaGuardia and Clayton Section 20.

107. United States v. United Mine Workers, 330 U.S. 258, 307 (1947). At least one Hutcheson critic was won back. See Gregory, *Government by Injunction Again*, 14 U. Chi. L. Rev. 363, 364 (1947): "Mr. Justice Frankfurter, who concededly is more familiar with the background and purpose of the Norris-LaGuardia Act than

any of his colleagues on the Court, says this last conclusion is not so. Furthermore, he says it in one of the most brilliant and distinguished opinions ever handed down from that bench."

108. A bystander at the time reports hearing Justice Frankfurter exclaim in the corridor of the Supreme Court building: "All the Chief will say is, 'Coal is important. Coal is important.'" Chief Justice Vinson wrote the opinion of the Court.

109. 330 U.S. 395, 413 (1947).

110. 259 U.S. 344 (1922).

111. 31 NEW REPUBLIC 328, 329 (1922). See also his observations in American Federation of Labor v. American Sash and Door Co., 335 U.S. 538, 545-546 (1949) quoted in text accompanying note 163, *infra*.

112. See Steele v. Louisville and Nashville Ry. Co., 323 U.S. 192 (1944); Graham v. Bro. of Locomotive Firemen, 338 U.S. 232 (1949).

113. See Bro. of R.R. Trainmen v. Chicago River R.R. Co., 353 U.S. 30 (1957); Order of R.R. Telegraphers v. Chicago Northwestern Ry. Co., 362 U.S. 330 (1960) (dissenting).

114. Sinclair Refining Company v. Atkinson, 370 U.S. 195 (1962).

115. In the course of argument in Teamsters Local 795 v. Yellow Transit Freight Lines, 370 U.S. 711 (1962), another case which raised the same issue, Justice Frankfurter observed: "You are leaving out the real purpose and drive behind the Norris-LaGuardia Act, which was not consideration for the parties but for the federal courts. Congress said the federal courts should not get into these controversies. . . . [S]how me a single sentence in the Taft Act that indicates that Congress changed its mind in 1947. . . . Show me one place where Congress set aside the Norris-LaGuardia Act without saying so. . . . Congress wished to keep the federal courts out of the labor dispute business. Don't you think they had collective bargaining agreements in those days? And don't you think the parties tried to enforce them? I can assure you they did." 30 U.S. Law Wk. 3118 (1961).

116. See discussion *infra* accompanying notes 188 and 190.

117. Lincoln Federal Labor Union v. Northwestern Iron and Metal Co., 335 U.S. 525 (1949) and American Federation of Labor v. American Sash and Door Co., 335 U.S. 538 (1949).

118. 335 U.S. at 544-545. By the same token a legislative validation

of a closed shop agreement must likewise be within legislative authority, for as Justice Frankfurter observed, quoting Holmes, "I could not pronounce it unwarranted if Congress should decide that to foster a strong union was for the best interest, not only of the men, but of the railroads and the country at large." Railway Employees' Department v. Hanson, 351 U.S. 225, 242 (1956) (concurring).

119. The credo with which the opinion concludes is central to the Justice's response to the task of constitutional adjudication: "Because the Court is without power to shape measures for dealing with the problems of society but has merely the power of negation over measures shaped by others, the indispensable judicial requisite is intellectual humility, and such humility presupposes complete disinterestedness. . . . Courts can fulfill their responsibility in a democratic society only to the extent that they succeed in shaping their judgments by rational standards, and rational standards are both impersonal and communicable. Matters of policy, however, are by definition matters which demand the resolution of conflicts of value, and the elements of conflicting values are largely imponderable. Assessment of their competing worth involves differences of feeling; it is also an exercise in prophecy. Obviously the proper forum for mediating a clash of feelings and rendering a prophetic judgment is the body chosen for those purposes by the people. Its functions can be assumed by this Court only in disregard of the historic limits of the Constitution." 335 U.S. at 557.

120. *Id.* at 550.

121. Carlson v. California 310 U.S. 106, 113 (1940) ("[P]ublicizing the facts of a labor dispute in a peaceful way through appropriate means, whether by pamphlet, by word of mouth or by banner, must now be regarded as within that liberty of communication which is secured to every person by the Fourteenth Amendment against abridgment by a State."); Thornhill v. Alabama, 310 U.S. 88, 95-96 (1940) ("Mere legislative preference for one rather than another means for combating substantive evils, therefore, may well prove an inadequate foundation on which to rest regulations which are aimed at or in their operation diminish the effective exercise of rights so necessary to the maintenance of democratic institutions").

122. American Federation of Labor v. Swing, 312 U.S. 321, 325 (1941). See also his opinions for the Court in Hotel and Restaurant

Employees' International Alliance v. Wisconsin Employment Relations Board, 315 U.S. 437 (1942); Cafeteria Employees' Union v. Angelos, 320 U.S. 293 (1943).

123. Douglas J., dissenting in International Bro. of Teamsters v. Vogt, Inc., 354 U.S. 284, 295 (1957).

124. Senn v. Tile Layers Protective Union, 301 U.S. 468 (1937). This was the Justice's own verdict. See Int'l Bro. of Teamsters v. Hanke, 339 U.S. 470, 476-477 (1950).

125. 257 U.S. 312 (1921).

126. Milk Wagon Drivers Union v. Meadowmoor Dairies, 312 U.S. 287 (1941).

127. Carpenters and Joiners Union v. Ritter's Café, 315 U.S. 722, 727-728 (1942).

128. The Justice was apparently drawing the same line here that he helped draw in the Norris-LaGuardia Act, which confined its immunities to cases involving "persons who are engaged in the same industry, trade, craft, or occupation; or have direct or indirect interests therein." Sec. 13(a). Yet, however sound as a matter of legislative policy, such a line seems hardly relevant to mark the boundaries of free speech, since, as Professor Jaffe rightly observed, "it is an essential and legitimate aim of 'communication' to reach neutrals." Jaffe, *The Judicial Universe of Mr. Justice Frankfurter*, 62 HARV. L. REV. 357, 405 (1949).

129. But compare Murphy J. in Thornhill v. Alabama, 310 U.S. 88, 106 (1940), quoting Schneider v. State, 308 U.S. 147, 163 (1939): "[O]ne is not to have the exercise of his liberty of expression in appropriate places abridged on the plea that it may be exercised in some other place."

130. Cf. Giboney v. Empire Storage and Ice Co., 336 U.S. 490 (1949).

131. Int'l Bro. of Teamsters v. Hanke, 339 U.S. 470, 474 (1950).

132. Hughes v. Superior Court of California, 339 U.S. 460, 465, 468 (1950).

133. See concurring opinion of Douglas J., joined by Black and Murphy JJ., in Bakery and Pastry Drivers v. Wohl, 315 U.S. 769, 775 (1942).

134. Giboney v. Empire Storage and Ice Co., 336 U.S. 490 (1949).

135. Hughes v. Superior Court of California, 339 U.S. 460 (1950).

136. Int'l Bro. of Teamsters v. Hanke, 339 U.S. 470 (1950).

137. Int'l Bro. of Teamsters v. Vogt, 354 U.S. 284 (1957).

138. *Id.* at 290.

139. Int'l Bro. of Teamsters v. Hanke, *supra*, at 478.

140. Hill v. Florida, 325 U.S. 538, 556 (1945) (dissenting).

141. See Frankfurter J. in San Diego Building Trades Council v. Garmon, 359 U.S. 236, 239-240 (1959).

142. United Mine Workers v. Arkansas Flooring Co., 351 U.S. 62, 76 (1956) (dissenting): "The various aspects in which this problem comes before the Court are seldom easy of solution. Decisions ultimately depend on judgment in balancing overriding considerations making for the requirement of an exclusive nation-wide regime in a particular field of legal control and respect for the allowable area within which the forty-eight States may enforce their diverse notions of policy." See also Bethlehem Steel Company v. New York State Labor Relations Board, 330 U.S. 767, 779-780 (1947) (separate opinion).

143. 359 U.S. 236, 241 (1959).

144. Hill v. Florida, 325 U.S. 538 (1945) (dissenting); Bethlehem Steel Company v. New York State Labor Relations Board, 330 U.S. 767 (1947) (concurring); Algoma Plywood and Veneer Co. v. Wisconsin Employment Relations Board, 336 U.S. 301 (1949); Amalgamated Association v. Wisconsin Employment Relations Board, 340 U.S. 383 (1951) (dissenting).

145. But see McCoid, *Notes on a "G-string": A Study of the "No Man's Land" of Labor Law*, 44 MINN. L. REV. 205, 217-221 (1959).

146. 325 U.S. 538 (1945) (dissenting).

147. DeVeau v. Braisted, 363 U.S. 144 (1960).

148. Cf. the observation of Justice Douglas in dissent: "I could more nearly comprehend the thrust of the Court's ruling in this case if it overruled Hill v. Flordia . . . and adopted the dissenting opinion in that case written by my Brother Frankfurter." And see the trenchant comments of Professor (now Judge) Hays, *The Supreme Court and Labor Law, October Term, 1959*, 60 COLUM. L. REV. 901, 907–908 (1960).

149. 356 U.S. 617 (1958).

150. San Diego Building Trades Council v. Garmon, *supra*, at 244.

151. United Automobile Workers v. Wisconsin Employment Relations Board, 351 U.S. 266, 275 (1956) (Douglas, Black JJ. and Warren C.J. dissenting).

152. Amalgamated Association v. Wisconsin Employment Relations Board, 340 U.S. 383, 399 (1951) (dissenting). The Supreme Court has recently unanimously reaffirmed the holding in that case. Division 1287 of the Amalgamated Association v. Missouri, 374 U.S. 74 (1963).

153. San Diego Building Trades Council v. Garmon, *supra*, at 244; Weber v. Anheuser-Busch, Inc., 348 U.S. 468 (1955).

154. San Diego Building Trades Council v. Garmon, *supra*, at 249, 250 (concurring opinion of Justice Harlan, joined by Justices Clark, Whittaker, and Stewart).

155. He suggested as much in Weber v. Anheuser-Busch, Inc., 348 U.S. 468, 479 (1955). But some of his language in International Association of Machinists v. Gonzales, 356 U.S. 617 (1958) appeared to reject the conflict-of-remedies rationale. That appearance was strengthened by his silent concurrence at the same time in International Union, United Automobile Workers v. Russell, 356 U.S. 634 (1958), which seemed squarely based on its rejection. In the next term, however, in San Diego Building Trades Council v. Garmon, *supra*, that rationale was unambiguously stated as the controlling one.

156. San Diego Building Trades Council v. Garmon, *supra*, at 243.

157. *Id.* at 245.

158. *Id.* at 249, 253 (concurring opinion of Justices Harlan, Clark, Whittaker, and Stewart).

159. In International Union, United Automobile Workers v. Wisconsin Employment Relations Board, 336 U.S. 245 (1949) a five-Justice majority, which included Justice Frankfurter, had so held. And see his dissenting observation in Hill v. Florida, 325 U.S. 538, 547-548 (1945): "The same regard for the harmonious balance of our federal system, whereby the States may protect local interest despite the dormant Commerce Clause, allows state legislation for the protection of local interests so long as Congress has not supplanted local regulation either by a regulation of its own or by an unmistakable indication that there is to be no regulation at all." For concerns which may have motivated his new caution, see Cox, *Labor Decisions of the Supreme Court at the October Term, 1957*, 44 VA. L. REV. 1057, 1063-1069 (1958).

160. Labor Injunction at 169.

161. Pennsylvania R.R. v. Rychlik, 352 U.S. 480, 498 (1957).

162. Brandeis J. dissenting in Duplex Printing Press Co. v. Deering, 254 U.S. 443, 488 (1921).

163. American Federation of Labor v. American Sash and Door Co., 335 U.S. 538, 544 (1949) (concurring). See text accompanying notes 109————, *supra.*

164. See *supra* note 112. See also International Association of Machinists v. Street, 367 U.S. 740, 807 (1960) (dissenting); American Federation of Labor v. American Sash and Door Co., *supra* at 546; Pennsylvania R.R. v. Rychlik, 352 U.S. 480, 498-499 (1957) (separate opinion).

165. American Federation of Labor v. American Sash and Door Co., *supra*, at 545-546. See also the Justice's separate opinion in United Steelworkers v. United States, 361 U.S. 39, 44, 52-54 (1961).

166. 325 U.S. 711 (1945).

167. *Id.* at 758-759. See also Pennsylvania R.R. v. Rychlik, 352 U.S. 480, 498 (1957) (separate opinion): "The governing outlook for construing the Railway Labor Act is hospitable realization of the fact that it is primarily an instrument of industrial government for railroading by the industry itself, through the concentrated agencies of railroad executives and the railroad unions. . . . The dominant inference that the Court has drawn from this fact is exclusion of the courts from this process of collaborative self-government." To similar effect, see the Justice's majority opinion in Pennsylvania R.R. v. Day, 360 U.S. 548 (1959), and his separate opinion in Order of Railway Conductors v. Swan, 329 U.S. 520, 530 (1947).

168. Elgin, Joliet & Eastern Ry. Co. v. Burley, 327 U.S. 661 (1946).

169. 334 U.S. 446, 477 (1948).

170. See Walling v. Youngerman-Reynolds Hardwood Co., 325 U.S. 419, 424-425 (1945): "The regular rate by its very nature must reflect all payments which the parties have agreed shall be received during the workweek, exclusive of overtime payments. It is not an arbitrary label chosen by the parties; it is an actual fact."

171. 334 U.S. at 493.

172. 63 Stat. 446, 912, 29 U.S.C. Sec. 207(d) (e) and (f) (1958).

173. Aeronautical Industrial Lodge v. Campbell, 337 U.S. 521, 527 (1949). See the Justice's comparable opinion on a related point in McKinney v. Missouri, Kansas & Texas R.R., 357 U.S. 265 (1958).

174. 348 U.S. 96 (1954).

175. 348 U.S. 437 (1955).

176. *Id.* at 457.

177. 367 U.S. 740 (1961).

178. Railway Employees' Department v. Hanson, 351 U.S. 225 (1956).

179. 367 U.S. at 801 (dissenting).

180. DeMille v. American Fed. of Radio Artists, 31 Cal. 2d 139, 150, 187 P. 2d 769, 776 (1947).

181. N.L.R.B. v. Insurance Agents, 361 U.S. 477, 506 (1960) (dissenting).

182. See generally Cox, *The Duty to Bargain in Good Faith,* 71 HARV. L. REV. 1401 (1958).

183. 351 U.S. 149, 154 (1956).

184. 361 U.S. 477, 501 (1960).

185. For example, the Court observed that the Board exceeded its power "by inferring a lack of good faith not from any deficiencies of the union's performance at the bargaining table by reason of its attempted use of economic pressure, but solely and simply because tactics designed to exert economic pressure were employed during the course of the good-faith negotiations." *Id.* at 490.

186. *Id.* at 507-508.

187. His voting pattern as well as his opinions reveal a preference for freedom of the bargaining process from Board control. See N.L.R.B. v. American National Insurance Co., 343 U.S. 395 (1952) (voted with majority to reject Board finding that it was a per se refusal to bargain for employer to hold out for a management functions clause covering a term of employment over which there was a duty to bargain); N.L.R.B. v. Wooster Div. of Borg-Warner Corp., 356 U.S. 342, 350 (1958) (joined dissent from Court's holding that employer's insistence on a clause covering a matter not within the subjects of mandatory bargaining constituted a refusal to bargain).

188. Assn. of Westinghouse Salaried Employees v. Westinghouse Electric Corp., 348 U.S. 437 (1955).

189. 353 U.S. 448, 465 (1957).

190. See discussion *supra*, accompanying note 176.

191. 353 U.S. at 462-463.

192. 361 U.S. 459 (1960).

193. So, for example, he concurred without protest in the so-called Steelworkers Trilogy, in which the doctrine of Textile Workers v. Lincoln Mills was further applied. United Steelworkers of America

v. American Manufacturing Co., 363 U.S. 564 (1960); United Steel-workers of America v. Warrior and Gulf Navigation Co., 363 U.S. 574 (1960); United Steelworkers of America v. Enterprise Wheel & Car Corp., 363 U.S. 593 (1960).

194. 313 U.S. 177 (1941).

195. While the Justice naturally did not include himself in a lengthy supporting footnote, it is clear that he could have.

196. N.L.R.B. v. Local 1229, I.B.E.W., 346 U.S. 464, 478 (1953).

197. N.L.R.B. v. United Steelworkers, 357 U.S. 357 (1958).

198. Compare Justice Frankfurter's similarly grounded rejection of the Board's per se refusal to bargain rules. See *supra* notes 183–187, and accompanying text. But see his opinion in Local 1976, United Bro. of Carpenters v. N.L.R.B., 357 U.S. 93 (1958) where he approved an automatic rule making it an unfair labor practice for a union to call the employees' attention to a hot-cargo clause, even though he recognized the ultimate issue to be whether the neutral employer was willing to abide by the clause.

199. The Justice's concurring opinion in Radio Officers' Union v. N.L.R.B., 347 U.S. 17, 55 (1954) manifests the same concern to leave judgment to the Board, the courts functioning primarily to insure the Board's attention to the considerations legally relevant. Where technical terms of art require definition the Justice regards the task as belonging solely to the Board. See N.L.R.B. v. Highland Park Co., 341 U.S. 322, 326 (1951) (dissenting opinion) ("national or international labor organization"); N.L.R.B. v. Coca-Cola Bottling Co., 350 U.S. 264 (1956) (union "officer").

200. Phelps Dodge Corp. v. N.L.R.B., *supra* note 194.

201. *Id.* at 210-211.

202. Polish National Alliance v. N.L.R.B., 322 U.S. 643, 648 (1944).

203. N.L.R.B. v. Seven-Up Bottling Co., 344 U.S. 344 (1953); N.L.R.B. v. Deena Artware Inc., 361 U.S. 398, 406 (1960) (separate opinion). Review of the Board's fact finding by Courts of Appeals must be left to the tillers of the fields of administrative law. See Universal Camera Corp. v. N.L.R.B. 340 U.S. 474 (1951); N.L.R.B. v. Walton Manufacturing Co., 369 U.S. 404, 409 (1962) (dissenting). Another important opinion of more direct relevance to administrative law is Addison v. Holly Hill Co., 322 U.S. 607 (1944), dealing with problems under the Fair Labor Standards Act.

204. N.L.R.B. v. Lion Oil Co., 352 U.S. 282, 294 (1957) (opinion concurring and dissenting in part).
205. Local 761, I.U.E.W. v. N.L.R.B., 366 U.S. 667 (1961).
206. Local 1976, United Bro. of Carpenters v. N.L.R.B., 357 U.S. 93 (1958).
207. Labor Injunction at 137.
208. 350 U.S. 270, 289 (1956) (dissenting).
209. Though certainly not all of these have been discussed. See, e.g., American Communications Association, C.I.O. v. Douds, 339 U.S. 382, 415 (1950) (opinion concurring in part and dissenting in part); United States v. International Union, U.A.W., 352 U.S. 567 (1957); United Steelworkers v. United States, 361 U.S. 39, 44 (1959) (concurring); Local Lodge No. 1424, I.A.M. v. N.L.R.B., 362 U.S. 411, 429 (1960) (dissenting). See also cases cited *supra* note 203.
210. Tiller v. Atlantic Coast Line R.R., 318 U.S. 54 (1943) (concurring); Johnson v. United States, 333 U.S. 46, 50 (1948) (partially dissenting); Wilkerson v. McCarthy, 336 U.S. 53, 64 (1949) (concurring); Urie v. Thompson, 337 U.S. 163, 196 (1949) (opinion concurring and dissenting); Rogers v. Missouri Pacific R.R., 352 U.S. 500, 524 (1957) (dissenting); Inman v. Baltimore and Ohio R.R., 361 U.S. 138, 141 (1959) (concurring).
211. Kirschbaum Co. v. Walling, 316 U.S. 517 (1942); 10 East 40th Street Bldg. v. Callus, 325 U.S. 578 (1945); Powell v. United States Cartridge Co., 339 U.S. 497, 522 (1950) (dissenting); Mitchell v. H. B. Zachery Co., 362 U.S. 310 (1960). Cf. Cox, *The Influence of Mr. Justice Murphy on Labor Law*, 48 MICH. L. REV. 767, 799–800 (1950); Mendelson, *Mr. Justice Frankfurter—Law and Choice*, 10 VAND. L. REV. 333, 344 (1957).
212. E.g., Bridges v. United States, 314 U.S. 252, 279 (1941) (dissenting); Tenn. Coal Co. v. Muscoda Local No. 123, 321 U.S. 590, 603 (1944) (concurring); Social Security Board v. Nierotko, 327 U.S. 358, 370 (1946) (concurring); United States v. Carbone, 327 U.S. 633, 642 (1946) (dissenting); D. A. Schulte, Inc. v. Gangi, 328 U.S. 108, 121 (1946) (dissenting); United States v. Petrillo, 332 U.S. 1, 13 (1947) (concurring); O'Leary v. Brown-Pacific-Maxon Inc., 340 U.S. 504 (1951); Staub v. City of Baxley, 355 U.S. 313, 325 (1958) (dissenting); United States v. Kaiser, 363 U.S. 299, 305 (1960) (concurring); Reed v. Penn. R.R., 351 U.S. 502, 508 (1956) (dissenting).

213. One of the stories of the proverbial banter between Justices Frankfurter and Jackson has it that Frankfurter once offered Jackson the compliment of wishing he possessed the latter's pen. To which Jackson replied: "But yours has more ink, Felix." Another was told by Frankfurter himself. As the New York *Times* reports it: "Supreme Court Justice Felix Frankfurter disclosed last night in a facetious introduction to a technical lecture before the Association of the Bar of the City of New York . . . that he has had his wife 'blue pencil all my non-judicial writings.' 'When I told that to Justice Jackson,' he continued, 'he said, "Why don't you extend the censorship?" ' " New York *Times*, March 19, 1947, p. 27, col. 3.

214. These are the words the Justice used of Justice Brandeis in the dedication to The Labor Injunction. See *supra* note 68.

215. Frankfurter, *The Supreme Court in the Mirror of Justices*, 105 U. Pa. L. Rev. 781, 794 (1957).

216. See Mendelson, Justices Black and Frankfurter: Conflict in the Court (1961) and Professor Kalven's review in 2 U. Chi. Law School Record 22 (1963).

217. The figure is Professor Kalven's, *supra*, at 25.

218. See *supra* note 160.

# Adventures in Administrative Law,
## *Louis L. Jaffe*

1. 309 U.S. 134 (1940).

2. *Id.* at 141.

3. Ashbacker Radio Corp. v. F.C.C., 326 U.S. 327 (1945).

4. His dissenting vote in CAB v. State Airlines, 338 U.S. 572 (1950) (dissenting opinion by Reed) is rather out of line with his Ashbacker attitude. The dissent emphasizes the failure of "opportunity to contest fairly for the selected route." The rationale of his dissent in Ashbacker would, it seems to me, amply justify the CAB's procedure.

5. 265 Fed. 17 (D.C. Mass. 1920).

6. Cf. Galvan v. Press, 347 U.S. 522 (1954); Flemming v. Nestor, 363 U.S. 603 (1960); but cf. Shaughnessy v. United States *ex rel.* Mezie, 345 U.S. 206 (1953) (dissenting).

7. People *ex rel.* Knauff v. Shaughnessy, 338 U.S. 537 (1950) (dissenting); People *ex rel.* Shaughnessy v. Accardi, 349 U.S. 280 (1955) (dissenting); Jay v. Boyd, 351 U.S. 345 (1956) (dissenting); Marcello v. Bonds, 349 U.S. 302 (1955) (dissenting); Heikkila v. Barber, 345 U.S. 229 (1953) (dissenting); but cf. Bridges v. Wixon, 326 U.S. 135 (1945) (dissenting).

8. 321 U.S. 284 (1944).

9. *Id.* at 312, 314. The non-availability of judicial review except as granted by statute is the basis of his dissents in United States v. I.C.C., 337 U.S. 426 (1949), Estep v. United States, 327 U.S. 114 (1946) (concurs on a special ground, dissents on principal issue).

10. 187 U.S. 94 (1902).

11. 239 U.S. 3 (1915).

12. United States v. Los Angeles & S. L. R. R., 273 U.S. 299 (1927); Chicago Junction Case, 264 U.S. 258 (1924); Alexander Sprunt & Son v. United States, 281 U.S. 249 (1929).

13. 316 U.S. 4 (1942).

14. *Id.* at 14, 17. His dissent in Ewing v. Mytinger & Casselberry, 399 U.S. 594 (1950) also emphasizes the general significance of the equity power in controlling administrative activity.

15. 341 U.S. 123 (1951).

16. *Id.* at 150.

17. Examples of his usually restrictive views on standing and ripeness are Stark v. Wickard, 321 U.S. 288 (1944); Columbia Broadcasting System v. United States, 316 U.S. 407 (1942); Eccles v. Peoples Bank, 333 U.S. 426 (1948); International Longshoremen's Union v. Boyd, 347 U.S. 222 (1954); United States v. Storer, 351 U.S. 192 (1956). These cases and his views are discussed in my article, *Ripeness and Reviewable Order*, 61 Mich. L. Rev. 1273 (1963). His refusal to go along in dissent with Harlan J. in Frozen Food Express v. United States, 351 U.S. 40 (1956) is a curious exception.

One of his earliest opinions, Rochester Tel. Corp. v. United States, 307 U.S. 754 (1939), on the other hand, considerably extended judicial review of the so-called "negative orders" of the ICC. The doctrine of the non-reviewability of "negative orders" had come to be seen as thoroughly unsound and riddled with unworkable distinctions.

18. Texas & Pacific R. Co. v. Abilene, 204 U.S. 426 (1907).

19. Far East Conference v. United States, 342 U.S. 570 (1952).

20. *Id.* at 575.

21. 316 U.S. at 446.

22. 309 U.S. at 146.

23. 320 U.S. 489 (1943).

24. Concurring in Trust of Bingham v. CIR, 325 U.S. 365, 378 (1945).

25. Concurring in Social Security Bd. v. Nierotko, 327 U.S. 358 (1946).

26. E.g., NBC v. United States, 319 U.S. 190 (1943); Secretary of Agriculture v. Central Roig Refining Co., 338 U.S. 604 (1950); East Texas Lines v. Frozen Food Express, 351 U.S. 49 (1956) (dissenting); FMB v. Isbrandtsen, 356 U.S. 481 (1957) (dissenting).

27. E.g., Addison v. Holly Hill Fruit Products, Inc., 322 U.S. 607 (1944); Packard Motor Car Co. v. N.L.R.B., 330 U.S. 485 (1947) (dissenting).

28. His opinions recognizing the broad range of law and policy-making power implied in administrative discretion are distinguished contributions to the subject. Board of Trade v. United States, 314 U.S. 534 (1942); O'Leary v. Brown-Pacific-Maxon, 340 U.S. 504 (1951); Brooks v. N.L.R.B., 348 U.S. 96 (1954); N.L.R.B. v. Seven-Up Bottling Co., 344 U.S. 344 (1953). But I find it difficult to follow his view that the questions in N.L.R.B. v. Highland Park, 341 U.S. 322 (1951) (dissenting) and Board of Governors v. Agnew, 329 U.S. 441 (1947) (concurring) were questions of discretion.

29. 318 U.S. 80 (1943).

30. *Id.* at 94. He had spoken to the same effect in Phelps Dodge Corp. v. N.L.R.B., 313 U.S. 177, 197 (1941). "The administrative process will be best vindicated by clarity in its exercise. . . . All we ask of the Board is to give clear indication that it has exercised the discretion with which Congress has empowered it."

31. 322 U.S. 194 (1947).

32. *Id.* at 216, 217. A more temperate attack on an administrative decision by Jackson (Frankfurter concurring) is the dissent in Boyce Motor Lines, Inc. v. United States, 342 U.S. 337 (1952) and the dissents of Jackson and Frankfurter in F.P.C. v. Hope Natural Gas, 320 U.S. 591 (1944).

33. As in the cases cited in note 27, *supra*.

34. 341 U.S. 412 (1951).

35. *Id.* at 421.

36. 319 U.S. at 224.

37. One of his most adroit and finished opinions is that in Universal Camera Corp. v. N.L.R.B., 340 U.S. 474 (1951), which gives sympathetic effect to the evident desire of the sponsors of the Administrative Procedure Act to widen the scope of judicial review of findings of fact. For good measure he leads the Court in establishing a subrule pursuant to which rulings of the Courts of Appeal will not be disturbed unless the standard of review "appears to have been misapprehended or grossly misapplied." This subrule has the effect of giving a certain leverage to those circuits which are unfriendly to the Labor Board. Frankfurter has been more willing to accept that consequence than a recent majority which has chastised the Fifth Circuit for overslipping the bounds of proper review. N.L.R.B. v. Walton Mfg. Co. 369 U.S. 404 (1962). A similar expression of sensitivity to the purposes of the APA is his joinder in the dissent with Black and Douglas in Ramspeck v. Fed. Trial Examiners Conference, 345 U.S. 128 (1953), his dissent, Black joining, in Heikkila v. Barber, 345 U.S. 229 (1953), and his dissent in United States v. L. A. Tucker Lines, 344 U.S. 33 (1952).